D0864810

Great Houses
of the National Trust

LYDIA GREEVES

 National Trust

LANCASHIRE COUNTY LIBRARY

3011813085144 1

First published in Great Britain in 2013 by

National Trust Books
10 Southcombe Street
London W14 0RA

An imprint of Anova Books Ltd

Copyright © National Trust Books 2013
Text © National Trust Books 2013

Based on *Houses of the National Trust* (new edition), 2013

The moral rights of the author have been asserted.

All rights reserved. No part of this publication may be
reproduced, stored in a retrieval system, or transmitted in any
form or by any means, electronic, mechanical, photocopying,
recording or otherwise, without the prior written permission of
the copyright owner.

ISBN: 978 1 907892 94 3

A CIP catalogue record for this book is available from the British
Library.

20 19 18 17 16 15 14 13
10 9 8 7 6 5 4 3 2 1

Reproduction by Mission Productions, Hong Kong
Printed by G. Canale & C. S.p.A., Italy

Picture credits

6 (top), 113 (top) © National Trust Images / David Garner; 6 (bottom) © National
Trust Images / John Blake; 7, 82 (top right and bottom right), 143, 157, 166–167 ©
National Trust Images / Nick Meers; 8–9, 59, 108 (right), 109, 155, 161 © National
Trust Images / Dennis Gilbert; 10 © National Trust Images / Stephen Robson; 11,
12, 23, 34, 36, 42, 44, 47, 50, 65, 73, 76, 92, 101, 113 (bottom), 114, 116, 120, 123, 127,
130, 139, 142, 150, 151 (left), 179, 185, 191 © National Trust Images / Andreas von
Einsiedel; 13, 14, 18, 38, 45, 51, 60, 72, 78, 82, 86, 87, 100, 106, 122, 131, 138, 184 ©
National Trust Images / Matthew Antrobus; 15, 27, 48, 52 (top and bottom), 67, 68,
74, 79, 80, 84, 95 (left and right), 107, 136, 164 (top and bottom), 177, 178, 181 ©
National Trust Images / Nadia Mackenzie; 16–17, 28, 56, 96, 144, 152, 154, 156, 171,
174 © National Trust Images / John Hammond; 19, 41, 110, 180 (bottom) ©
National Trust Images / James Mortimer; 20, 21, 25, 32, 63, 86, 108 (left), 119, 146,
162, 169, 173, 186, 187 (top), 188 © National Trust Images / Andrew Butler; 22 ©
National Trust Images / Raymond Lea; 29, 97, 158, 183 © National Trust Images /
Mike Williams; 30 © National Trust Images / Alasdair Ogilvie; 31, 141, 153 (top and
bottom), 159, 176 © National Trust Images / David Sellman; 33 © National Trust
Images / George Wright; 35, 46, 54, 66, 69, 77, 85, 103, 112, 115, 134, 151 (right), 165,
172 © National Trust Images / Rupert Truman; 37 © National Trust Images / Mark
Bradshaw; 39 © National Trust Images / Patrick Prendergast; 40 © National Trust
Images / Chris Gascoigne; 49, 192 © National Trust Images / Arnhel de Serra; 53 ©
National Trust Images / John Miller; 55 © National Trust Images / Paul Mogford; 57
© National Trust Images / Dave Zubraski; 58 © National Trust Images / Brian and
Nina Chapple; 61 © National Trust Images / Joe Cornish; 62, 93, 98 (right), 124
(right), 133 © National Trust Images / Derek Croucher; 64, 81, 94, 104, 105 ©
National Trust Images / Robert Morris; 70, 135, 140 © National Trust Images / Bill
Batten; 71 © National Trust Images / Michael Caldwell; 75 © National Trust Images
/ Magnus Rew; 83 © National Trust Images / Angelo Hornak; 88 (top and bottom)
© National Trust Images / Aerial-Cam; 90, 91 © National Trust Images / Nick
Guttridge; 99 © National Trust Images; 111 © National Trust Images / James
Dobson; 118 © National Trust Images / David Dixon; 121, 148 © National Trust
Images / John Millar; 124 (left) © National Trust Images / Neil Campbell-Sharp; 125
© National Trust Images / W H Rendell; 129 © National Trust Images / Peter
Aprahamian; 137 © National Trust Images / Keith Hewitt; 140, 187 (bottom) ©
National Trust Images / John Bethell; 145, 163 © National Trust Images / Geoffrey
Frosh; 147 © National Trust Images / Erik Pelham; 149 © National Trust Images /
Alan Novelli; 160 © National Trust Images / Stuart Cox; 170 © National Trust
Images / Andy Marshall; 180 (top) © National Trust Images / Derrick E Witty; 189
© National Trust Images / Paul Raeside.

Images produced by kind permission of: Sir Evelyn de Rothschild (pages 16–17): ©
Estate of Rex Whistler. All rights reserved, DACS 2012 (page 127).

LANCASHIRE COUNTY LIBRARY	
3011813085144 1	
Askews & Holts	28-Jan-2015
728.80942 GRE	£15.99
NTH	

Contents

Introduction

The National Trust cares for a large and wonderfully diverse collection of buildings. Between them, they span almost a thousand years of history, from the time of William the Conqueror to the present day. Among the earliest is the remarkable one-storey Norman hall at Horton Court, deep in the Cotswolds, and Corfe Castle, now a dramatic ruin standing high on the Purbeck Hills, but once an impregnable stronghold built by William the Conqueror. The most recent buildings include the terraced house on a post-war Liverpool estate where Paul McCartney and John Lennon worked out their first songs and two examples of modernist domestic architecture: 2 Willow Road, looking over London's Hampstead Heath, and The Homewood, in leafy Surrey.

Although the preservation of buildings and their contents is now seen as a core aspect of the Trust's work, this has not always been so. For the first forty or so years of its existence, from 1895, the Trust was primarily concerned with the acquisition and protection of the countryside, a focus which partly reflects the principal aims of its founders, Octavia Hill, Robert Hunter and Canon Hardwicke Rawnsley.

Significantly, many of the early buildings acquired by the Trust came to them without any contents and this was also true of Barrington Court, the Trust's first substantial property, which was bought in 1907. The purchase price and bill for initial repairs together came to the then massive sum of £11,500. Maintaining this property, which was a constant drain on the Trust's slender resources, proved to be a salutary lesson in the pressures and difficulties involved in caring for houses of this size and the need for endowments to cover ongoing expenditure. Fortunately, in the years before the Second World War, just at the time when owners of great country houses were being faced with ruinous increases in taxation, death duties and running costs, a change in the Trust's status in 1937, which enabled the Trust to hold land and investments to provide for property upkeep, and the

introduction of the Country Houses scheme in 1940, by which owners could transfer their houses to the Trust, together with a suitable tax-free endowment, while continuing to live there, paved the way for a number of the finest properties, together with their contents, to be gifted. Blickling was given to the Trust in 1940, Wallington was acquired in 1941, Cliveden in 1942, West Wycombe in 1943, Polesden Lacey and Lacock Abbey in 1944. Many more followed after 1946, when the government decided to accept houses and land in lieu of death duties and to hand suitable properties over to the Trust.

These great houses, and many more modest acquisitions, offer a unique record of changing tastes and fashions in architecture and decoration and house an unrivalled collection of precious and beautiful things. Moreover, the paintings, furniture, books and other contents in Trust properties are often intimately connected with the history of the house and of the family, or families, who have lived there and, in many cases, continue to live there. Bess of Hardwick herself probably worked on some of the Elizabethan embroideries and other hangings at Hardwick Hall; luminous landscapes by Turner at Petworth reflect the artist's friendship with the 3rd Earl of Egremont, who arranged for Turner to have a studio in the house; and a shoal of tiny glittering fish displayed at Ickworth, each a beautifully crafted silver scent bottle or vinaigrette, was acquired by the 3rd Marchioness of Bristol. Gifts and loans of furniture and paintings and the donation of particular collections have further enriched what is on offer and have enabled the Trust to refurnish those properties where the contents have been lost or diminished. In recent times, too the Trust has benefited enormously from the loan of portraits from the National Portrait Gallery, whose paintings are seen at Montacute in Somerset and Beningbrough Hall in Yorkshire.

But grandeur is only one side of the story. At many houses, visitors are also able to see the extensive quarters where an army of servants kept the establishment going, cooking meals of many courses for the dining room, cleaning clothes and linen, brewing beer and making butter, cream and cheese from milk brought in from the home farm. Some 40 servants were employed at Penrhyn Castle in the late nineteenth century, among them the men who tended to the 36 horses in the stables and the French chef who presided over the gastronomic dinners served to the Prince of Wales and his entourage during their visit to the house in 1894. A property may have a prettily tiled dairy, and at Ham House there is even a late seventeenth-century still house, where soaps, sweet-scented waters and ointments were prepared. These rare survivals are typical examples of the Trust's extensive collection of the kind of everyday objects that were once seen everywhere but are now uncommon, among them such things as leather fire buckets, double-handled creamware pottery jugs used for carrying milk from the dairy to the house, spits and other equipment for roasting meat over an open fire, and a range of carts, carriages and other conveyances. Particularly memorable is the large collection of early bicycles that now hangs in one of the attics at Snowshill Manor.

Today the Trust is huge, but the philosophy and principles on which it rests remain unchanged. Most importantly, as its founders recognised, it is completely independent of government subsidy, relying for its income on the generosity of the public together with support from bodies such as the Heritage Lottery Fund, Historic Buildings Council and the National Heritage Memorial Fund, which may recommend a grant to make up an endowment or help meet the cost of a major acquisition. Increasingly, too, local authorities have provided financial assistance. Nevertheless, although rich in terms of what it holds, the Trust is always short of money. When Tyntesfield, a major example of Victorian Gothic architecture, was due to be sold by public auction in 2001, the necessary funds were only secured by a whirlwind appeal. The sum of over £20 million was raised.

Secondly, as a result of an Act of 1907, the Trust has the unique power to declare its properties and land inalienable, which means they cannot be sold or mortgaged. This is a priceless asset, which effectively means that anything gifted will be safeguarded for ever. Thirdly, the Trust exists to conserve buildings and countryside for the nation, for all of us to enjoy. With the massive growth in membership and visitor numbers in recent years, this has inevitably led to a conflict between the demands of access and conservation. This raises dilemmas of which the Trust is acutely aware and accounts for, for example, very low light levels in some rooms and restrictions on visitor numbers.

Today, tourism, and the visiting of historic properties, is a major activity. But there is nothing new about it. As Jane Austen shows so clearly in *Pride and Prejudice*, when Elizabeth Bennet and her uncle and aunt go to visit Pemberley, Mr Darcy's grand country house, it was understood that people would turn up at these places and ask to be shown round. Elizabeth and the Gardiners are attended to by the housekeeper, 'a respectable-looking elderly woman', and it was part of a housekeeper's duties to act in this way when the owners were absent, a task that usually brought them a generous tip. Jane Austen was describing the world she knew, of the late eighteenth and early nineteenth century, but interest in country seats goes back at least another hundred years. As Boswell recorded in his journal, he and Dr Johnson were taken round Kedleston in 1777 by the elderly Mrs Garnett, who was housekeeper there for over 30 years and whose portrait by Thomas Barber hangs in the house. When talking to visitors, she presumably referred to the printed catalogue of pictures and statues which she is shown holding in her hands. Some 240 years later, the Trust's guidebooks are the descendants of such catalogues.

A La Ronde

Devon
2 miles (3.2 kilometres) north of
Exmouth on the A376

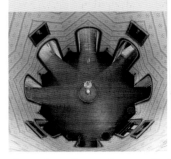

On the northern fringes of Exmouth, with views across the Exe estuary, is a delightfully uninhibited late eighteenth-century *cottage ornée*. Looking rather like a dovecote for humans, A La Ronde is a small, sixteen-sided, three-storey house, with rough limestone walls and a steeply pitched conical roof – now tiled but originally thatched – topped off with tall brick chimneys. Dating from a time when Exmouth was a fashionable resort, it was built, almost certainly to designs by the Bath architect John Lowder, for two resourceful spinsters: Jane Parminter, daughter of a Barnstaple wine merchant, and her younger cousin Mary, who had both just returned from a nine-year Grand Tour. The design of the house, with wedge-shaped main rooms divided by triangular lobbies, and curious diamond-shaped windows on the exterior angles, is unusual enough; even more so are the decorative schemes of the Parminters.

These are rare survivals of the kind of time-consuming, intricate techniques involving paint and paper, shell and feathers, sand and seaweed, which were much indulged in by Regency ladies but which, due to their fragility, have mostly been lost. The interior of the property stands out, too, for the skilful use of awkward angles and corners, and for the survival of its original contents.

The main rooms are arranged around a central octagon. The eight doors off have marbled yellow and green architraves, ingenious seats fold down over the openings and there are unique painted chairs with octagonal seats. The west-facing drawing room has its eighteenth-century tub chairs and sofa, the original marbled skirting and painted pelmet and the Parminters' feather frieze, with a delicate pattern of downy concentric circles.

Pictures here include a large silhouette group of the Parminter family in 1783 and landscapes of paper, sand and seaweed, with feathery trees stretching out their microscopic branches. A chimney board with shellwork surrounding a watercolour of St Michael's Mount is a prelude to the gallery at the top of the house. Alas, so fragile that it can only be viewed on video, this is the Parminters' *tour de force*, with shell-encrusted recesses and a zigzag frieze setting off feathery bird portraits resting on moss and twigs.

Jane died in 1811, Mary in 1849. Partly due to Mary's will, which aimed to keep the house as it was and to allow only unmarried kinswomen to inherit, A La Ronde survived remarkably unaltered, despite the attentions of its only male owner, the Rev. Oswald Reichel, who added the third-storey dormer windows and roofline catwalk and introduced a dark Victorian note to some of the rooms. The family struggled to keep the property intact until increasing difficulties brought it to the National Trust in 1991.

ABOVE LEFT The intricate decoration of the Shell Gallery took years of work to complete.
LEFT A La Ronde: this whimsical sixteen-sided house on the outskirts of Exmouth was built in the 1790s for Jane and Mary Parminter, who were cousins, and originally had dovecotes hanging from the eaves.

Anglesey Abbey and Lode Mill

Cambridgeshire
In the village of Lode, 6 miles (9.6 kilometres) north-east of Cambridge on the B1102

An interest in horse racing led Huttleston Broughton, later 1st Lord Fairhaven, and his brother Henry to purchase Anglesey Abbey in 1926. A typical stone Jacobean manor house with mullioned windows and tall chimneys, it was conveniently placed for Newmarket and the family stud near Bury St Edmunds and set in good partridge-shooting country. Apart from the vaulted monks' parlour, now the dining room, few traces remained of the Augustinian priory established here in the early thirteenth century from which the house takes its name.

Although his sporting interests were never neglected, over the next 40 years Lord Fairhaven transformed the house, of which he was sole owner from 1932, and filled it with a wide-ranging collection of works of art. His taste had been formed as a child in New York where his American mother, the oil heiress Carla Leyland Rogers, had furnished the family house with exquisite things, and where his parents moved in the same circles as the Fricks, Rockefellers and Vanderbilts. And there was no shortage of money. Lord Fairhaven's great wealth came not only from his mother but also from his English father, who made a fortune in American railroads.

Comfortable, intimate interiors, where log fires were kept burning all day, were created with the help of the architect Sidney Parvin, who introduced panelling, antique stone fireplaces, a vaulted corridor, a stone spiral staircase and other 'period' touches. These rooms are the setting for carefully arranged groupings of fine furniture, clocks, silver, tapestries, small bronzes and other statuary, and paintings. In the dining room, the medieval vaulting is complemented by a massive refectory table, at which the family still eat, and by a sixteenth-century carved oak cabinet, but elsewhere objects of very different date and character are set harmoniously together. In the living room a goat modelled by the great eighteenth-century sculptor Michael Rysbrack sits on an inlaid Italian cabinet, a Regency clock devised as a pagoda stands against a French tapestry, and there are eighteenth-century English landscapes on the walls.

Lord Fairhaven's exceptional collection of books is housed in the spacious library, built on by Sidney Parvin in 1937–8. The 9,000 or so volumes now here, overlooked by John Constable's riverscape showing the opening of Waterloo Bridge in 1817, include rarities such as Saxton's atlas of the English counties of 1574–9 and many spectacular illustrated books from the period 1770–1820. Intriguingly, the shelves are made of elmwood taken from Waterloo Bridge when it was demolished in 1934.

ABOVE The Jacobean south front of Anglesey Abbey, with square-headed mullioned and transomed windows, dates from c. 1600, although the period porch was added in the twentieth century.

Lord Fairhaven had a particular liking for nudes by the fashionable Victorian painter William Etty, about 20 of which now hang in the house. He also acquired a unique collection of views of Windsor, where he lived for a time in the Great Park. Displayed in the two-storey gallery designed by Sir Albert Richardson that was built onto the house in 1955, these paintings faithfully record changes in landscape and architecture over 350 years and range in style from the toy castle depicted in an early seventeenth-century canvas to William Daniell's mistily romantic view down the Long Walk, executed in the early nineteenth century. On the lower floor hang the three paintings for which this space was primarily created, a biblical scene by Aelbert Cuyp and two of the sublime landscapes by Claude Lorraine that inspired the naturalistic gardens of the eighteenth century. In *The Landing of Aeneas*, each slave rowing the boat carrying the Trojan leader is an individual, two looking over their shoulders to see how far they are from the shore. Displays of fine silver in the gallery include the sculptor John Flaxman's *Shield of Achilles*, which was inspired by a description in Homer's *Iliad*.

To set off his house, Lord Fairhaven transformed 40 acres of unpromising fen into a garden on the scale of an eighteenth-century landscape. A composition in trees and grass against the backdrop of towering East Anglian skies, this is a place of long vistas punctuated by an urn, a statue or some other eye-catcher. Broad avenues and walks provide a bold geometric framework, within which are some areas of very different character. Some are grand set pieces, like the curved border in the herbaceous garden, with its spectacular summer displays; others are more intimate and enclosed, such as the small sheltered lawn where William Theed's *Narcissus* contemplates his image in the still waters of a pond. Several vistas focus on the water-mill on the River Lode at the northernmost tip of the garden. A white weather-boarded building with a projecting lucarne (dormer window) on the fourth floor, the present structure dates from the eighteenth century, but there has probably been a mill here since the time of Domesday Book. The mill is once again a working water-mill, used for grinding flour.

RIGHT Lord Fairhaven's winter drawing room, where the paintings hung against Jacobean oak panelling include a serene landscape by Claude.

Antony

Cornwall
5 miles (8 kilometres) west of
Plymouth via the Torpoint car ferry,
2 miles (3.2 kilometres) north-west
of Torpoint, north of the A374,
16 miles (25.7 kilometres)
south-east of Liskeard, 15 miles
(24 kilometres) east of Looe

Antony stands at the end of the long neck of land forming the far south-eastern corner of Cornwall, an isolated peninsula bounded by the estuaries of the rivers Tamar and Lynher to the east and north, and by the sea to the south. The best way of approaching Antony is by boat, as it has been for centuries, crossing to Cornwall by the car ferry from Plymouth to Torpoint rather than taking the much longer route by road over the Tamar Bridge. The house is beautifully set. The entrance front faces up a slight rise crowned by a wrought-iron screen, but at the back the ground falls away across terraces to a sweep of grass and woodland beyond. Attractively grouped clumps of trees frame glimpses of the Lynher and of the arches of Brunel's Saltash railway bridge crossing the Tamar estuary.

The Antony estate has been the property of the Carews, and their descendants the Pole-Carews and Carew Poles, since the early fifteenth century. The main block of the present house, an elegant two-storey rectangle faced with beautiful silvery-grey stone and ornamented only with the plainest of pediments marking the central bay and with pilasters framing the front door, was built by Sir William Carew between 1718 and 1724. The architect is as yet unknown. Red-brick colonnaded wings enclosing a courtyard on the south front, thought to have been designed by James Gibbs, were added a little later. It is a charming and entirely satisfying house, one of the best of its date in the West Country, and was built to be lived in, not as a show place: modest, oak-panelled rooms lead off the hall and upstairs there are only five principal bedrooms, the space for a sixth being taken up by the huge and elegant staircase.

Antony is exceptional for the quality of its furnishings and for the collection of family and other portraits. Queen Anne pier glasses in the saloon and a Soho tapestry hanging in the room next door were made for the house, and other pieces that have always been here include a set of early eighteenth-century walnut-framed settees and chairs. At the same time, each generation of the family has continued to enrich the house, a recent acquisition being the endearing Chinese ceramic army from the Ming period (1368–1644) displayed over the fireplace in the tapestry room.

The portraits, including several works by Reynolds, enhance every room. Most memorable is the likeness of Charles I painted at his trial that hangs in the hall. The king is shown dressed in black wearing a large beaver hat, his sad eyes pouched with weariness. This is the last of a number of portraits that record Charles's final days and only here has the famous pointed beard turned grey. John Carew, who had sat in judgement on Charles, was himself executed at the Restoration. His tragic elder brother Alexander, whose portrait hangs in the library, suffered the same fate at the hands of the Parliamentarians, dying with a troubled and divided mind, uncertain which cause was right.

Antony's landscaped setting is partly due to Humphry Repton, who was consulted in 1792 and produced one of his earliest Red Books at the house. The terraces above the lawns were once planted with parterres and there is a more formal garden to the west with clipped yew hedges, espaliered fruit trees, a sheltered flower garden and a knot garden. An eighteenth-century dovecote squats by the house; some striking modern sculptures, by William Pye and others, were commissioned by Sir Richard Carew Pole, who lives at Antony; and hidden in a tangle of woodland beside the Lynher (not owned by the National Trust) is a bath house of 1784, with a plunge bath.

BELOW Antony's elegant north front looks across a sweep of grass to tree-framed vistas of the Lynher estuary.

ABOVE The library at Antony is hung with portraits of the Carew family and the large, lidded Chinese vase standing on one of the bookcases is part of a fine collection of ceramics in the house.

Ardress House

Co. Armagh
7 miles (11.2 kilometres) from
Portadown on the B28 Moy road,
5 miles (8 kilometres) from Moy,
3 miles (4.8 kilometres) from
Loughgall, intersection 13 on
the M1

Ardress House is not quite what it seems: the apparently Georgian entrance front disguises what was originally a seventeenth-century farmhouse, one room deep, the roof of which still rises above the urn-studded parapet. Moreover, the long two-storey facade with an impressive array of sash windows is partly a sham, one end of it being nothing more than a screen wall with false openings added in the interests of symmetry. There is a pedimented portico giving dignity and importance to the front door but it is not placed centrally between the windows on either side. The interiors of Ardress similarly reflect the gradual evolution of the house: intimate and homely rooms, and a worn flagged floor in the hall, contrast with grander later additions.

This piecemeal gentrification was partly the work of the architect George Ensor, who married the heiress of Ardress in 1760 and moved here from Dublin some 20 years later. Although he doubled the size of the house, a full remodelling was beyond his means and, apart from adding the classical portico on the entrance front, he concentrated his resources on an elegant new drawing room. Ardress's finest feature, the room is dominated by exceptional Adam-style plasterwork. An intricate pattern of intersecting circles and arcs round the central medallion on the ceiling, one of several showing figures and scenes from classical mythology, is picked out in muted tones of yellow, mauve and grey, with a rich blue as contrast. Whirls of foliage here are echoed in more extravagant loops and chains framing more medallions on the walls. Playful plaster cherubs along the frieze stand with the right leg crossed behind the left, except in one corner of the room, where the stance is reversed. This exceptional plaster decoration, among the finest in Ireland, was the work of the outstanding stuccadore Michael Stapleton, who is known for the magnificent interiors he created in eighteenth-century Dublin, where Ensor's brother John was a leading architect. Stapleton and Ensor would have known each other, and may even have worked together.

The lawyer and author George Ensor II's additions to the house in the early nineteenth century, including the extended entrance facade and curving screen walls framing the garden front, are a more mixed bag. His new wing at the back of the house contains a cavernous dining room which can only be reached from outside, because an internal door would have upset the Stapleton plasterwork in the drawing room next door. The dining room is now hung with seventeenth-century Dutch and Flemish paintings on loan from the collection of the Earl of Castle Stewart, among them a rare signed picture by the Flemish artist J. Myts. The diminutive haloed figure of Our Lord on the road to Emmaus is portrayed in a Northern European setting, with gentlemen in frock coats and a cluster of steep-roofed half-timbered houses marking a little town in the distance.

Fine period furniture includes a locally made oak and applewood bureau-bookcase of 1725 in the little parlour, an oak Irish Chippendale sideboard with characteristic five-clawed feet and lion's mask decoration in the dining room and a pair of Neo-classical settees in the drawing room. A late

LEFT The intricate plaster ceiling in the drawing room at Ardress House was devised as a kaleidoscopic pattern of circles and segmental curves.
OPPOSITE Gentrification of Ardress House in the mid-eighteenth century accounts for the Georgian entrance front, which conceals an older building behind.

eighteenth-century table made for the Speaker of the Irish Parliament is the one on which George V signed the Constitution of Northern Ireland when Ulster was formally separated from the rest of the country in 1921.

A cobbled yard behind the house is a reminder of the working farm Ardress once was, the outbuildings here including a dairy, a smithy, a cow byre, a threshing barn complete with horse-powered thresher, and a boiler house where large quantities of potatoes were cooked for the pigs. There is a formal garden and landscaped woodland near the house; beyond, the farmland, orchards and woods of the estate slope down to the Tall River.

Arlington Court

Devon
7 miles (11.2 kilometres) north-east
of Barnstaple on the A39

The plain, grey stone facades of this Neo-classical house are no preparation for the cluttered Victorian interior, where boldly patterned and coloured wallpaper sets off mahogany furniture and display cabinets overflowing with shells, snuffboxes, model ships, pewter and precious objects. The house was built in 1820 for Colonel John Chichester by the Barnstaple architect Thomas Lee and still has some decorative schemes of 1839, by the London firm of John Crace and George Trollop. But the collections are all the work of Rosalie Chichester, the last of the Chichesters of Arlington, who lived here for 84 years until her death in 1949.

Only child of the flamboyant and extravagant Bruce Chichester, who created the opulent staircase hall hung with yachting pictures more suited to a gentleman's club than a private house, Rosalie had been taken on two world cruises in her father's schooner *Erminia* before she reached her teens. Perhaps fired by these early experiences, she was always an enthusiastic traveller, one of the many delightful photographs on display showing her with Chrissie Peters, her diminutive companion, in New Zealand, both of them in sensible shoes and heavy suits with skirts down to their ankles. The Pacific shells and other mementoes she brought back from her travels were added to her growing collections, among them such things as model ships, tea caddies, candle snuffers and paperweights as well as more exotic items. Although her stuffed birds, Maori skirts and African clubs are no longer in the house, and the National Trust had to make the rooms less crowded before they could be opened to visitors, Arlington is still full of Rosalie's treasures, including the largest collection of pewter held by the Trust. Her favourite piece, a slightly malevolent red amber elephant from China, is prominently displayed in the White Drawing Room, one of three sunny rooms that interconnect along the south front. Also in the

BELOW The main block of Arlington Court, marked by the single-storey porch, was built in a plain Greek Revival style in 1820; the service wing to the right was added in 1865.

drawing room is a thirteenth-century Flemish psalter and in the ante-room next door hangs a mystical watercolour by William Blake, which was found on top of a pantry cupboard in 1949.

Shady lawns surrounding the house are planted with specimen trees, including an ash collection. Some distance away is a small formal garden laid out in 1865, where a conservatory against a high brick wall looks down over three grass terraces and a fountain pool guarded by metal herons, the birds of the Chichester crest. To the west of the house, beyond the little parish church filled with Chichester memorials, is the colonnaded stable block constructed by Rosalie's father. A modern extension here now displays one of the finest carriage collections in Britain. Largely dating from the nineteenth century, and brought together after the Trust took over the house, the exhibits range from carriages made

for children and a pony carriage made for Queen Victoria to a travelling chariot that is known to have been driven to Vienna.

Arlington is the centre of a thriving agricultural estate, as it has been ever since the Chichester family came here in the sixteenth century. A walk leads down to the thickly wooded valley of the River Yeo, where two great piers on the lake below the house are all that was built of the suspension bridge Rosalie's father had planned to carry a grand new drive. The lake and woods, which have been rejuvenated by the Trust, are a haven for wildlife, and the Jacob sheep and Shetland ponies in the park are descendants of those she established here as part of her wildlife sanctuary.

ABOVE The Morning Room at Arlington Court forms one end of a long sunny gallery running down the south front.

Ascott

Bedfordshire
½ mile (0.8 kilometre) east of
Wing, 2 miles (3.2 kilometres)
south-west of Leighton Buzzard,
on the south side of the A418

Entrepreneurial talent rarely passes from generation to generation, but Mayer Amschel Rothschild (1744–1812), who founded the family banking business in Frankfurt during the Napoleonic Wars, was blessed with five sons whose drive and ambition matched his own. While one inherited his father's mantle, the others dispersed to Paris, Naples, Vienna and London to set up branches of the firm. The wealth generated by the activities of this extraordinary clan financed the collection in this rambling neo-Jacobean house overlooking the Vale of Aylesbury as well as the more flamboyant magnificence of Waddesdon Manor a few miles away.

Ascott is the creation of Leopold de Rothschild, great-grandson of the founder of the family fortunes and son of Baron Lionel, the first Jewish British MP. The little Jacobean farmhouse he took over in 1876 is now buried in the gabled ranges, all black-and-white half-timbering and diamond-paned windows, added by the architect George Devey, and his assistant James Williams, in the years that followed, transforming the house into a massively overgrown cottage. But, despite Ascott's size, the rooms are pleasingly domestic in scale. Rothschilds live here still and the atmosphere is that of a beautifully furnished private house. Leopold's son Anthony removed most of the original Victorian décor in the 1930s and recently Sir Evelyn de Rothschild, Anthony's son, has again redecorated the rooms on show.

Predominantly Dutch and English paintings include Aelbert Cuyp's panoramic *View of Dordrecht*, its wide shallow canvas filling one wall of the low-ceilinged dining room. The town lies on the left, a low sun lighting up a row of gabled houses on the glassy river and giving a warm glow to the clouds heaped overhead. A faint mark in the centre of the painting shows where the canvas was once divided to be sold in two halves. A striking woman by Gainsborough, thought to be a likeness of the Duchess of Richmond, her flaming red curls set off by the silky sheen of her blue satin dress, is one of a number of fine English portraits at Ascott. There are three of Stubbs's distinctive horse studies, including the only known canvas in which he shows mares without any foals (shown

above), and a major work from the Italian Renaissance, Andrea del Sarto's arresting *Madonna and Child with St John*. Elegant eighteenth-century English furniture, such as the two oval pie-crust tables and the walnut and mahogany chairs covered with tapestry and needlework in the oak-panelled library, contrast with the contemporary French pieces elsewhere.

Anthony de Rothschild added paintings and English furniture to his father's collection and also introduced the oriental ceramics that are now such a prominent feature of the house.

The earliest pieces are ceramics from the Han (206BC–AD220), Tang (618–906) and Sung (906–1280) dynasties, with the cream of the collection, in deep rich colours, from the Ming (1368–1644) and Kangxi (1662–1722) periods. These were the centuries that produced sophisticated, three-colour ware in vibrant shades of blue, purple and burnt yellow, such as the elegant vases decorated with flowing chrysanthemums.

But it is the paintings, one of the best small collections in Britain, that make a visit to Ascott so rewarding. And

afterwards visitors can enjoy panoramic views to the Chilterns from the terraced lawns that fall away from the house.

ABOVE This serene picture by George Stubbs, the only known canvas in which this renowned horse-painter showed mares without their foals, is part of the exceptional Rothschild art collection at Ascott.

Attingham Estate

Shropshire
4 miles (6.4 kilometres) south-east
of Shrewsbury, on the Telford road

Few family mottoes can be more apposite than that of Noel Hill, 1st Lord Berwick: 'Let wealth be his who knows its use.' This wily politician, who obtained his peerage through expedient loyalty to William Pitt the Younger, poured the fortune he inherited into this grandiose classical house, set, like Wallington, in full view of a public road, from which it was devised to look as magnificent as possible.

Designed in 1782 by the individual Scottish architect George Steuart, and a rare survival of his work, Attingham consists of a main three-storey block linked by colonnaded corridors to pavilions on either side, with a classical portico rising the full height of the house on the entrance front. Seen from the bridge taking the road over the River Tern, the facade stretches 122 metres (400 feet) from pavilion to pavilion, while inside there are 80 rooms, an unusually large number for a house of this period. The layout of the interior is equally singular, with the rooms on the west side, including the library and dining room, making up a set of masculine apartments, and those on the east, including the drawing room, a set of feminine rooms.

On the 1st Lord's untimely death at the early age of 44, with Attingham not yet completed and furnished, the house passed successively to his two elder sons, who were responsible for the splendid Regency interiors. Acquisitions during a lengthy Grand Tour in Italy formed the basis of an extensive art collection built up by the 2nd Lord, who commissioned John Nash to add the grand picture gallery in 1805–7. One of the first to be built in a country house, this room is notable for the revolutionary use of curved cast-iron ribs to support the windows in the roof, an innovation that was to be used in the design of the Crystal Palace. Although the 2nd Lord's paintings were largely dispersed in the sale that followed his bankruptcy in 1827, a financial disaster that was precipitated by his marriage, at the age of 43, to a 17-year-old courtesan who helped him spend his fortune, the mixture of Italianate landscapes and copies of Old Masters now hanging two and three deep in the gallery conjures up the splendour of the original collection.

A pair of Neapolitan landscapes by Philipp Hackert (1737–1807) includes a view of Pompeii showing the small extent of the excavated area at the end of the eighteenth century and the garlanded vines that can still be seen in this part of Italy.

Nash was also responsible for the theatrical staircase, with a mahogany handrail inlaid with satinwood and ebony, which rises confidently to a half landing. In the drum-like space available, however, there was not room for the two flights into which the stairs divide to continue elegantly to the first floor, and Nash hid his unsatisfactory solution behind jib doors.

The Regency flavour continues in the dining room. Boldly decorated in deep red and gold, with gilded mouldings framing a show of portraits, the room is dominated by George Steuart's plasterwork design on the ceiling, with its gilded wreath of lacy vine leaves, and there are more vines decorating an original set of mahogany dining chairs. The tiny feminine boudoir on the other side of the house, with a domed ceiling painted with frail tendrils of foliage and medallions depicting cherubs set against rose-tinted clouds, has one of the most delicate late eighteenth-century schemes to survive in England and may be one of the few rooms to have been completed before the 1st Lord's death.

The paintings and furniture now seen in the house were largely collected by the diplomatist 3rd Lord – described by Byron as the only Excellence who was really excellent – during his 25 years in Italy. He was responsible for the elegant pale-blue drawing room filled with white and gold Italian furniture, some of which may have come from Napoleon's sister's Neapolitan palace, and for the glittering silver displayed in the old wine cellars, once stocked with some 900 bottles of sherry, port and Madeira.

Parkland dotted with mature oaks, elms, beeches and pines slopes gently down to the Tern. The initial layout, of 1769–72, was by Thomas Leggett, but the planting schemes reflect the hand of Humphry Repton, who produced a Red Book for Attingham in 1797. A grove of Lebanon cedars marks the start of Leggett's Mile Walk, which loops down to the river and returns past the walled garden.

OPPOSITE The Scottish architect George Steuart designed Attingham's grandiose entrance front, dominated by a three-storey portico.
RIGHT Delicate decoration featuring Venus and cupids in the boudoir reflects the real affection between the 1st Lord and Lady Berwick, who married for love, not money.

Baddesley Clinton

Warwickshire
¾ mile (1.2 kilometres) west of the
A4141 Warwick–Birmingham road,
at Chadwick End, 7½ (12 kilometres)
miles north-west of Warwick,
15 miles (24 kilometres) south-east
of central Birmingham

This exceptional medieval manor house set in an ancient park lies in a remnant of the Forest of Arden. Although only 15 miles (24 kilometres) south of Birmingham, the surrounding countryside, criss-crossed by a network of sunken lanes, still has an essentially medieval character, with the waves of former ridge and furrow showing in fields that are now under grass.

The present house, built round three sides of a courtyard, dates from the fifteenth century, but it is encircled by a moat that is probably much older and was dug to surround an earlier building. The only way into the manor is over the two-arched, eighteenth-century bridge that leads to the crenellated gatehouse. Grey walls punctuated with mullioned windows fall sheer to the water on either side and there are tall red-brick Elizabethan chimneys that form splashes of colour against the roof. Despite its guarded appearance, this is not a forbidding place. Its small panelled rooms, filled with mostly seventeenth- and eighteenth-century oak furniture, are intimate and homely.

Baddesley Clinton is a remarkable survival. From the early sixteenth century until 1980, when it came to the National Trust, this romantic moated house was lived in by generation after generation of the Ferrers family who, despite financial pressures, managed to preserve the manor and the estate. In 1940, when the house was first offered for sale, the estate lands were the same as those shown on a map of 1699. Succeeding generations have left their mark on the manor. Henry Ferrers, the Elizabethan antiquary who owned the house from 1564 to 1633, did much to embellish it, rebuilding the south range and introducing oak panelling, carved heraldic overmantels and richly coloured armorial stained glass. Much of this decoration survives, although some, such as the great stone chimneypiece now in the great hall, was once elsewhere. Although a Catholic, Henry seems to have avoided penalties for recusancy, despite the fact that the widow to whom he let the house in the late sixteenth century,

when persecution was at its height, sheltered Jesuit priests here and created hiding places for them. One of these, formed out of an old sewer and viewable through a glass panel in the kitchen floor, is where eight men evaded capture in October 1591, standing motionless with their feet in water for four hours. Then, in 1604, Henry was unwittingly involved in the Gunpowder Plot when his Westminster house, which he had let to one of the plotters, was used to store the gunpowder for blowing up Parliament. Although he was never penalised for his religion, Henry died heavily in debt and the family was further impoverished by taxation and appropriations during the Civil War. But this shortage of funds is probably the reason why Baddesley survived unchanged.

At the end of the nineteenth century, the manor's medieval character was further enhanced by an artistic quartet. In 1867 Marmion Edward Ferrers had married Rebecca Dulcibella Orpen, whose romanticised portraits of her friends and life at Baddesley are now a feature of the house. Two years later the couple were joined by Rebecca's aunt, Lady Chatterton, a romantic novelist, and her husband Edward Dering, who devoted his fortune to the house and estate. All four revelled in the antiquity of the place, added further stained glass and other embellishments and created the Catholic chapel, sumptuously fitted out with leather hangings decorated with flowers and birds. Both Lady Chatterton and Rebecca liked to paint in the great parlour on the first floor of the gatehouse. Today, the high barrel ceiling, sparse furnishings and rippling reflections from the moat create a sense of airy spaciousness that contrasts with the dark intimacy of the rest of the house.

OPPOSITE An early eighteenth-century brick bridge is the only way across the moat.
RIGHT The former courtyard was transformed into a garden in 1889.

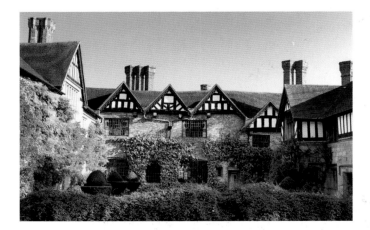

Basildon Park

Berkshire
Between Pangbourne and Streatley, 7 miles (11.2 kilometres) north-west of Reading, on the west side of the A329

This Neo-classical mansion standing high above the River Thames a little way upstream from Reading was built between 1776 and 1783 by the Yorkshire architect John Carr. One of Carr's best works and his only house in the south of England, it was commissioned by another Yorkshireman, Francis Sykes, who had bought the Basildon property in 1771. Sykes, later 1st Baronet, was one of those ambitious self-made men who returned from India with vast fortunes accumulated in the service of the East India Company. Although less corrupt than many, he appears to have been particularly wealthy and was able to spend lavishly on his new house. Several other men who had made themselves rich in India lived in the tranquil countryside round about, among them his friend Warren Hastings.

John Carr's Palladian villa, built of beautiful honey-coloured Bath stone, is both restrained and suitably grand.

BELOW A fortune made in Bengal in the service of the East India Company enabled Sir Francis Sykes to build Basildon Park, an outstanding Georgian mansion set high above the Thames.

A pedimented portico, its massive columns standing out against a deep shadowy recess behind, dominates the three-storey entrance front. To either side, linked to the main house by screen walls that hide service courtyards, are two-storey pavilions, their pedimented facades echoing the design of the central block. Originally, all three parts of the house were linked internally but this is no longer so, the windows and doors on the screen walls being only dummies.

Carr's Neo-classical decoration in the hall, with its delicate plasterwork ceiling subtly coloured like expensive wrapping paper in pink, lilac, green and stone, survives unaltered. His magnificent staircase, lit from above by graceful lunettes and with an elegant wrought-iron balustrade that curves gently upwards, is little changed. But Francis Sykes did not finish his new house, perhaps because he never recovered from the investigation into his dealings in India which lost him his parliamentary seat and left him £11,000 poorer, or because of his disappointment in his sons, one dying young, the other a spendthrift. In 1838 the decline in the family fortunes forced his grandson to sell to the Liberal MP James Morrison, a similarly self-made man whose upward path in life had been eased by marriage to his employer's daughter. Now a merchant prince, he needed a suitably grand setting to display his considerable collection of pictures. Morrison employed his architect-friend J.B. Papworth to complete the house and he and his ten children lived here in style. This was Basildon's golden age. A fast train link with London brought many distinguished visitors, J.M.W. Turner and Bishop Samuel Wilberforce among them.

Sadly, with the death of Morrison's daughter Ellen in 1910, the contents were dispersed and the house remained empty for over 40 years. During this period Basildon survived a scheme to re-erect it in America (no purchaser could be found) and lost some sections of plasterwork which were sold to the Waldorf Astoria Hotel in New York. It was saved by the 2nd Lord and Lady Iliffe, who bought it in 1952, restored it with great skill and filled it with period furnishings and paintings, including portraits by Lely, Hoppner and Myters as well as one or two twentieth-century works, such as Frank Salisbury's lovely painting of Lady Iliffe in a simple white dress, or Graham Sutherland's portrait of Lord Iliffe and watercolour studies for 'Christ in Glory', the tapestry that

ABOVE The richly decorated hall at Basildon Park would have been used for the kind of grand entertaining that was a feature of country-house life in the eighteenth century.

hangs behind the altar in Coventry Cathedral. The grandest interior, at the centre of the garden front, is the Octagon Drawing Room, its three great windows looking out over the Thames and the beech woods beyond. Pompeo Batoni's vivid portrayals of seven of the apostles and God the Father clustered round the doors on either side of the room are typical of the fine seventeenth- and eighteenth-century Italian paintings that Sir Francis Sykes might have acquired on a Grand Tour, and the deep red of the walls on which they are displayed is in accord with eighteenth-century taste.

Parkland studded with carefully placed chestnuts, beeches and limes still comes right up to the entrance front, as it did in

Sir Francis Sykes's day. James Morrison added the balustraded terrace walk that now frames a lawn at the back of the house, and he also introduced the pair of carved stone dogs on the north side of the grass, which he bought on a trip to Italy in 1845–6. Lord and Lady Iliffe were responsible for most of the other garden ornaments and the present sympathetic planting, such as the white rambling rose on the terrace balustrade and the magnolia on the house.

Belton House

Lincolnshire
3 miles (4.8 kilometres)
north-east of Grantham on the
A607 Grantham–Lincoln road

Belton is at peace with the world. Built in the last years of Charles II's reign to an H-shaped design by the gentleman-architect William Winde, its simple Anglo-Dutch style seems to express the confidence and optimism of Restoration England. Symmetrical honey-coloured facades look out over the tranquil, wooded park, the grandeur of the broad flight of steps leading up to the pedimented entrance front offset by domestic dormers in the steeply pitched roof and a delightful crowning cupola.

The interiors reflect Belton's long association with the Brownlow and Cust families, descendants of the ambitious and wealthy Elizabethan lawyer who bought the estate in 1609. Family portraits hang in almost every room, from Reynolds's imposing study of Sir John Cust, Speaker of the House of Commons from 1761–70, which greets visitors in the marble hall, to Lord Leighton's magical portrait at the top of the stairs of the last Countess Brownlow as a young woman, the colour of the bouquet she holds against her long white dress echoed in the autumnal trees behind.

High-quality decorations and furnishings, including magnificent wall mirrors, a brilliant-blue Italian lapis lazuli cabinet and the remnants of an extensive collection of Old Masters, speak of wealth well spent. Glowing panelling lines the formal seventeenth-century saloon in the middle of the house, setting off delicate limewood carvings with minutely realised fruit and flowers that suggest the hand of Grinling Gibbons. Early eighteenth-century gilt wall mirrors between the three long windows looking onto the garden reflect two sets of Charles II walnut chairs arrayed on the pink and green Aubusson carpet, their seats and backs upholstered in faded crimson velvet and a host of cherubs adorning the frames. Two more cherubs, their grumpy expressions perhaps due to their rather precarious position, perch uncomfortably on the monumental reredos in the largely unaltered north-facing chapel, where an exuberant baroque plaster ceiling by Edward Goudge contrasts with James Wyatt's Neo-classical compositions of the 1770s in other parts of the house.

Apart from the silver awarded to Speaker Cust for his service to the House of Commons, and the fine porcelain seen in almost every room, such as the massive blue and white Chinese Kangxi vases in the marble hall, some of the most prized pieces at Belton are the vast garden scenes by Melchior d'Hondecoeter acquired by the 3rd and last Earl. He and his wife presided over a golden age in the late nineteenth century, when Belton was sympathetically restored. The last Earl also made changes to the garden, adding a final layer to the harmonious blend of styles and periods that characterises the grounds. To the north of the house is his re-creation of a baroque Dutch layout, a formal composition of clipped yew and gravel walks punctuated by urns and pieces of sculpture, among them an eighteenth-century sundial clasped by Father Time. Further from the house is the more extensive sunken Italian garden dating from 1810 that was designed by Jeffry Wyatville and is overlooked by Wyatville's elegant orangery of 1820.

The last Earl's Dutch garden was based on an engraving of the original elaborate baroque layout. A lime avenue sweeping east across the park to a tall prospect tower silhouetted against the sky is a remnant of this scheme. A little Palladian temple facing across a short canal on the east side of the garden and an unrestored Picturesque wilderness to the west are also survivals of earlier layouts, as depicted in a number of eighteenth-century paintings of the house and grounds in the breakfast room. Twentieth-century portraits hanging here include a likeness of the 6th Lord Brownlow, Lord in Waiting to Edward VIII during his brief reign and a close friend of the king. Edward VIII stayed several times at Belton, perhaps deriving strength from the serenity of his surroundings.

OPPOSITE Grinling Gibbons may have carved the limewood garland framing this portrait of 'Old' Sir John Brownlow, the seventeenth-century sheep farmer who founded the family fortunes.

ABOVE A fortune made from sheep farming and the law financed the building of Belton House in 1685–88. The north front looks over nineteenth-century formal gardens.

Beningbrough Hall and Gardens

North Yorkshire
8 miles (12.8 kilometres)
north-west of York, 2 miles
(3.2 kilometres) west of Shipton,
2 miles (3.2 kilometres)
south-east of Linton-on-Ouse

This great baroque house is set on a slight rise above the water meadows of the Ouse. Built of red brick and stone, with long sash windows lighting the two principal floors and little pavilions crowned with cupolas either side of the main block, it is a product of the cultivated, secure decades of the early eighteenth century and was largely complete by 1716. Ornate stonework, including two lifelike horses struggling to escape sculptured drapery, marks the central bay, a splayed flight of steps rises to the entrance and tiny casements in the attic storey are squeezed in between the massive console brackets supporting the prominent cornice.

Beningbrough was built for John Bourchier, whose family had acquired the property by marriage in the previous century, but it is not known exactly who designed the house. The talented local carpenter-architect William Thornton, who oversaw construction, may have done more than just supervise the work; there may have been advice from the architect Thomas Archer, who had studied continental baroque at first hand; and Bourchier, who had seen contemporary buildings in Italy, may also have played a part. Certainly, much of the exterior detailing, such as the paired brackets supporting the cornice, is taken from Italian baroque buildings, and the treatment of the imposing stone-flagged entrance hall, rising through two storeys on the north side of the house, may well have been influenced by the grand baroque palaces Bourchier saw in Rome.

The interior plan, with its formal, strongly axial layout, is marked by the kind of spatial effects characteristic of baroque architecture. There are long vistas down the corridors running the length of the house on both floors, the lower closed by the greenery of the conservatory at one end, the upper with openings into the entrance hall. Another feature is the exceptional woodcarving that stands out in high relief on the friezes and overmantels of the pine-panelled rooms, decoration that was usually executed in plaster being here realised in wood. This was probably the work of French Huguenot craftsmen employed by Thornton, who was closely associated with a group that had established themselves in the north of England. Despite the sale of the contents in 1958, the interior is furnished in period style. Some exceptional pieces and pictures were bought back by the National Trust, while others are from a bequest by Lady Megaw, and the house has benefited from the loan of oriental porcelain by the Ashmolean Museum and from an imaginative partnership with the National Portrait Gallery, as a result of which Beningbrough's eighteenth-century interiors now display an outstanding collection of period portraits.

Running across five bays on the first floor of the garden front is the impressive saloon. Decorated in grey and gold and hung with portraits, this grand architectural space would have been used for balls and large family gatherings. The formality of early eighteenth-century life comes through in the apartments on the ground floor, where suites of rooms were used for receiving visitors as well as sleeping. There is magnificent upholstery on a trio of state beds and stepped shelves over the fireplaces in the intimate closets at the corners of the house, where only the closest friends would have been admitted, are crowded with oriental porcelain. Contemporary taste for the eastern and exotic is also reflected in pieces of lacquer work, among them a Chinese cabinet in one of the dressing rooms.

The paintings, illustrating many of the great figures of the day and work by most of the leading portraitists, are a feature of all the furnished rooms. Here are canvases by Ramsay, Angelica Kauffman, Highmore, Hudson, Reynolds, Gainsborough, Batoni and, above all, Kneller, whose studies of members of the politically influential Kit-Cat Club, all painted to the same format and in identical frames, hang two deep in the dining room. Like the show of eighteenth-century royalty in the entrance hall, these Kit-Cat portraits, nearly half of those Kneller produced, are among the paintings on loan from the National Portrait Gallery. So, too, is the poignant portrait of the bedridden actress Peg Woffington, who was stricken with palsy during her last performance.

A door in the wall of the cobbled yard opposite the nineteenth-century laundry leads into the garden. Two formal layouts are enclosed by yew hedges and set round a fountain pool and the walled garden is planted with fruit trees and box-edged beds. The view south over the ha-ha to the water meadows has a feeling of the eighteenth-century landscaped park that once surrounded the house.

Berrington Hall

Herefordshire
3 miles (4.8 kilometres) north
of Leominster on the west
side of the A49

Berrington is the creation of Thomas Harley, the 3rd Earl of Oxford's remarkable son, who made a fortune from banking and from supplying pay and clothing to the British army during the American War of Independence. He became Lord Mayor of London in 1767 at the age of 37. The architect of his austere three-storey house, with its domestic quarters clustered round a courtyard behind, was the young Henry Holland, who was to go on to build Carlton House for the Prince Regent.

The house is set above the wide valley of a tributary of the River Lugg, with views west and south to the Black Mountains and Brecon Beacons. This was the site advised by 'Capability' Brown, whom Harley took to see the estate in 1775, shortly after he had acquired it, and who was to landscape the park, creating the lake with its artificial island (Berrington is one of the best examples of his work). Holland, who was Brown's son-in-law, started on the house three years later.

Approached through an entrance lodge built in the form of a triumphal arch, the rather plain Neo-classical exterior with a wide flight of steps leading to the pedimented portico on the entrance front gives no clue to the lavishness of the interior. Feminine plaster ceilings now decorated in muted pastel colours adorn the principal rooms. Holland is at his most fanciful in the drawing room, where painted roundels on the ceiling, thought to be by Biagio Rebecca, are set off by white plaster cherubs leading seahorses by blue ribbons over a lavender background. Biagio Rebecca probably also executed the prominent grisaille panels in the library, deep shadows in those showing eminent Englishmen of letters on the ceiling giving them a three-dimensional quality, as if they were made of plaster. Bacon and Chaucer are easily recognisable; Alexander Pope is the only one of the eight to be shown in full profile.

Holland's most original interior at Berrington is the staircase hall. Rising to a delicately treated glass dome, it shows an extraordinary ability to use perspective and space to dramatic effect, as in an engraving by Piranesi. The rooms are set off with a collection of French furniture, including pieces that belonged to the Comte de Flahault, the natural son of Talleyrand, and Napoleon's stepdaughter Hortense.

ABOVE The finest of the interiors created by Henry Holland at Berrington is the staircase hall, with its screens of scagliola columns, delicate glass dome and bold spatial effects.

In the dining room, four panoramic sea paintings, three of them by Thomas Luny, are a tribute to the distinguished Admiral Rodney. Father-in-law of Harley's daughter Anne and one of the most eminent admirals of the eighteenth century, he played a prominent role in the American War of Independence. The paintings show important incidents in the war at sea, in which Rodney was in action against the French and Spanish, who had allied themselves with the rebellious Americans. Two large pictures at either end of the room are of the Battle of the Saints on 12 April 1782, an engagement that Luny, who served as a purser, may have witnessed. One is a morning scene showing Rodney breaking the French line; the other depicts the surrender of the French flagship in the evening of the same day.

More poignant reminders of members of the Cawley family, to whom the estate was sold in 1901, hang in Lady Cawley's room. One of the photographs shows the 1st Lord Cawley and his four sons on horseback in front of the house, ready for a day's hunting. A few years later three of the young men had lost their lives in the First World War.

Blickling Estate

Norfolk
On the north side of the B1154,
½ mile (0.8 kilometre) north-west
of Aylsham on the A140, 15 miles
(24 kilometres) north of Norwich,
10 miles (16 kilometres) south of
Cromer

A winding road from Aylsham leads to this serene Jacobean mansion set in almost 2,000 hectares (4,800 acres) of gently undulating park and estate in a loop of the River Bure. Built of warm red brick with stone dressings, Blickling has curving Dutch gables, generous leaded windows, massive chimneystacks and corner turrets carrying gilded weather vanes. On the southern entrance front, long, low service wings, their lines continued by yew hedges, frame the approach. The house was designed for Sir Henry Hobart, James I's distinguished Chief Justice of the Common Pleas, by Robert Lyminge, who transformed an existing medieval and Tudor manor. No trace of this manor can be seen, but its ghost lives on in the dry moat ringing the house and in many features of the layout and dimensions of the new building, such as the double courtyard plan. Further remodelling in the eighteenth century by Thomas and William Ivory for John Hobart, the 2nd Earl of Buckinghamshire, resulted in a house that is a harmonious combination of Jacobean and Georgian, the later work, to the north and west ranges, blending beautifully with the earlier, more solid styling.

Rich and showy Jacobean decoration and fittings show Sir Henry spared no expense in creating interiors to match his status. The 1620s staircase, with carved figures on the newel posts, is a striking feature of the portrait-hung great hall, to which it was moved in 1767, while the south drawing room at the end of the east range, once the great chamber of the Jacobean house and the room where Charles II was entertained in 1671, still has its outstanding plasterwork ceiling by Edward Stanyon and the original ostentatious chimneypiece. An ante-room off the drawing room leads into Sir Henry's spectacular Long Gallery, adorned with another intricate plaster ceiling by Stanyon. Here, his decoration intermingles heraldic motifs with delightful depictions of the senses. In one panel a stag listens entranced to a man playing the mandolin, his lady following the music for him with her finger; in another, a woman lifts a brimming glass to her lips, her lap full of luscious fruit. In about 1745 the gallery was converted into a library to accommodate the books inherited from Sir Richard Ellys, a

ABOVE Blickling has fine collections of family portraits, books, tapestries and mainly English furniture, although this carved late seventeenth-century seat may be Dutch.
OPPOSITE Blickling's Jacobean east front, with large windows lighting the Great Chamber and Long Gallery, looks over a formal parterre to a terrace walk.

distinguished theologian and antiquary who, with an eye for the rare, curious, old and beautiful, assembled an outstanding collection of works. The 12,000 volumes housed at Blickling, which form one of the most remarkable country-house libraries in England, include a very rare Eliot Indian bible printed in Massachusetts in 1663, a unique maritime atlas of the same period, spectacular books of engravings and books from the Aldine Press in Venice, several of which are in contemporary bindings. J.H. Pollen's delicately painted frieze above the bookcases, full of timid rabbits and other wildlife of the Norfolk countryside, is part of the Pre-Raphaelite mural decoration commissioned by the 8th Marquess of Lothian shortly after he inherited the house in 1850.

A door from the gallery leads into one of the rooms fitted out in 1778–82 to display the works of art acquired by the 2nd Earl during his congenial three-year posting as Ambassador to the court of Catherine the Great. There are only three paintings here now, but the room still displays the magnificent tapestry, given to the 2nd Earl by the empress as a

parting present, which shows Peter the Great triumphing over the defeated Swedish army at Poltawa in 1709.

An RAF museum in the east wing, with displays of photographs and of equipment, clothing and other memorabilia, is a reminder of the role Blickling played in the Second World War, when aircrews from RAF Oulton, a satellite Bomber Command airfield just to the west of the estate, were billeted in the house and in Nissen huts in the grounds.

A formal garden remodelled by Norah Lindsay in the 1930s and flanked by formal wilderness areas with wooded walks borders the Jacobean east front, and a path leads on from here to a little early eighteenth-century temple set high on a massive terrace. Rolling wooded parkland landscaped in the eighteenth century stretches away to the north and west of the house, with beeches, sweet chestnuts and huge mature oaks framing a long, sinuous lake.

Bodiam Castle

East Sussex
3 miles (4.8 kilometres) south of Hawkhurst, 1 mile (1.6 kilometres) east of the B2244

By 1372, halfway through the Hundred Years War, England had lost control of the Channel and had begun to suffer devastating French raids. The Sussex ports of Winchelsea and Rye had both been destroyed a few years earlier; the manor of Bodiam, lying only some 10 miles (16 kilometres) from the coast and at the furthest navigable point of the River Rother, must have seemed similarly vulnerable. In 1385, Sir Edward Dalyngrigge, a veteran of the wars in France and an important figure in the defence of Sussex, asked Richard II for permission to fortify his house.

Rather than improving his manor, Dalyngrigge chose to build anew, on a site that gave a view of the river and a strategic bridge. Work started in 1385 and the fine, four-square castle which still stares south across the Sussex marshes was completed some three years later. Built just before siege artillery changed the approach to castle design, Bodiam's strength lay in the height and might of its tower-studded circuit walls, which rise sheer from a broad moat. The massive gateway, bristling with machicolations and gunports, is reached from the north bank across three bridges and two islands. Originally, to repel any attacker, this approach involved a dog-leg to the west bank, three drawbridges and an outlying barbican, the remains of which stand on one of the islands. A ground-hugging Second World War pillbox by the path up from the car park shows how much defensive thinking has changed.

Although now in ruins, enough of the interior survives to give a vivid picture of the realities of castle life. The deep well and the remains of a pigeon loft suggest the preoccupations of a garrison expecting to be besieged, but in fact the French threat soon receded and the remnants of traceried windows and a number of fireplaces tell a different story. Like many contemporary buildings in France and England, which Dalyngrigge must surely have seen, Bodiam combines domestic comfort with the trappings of defence and it is very likely the castle was built to be a status symbol as much as a fortress. The great courtyard beyond the gatehouse is surrounded by the outlines of domestic accommodation, including a traditional great hall with adjoining buttery, pantry and kitchen, such as would have been found in any mansion of the period, and personal chambers for Dalyngrigge and his wife. Separate quarters, each suite with its own fireplaces and garderobe, were provided for his household, with additional provision for a military garrison. A chapel catered for the spiritual needs of the retinue and their lord. The emphasis on the castle as a grand residence also comes through in the recently identified remains of landscape gardens beyond the moat. Dips and hollows in the grass mark what was a series of ponds and there was a terrace on the hill above from which to admire the castle and its setting.

ABOVE These three arches connected the great hall to the kitchen range. The two outer doorways gave access to the buttery and pantry, the taller central one to a passage leading to the kitchen.
OPPOSITE Bodiam looks everything a castle should be, with a massive gatehouse protecting the entrance on the north front and a wide moat, here frozen and snow-covered.

Buckland Abbey

Devon
6 miles (9.6 kilometres) south of Tavistock, 11 miles (17.7 kilometres) north of Plymouth

Francis Drake's tiny *Golden Hind* left Plymouth on a cold winter's day in December 1577 and did not return until nearly three years later, on 26 September 1580. This historic voyage was the first circumnavigation of the globe by an Englishman, involving what must have been a terrifying passage across the unknown expanses of the Pacific Ocean. A national hero on his return, Drake needed a house that reflected his newly acquired status, ironically choosing to purchase the abbey that had been so recently converted by his rival, Sir Richard Grenville. It was from here that Drake planned his assault on the Spanish Armada a few years later.

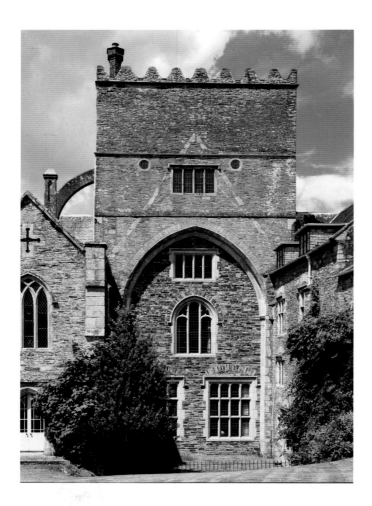

Set among sloping green lawns and exotic trees and shrubs on the edge of the sleepy Tavy valley, Buckland Abbey is rich in associations with Drake. There are many echoes too of the great Cistercian monastery that was founded here in 1273 and which was dissolved in 1539, passing to Richard Grenville two years later. Like Lord Sandys at Mottisfont, Grenville chose to convert the thirteenth-century abbey church rather than using the domestic buildings of the community. The abbey's great crossing tower, its south wall marked clearly with the roofline of a demolished transept, dominates the house, there are blocked arches and traces of monastic windows and, inside, the tracery of the chancel arch and ancient mouldings can be seen.

Presented in association with Plymouth City Museum and Art Gallery, the interior is a mix of museum-like exhibits and furnished rooms. Imaginative displays in the long gallery running the length of the top floor outline the history of the abbey from medieval times to the present day. Carved stones, pieces of tracery and floor tiles help recall the monastic community that lived here for some 300 years, growing gradually richer on an income derived from tin mines in the Tavy valley as well as from the tenants on their estates. Drake's coat of arms over the fireplace, on which a fragile ship is guided by the divine hand of providence, heralds the displays on the floor below. Gorgeous flags, one showing the golden leopards of England on a red ground, may have flown on the *Golden Hind*. Other cases contain Elizabeth I's commission of 5 March 1587, giving Drake command of the fleet with which he 'singed the King of Spain's beard'; Armada medals, the first ever struck to commemorate a historical event; and finds from Spanish ships that foundered off Ireland. A fascinating document details the Armada accounts from December 1587, early entries covering payments – 'to drummers, carpenters, cooks, mariners, surgeons' – concerned with preparations to meet the Spanish, later months including terse references to engagements. Marginal notes in Treasurer Lord Burghley's thin, spidery hand record sums reimbursed, such as the payment in October 1588 to cover the loss of a fireship. Here, too, is Drake's drum, which was with him on his epic voyage

LEFT At Buckland Abbey, Sir Richard Grenville converted the monastery church into a country house, leaving the outline of a demolished transept on what had been the church tower.

and when he died of dysentery off Panama in 1596. It is said to beat if England is ever in danger.

The only complete interior surviving from these times is the sixteenth-century great hall. Dating from Sir Richard Grenville's conversion of the abbey, it is warmly panelled in oak and decorated with an elaborate ceiling and a holly and box frieze adorned with carved figures. Contemporary plasterwork on the end walls symbolising Grenville's retirement to Buckland shows his shield hanging on a tree and a large pile of discarded arms. A Georgian dining room hung with two characteristic seascapes by Van de Velde the Younger and other seventeenth-century Dutch works, and the elegant staircase curling up through four floors were added as part of late eighteenth-century improvements.

A picturesque group of granite outbuildings with lichen-stained roofs includes an ox-shed introduced by the agricultural improver William Marshall, who spent four years at Buckland in 1791–4. Close by the abbey is the huge, heavily buttressed monastic barn, built in about 1300. Almost 49 metres (160 feet) long, it is one of the largest in Britain, eloquently suggesting the wealth of the community. Sinuous box hedges like window tracery enclose a little herb garden planted beside the barn, where it is easy to imagine white-robed figures moving silently from bed to bed collecting lovage, balm or sweet cicely. There is a re-creation of an Elizabethan garden too.

BELOW Georgian alterations at Buckland Abbey included the insertion of this splendid staircase, which rises right through the house. A gate on one of the half-landings kept dogs from the upper floors.

Calke Abbey

Derbyshire
9 miles (14.4 kilometres) south
of Derby, on the A514 at Ticknall
between Swadlincote and
Melbourne

Set some distance from any public road, Calke Abbey lies hidden in a fold of the landscape in a beautiful eighteenth-century park, insulated from the world by thousands of trees grouped in picturesque clumps and windbreaks and framing a chain of ornamental ponds. Built in 1701–4, it is an imposing three-storey baroque house set round a courtyard and with corner pavilions decorated with fluted pilasters. But behind the symmetrical grey sandstone facades are substantial remains of an Elizabethan building and the abbey's low-lying position, in a hollow of the park, reveals its earlier, monastic origins, some of the fabric having probably been recycled from the priory of Austin canons that was established here in the early twelfth century. Substantial remodelling by William Wilkins the Elder between 1789 and 1810 for Sir Henry Harpur, 7th Baronet, accounts for the pedimented entrance portico, the roofline balustrade and the suite of reception rooms on the first floor, of which only the dining room, with its Neo-

classical decoration, and the library, where the rolled-up maps attached to the bookshelves are among the fittings supplied in 1806–7, are as he designed them.

Like Kedleston Hall only a few miles to the north, Calke has been in the hands of the same family for hundreds of years, each generation of the Harpurs and Harpur Crewes contributing to the extraordinary individuality of the house. More remarkably, little has been changed since the mid-nineteenth century, providing a unique insight into mid-Victorian England.

William Wilkins's drawing room still has the striking gold and white wallpaper that was hung in 1841–2 and it is still as cluttered as it appears in a photograph of 1886, crowded with chairs and stools, numerous occasional tables and ornaments under glass domes. Display cases full of glistening polished stones are no preparation for the contents of the room next door, the saloon remodelled by Henry Isaac Stevens in 1841. Stevens's coffered ceiling decorated with the Harpur boar and his elegant panels hung with family portraits fade into insignificance beside the cases of stuffed birds and geological specimens and the stag trophies mounted on the walls. A noble head even looks down on Tilly Kettle's charming portrait of Lady Frances Harpur and her son, the future 7th Baronet, painted in c.1766.

These unusual exhibits reflect the interests of Sir Vauncey Harpur Crewe, the idiosyncratic recluse who inherited Calke in 1886 and filled the house with his collections. Increasingly unpredictable, Sir Vauncey took to communicating with his servants by letter, would make off into the woods when his wife entertained, and forbade his tenants to cut the hedges so as to provide maximum cover for the birds. Carriages now displayed in the stable yard reflect his insistence that motor vehicles should not be allowed on the estate.

Sir Vauncey seems to have had nothing in common with the three Georgian baronets, two Sir Henrys and Sir Harry, whose keen interest in the turf is commemorated by paintings of racehorses by Sartorius and Sawrey Gilpin in the library, by three florid eighteenth-century racing cups and, in the case of Sir Harry, by the riding school added to the impressive brick stable block in 1767–9. Lady Caroline, wife of the 5th Baronet, one of the Henrys, was given the sumptuous early eighteenth-century

LEFT This cluttered bedroom, still much as it was when occupied by the eccentric Sir Vauncey Harpur Crewe in the mid-nineteenth century, typifies Calke's unusual interiors.

state bed, its beautiful Chinese silk hangings, embroidered with dragons, birds, deer and other traditional motifs in rich blues, reds, greens and oranges, still as fresh as when it arrived. This exceptional survival was found in a packing case in the former linen closet, and many more treasures lay forgotten behind closed doors or languishing in outhouses, among them Victorian dolls in mint condition, books full of dried flowers, a Georgian chamber organ and a harpsichord by Burkat Shudi. Household objects that would have been thrown away long ago in other establishments, such as an array of lamps that was in use until electricity was installed in 1962, have also survived here.

After Sir Vauncey died in 1924, apart from a brief period during the Second World War, when some evacuees and, later, soldiers were billeted here, the house slowly shut down. Charles Harpur-Crewe, who inherited in 1949, was even more socially retiring than Sir Vauncey and, increasingly, only a core of habitable rooms was occupied. The extensive servants' quarters were shut up, and other rooms became filled with the wreckage of unwanted things. These rooms, and the long bleak corridors connecting them, are shown as they were found and are deeply atmospheric. Wallpaper is stained and peeling, great cracks snake across ceilings, and paintwork is chipped and flaking. Seen with the shutters largely closed, the effect is of a place turned in on itself, of abandonment as much as decay. In the bowels of the building is the old kitchen and a series of cave-like wine and beer cellars and, from the north side of the courtyard, a long, dimly lit tunnel winds far underground to emerge in the brewhouse in the stable block.

Several members of the family lie buried in the graveyard and vaults of the little church, which crowns a rise to the south of the house. Although apparently of the nineteenth century, its appearance is due to a remodelling, in 1827–9, of a simple Elizabethan building, some parts of which, such as the roof trusses, were re-used. Nearby, hidden by a screen of trees, are the late eighteenth-century walled gardens, a combination of the ornamental and the practical. A vast grassy arena at the top of the slope with an orangery on the north side and views over Staunton Harold reservoir was once the kitchen garden.

When Charles Harpur-Crewe died in 1981, while setting mole traps in the park, his brother Henry, who inherited the estate, faced death duties of £8 million. Despite the problems involved, including interest mounting up at the rate of £1,500

ABOVE The plain baroque south front of Calke Abbey, completed in 1703, was embellished with a classical portico in 1806–8.

a day, Henry was determined to preserve Calke and, four years later, after special grants from the National Heritage Memorial fund and English Heritage, a successful public appeal and an anonymous donation, it was successfully transferred to the National Trust. Essential repairs meant that it was 1989 before the house could be opened to the public.

Canons Ashby

Northamptonshire
On the B4525
Northampton–Banbury road

Set in the rolling, thinly populated country of south Northamptonshire, this ancient courtyard house reflects the bookish, conservative and never very wealthy family who lived here for 400 years, gradually altering and adding to the place but never rebuilding it. Little has changed since the early eighteenth century when the motto 'Antient as the Druids' was inserted over the drawing room fireplace. A lime avenue from the garden leads to an unexpectedly grand church, all that remains of the Augustinian priory that gave Canons Ashby its name and which once dominated a thriving medieval village, now only bumps and furrows in the grass. Although reduced to a quarter of its former length, the church is impressive; there is a striking red and white arcade on the west front and the massive pinnacled tower can be seen for miles.

John Dryden's modest H-shaped Tudor manor, built with material from the demolished east end of the church, now forms the great-hall range of the house, with its unusual squat tower like an echo of a Cumbrian pele rising over the south front. The wings to the east, enclosing the cobbled internal courtyard, were added by his son Sir Erasmus, the 1st Baronet, in the 1590s. Unlike the finished stone and brickwork of the exterior, the courtyard walls are rough and irregular, patterned with lichen and moss and set with leaded casement windows.

Painted decoration uncovered by the National Trust in the 1980s dates from Sir Erasmus's time. Some of it, such as the illustration of a story from the Old Testament with a great sailing ship at anchor in front of a walled city, is in grey-blue monochrome, but the array of crests and devices in the servants' hall is in full colour. Intriguingly, some of the symbols here, such as set squares and dividers, point to a connection with early freemasonry in Scotland, over a century before it was organised in England. Sir Erasmus was also responsible for the vast chimneypiece in the drawing room, but it was his son who added the striking domed ceiling, every inch of it crowded with elaborate plasterwork featuring thistles and pomegranates on stylised curving branches. Three long sash windows lighting this room, added when Edward Dryden remodelled the south front in 1710, look out over a rare survival of a formal garden of the same date, with a vista down a flight of terraces falling away from the house to a grand baroque gateway and across the park beyond. Enclosing walls are all of a piece.

Edward Dryden was also responsible for Canons Ashby's dignified west front. This now faces onto a grassy court but for centuries, from 1550 to c.1840, it was used as the main entrance to the house. An imposing baroque doorway dominates the facade, and Edward probably commissioned the sculptor Jan Van Nost to supply the leadwork coat of arms above the entrance and figures for the garden, of which only a statue of a shepherd boy survives. He also purchased the exquisite needlework-covered furniture in the Tapestry Room, with flowers and pastoral scenes embroidered on the seats and backs.

The present approach to the house, across the cobbled courtyard and up steps into the great hall, was arranged by Sir Henry Dryden, the much-loved Victorian squire of Canons Ashby who was known as the Antiquary. Fired by a lifelong interest in medieval architecture, Sir Henry measured and recorded all aspects of the house, down to the catches on the casement windows, and largely preserved it as it was, his only major addition being the oak bookcases in the little library where he wrote his learned articles. Leather-bound volumes now filling the shelves include the works of the three important literary figures associated with the house: the poet Edmund Spenser (1552–99), author of *The Faerie Queene*, who was a cousin of Sir Erasmus Dryden's wife; the poet laureate John Dryden, who visited the house as a very young man in the 1650s to pay court to his cousin, daughter of the 3rd Baronet; and the playwright and novelist Samuel Richardson (1689–1761), who is said to have written much of *Sir Charles Grandison*, his improbable moral tale about a virtuous paragon, at Canons Ashby.

The house is shown through Sir Henry's life and times and his meticulous records and period photographs have been used to re-create the Victorian planting of the terraces, with island beds and topiary yew on the grassy upper levels giving way to fruit and vegetable gardens framed by apples and pears on the lower terraces.

OPPOSITE A huge pendant hangs from the centre of the plasterwork ceiling
that was added to the drawing room in the 1630s.
ABOVE Sixteenth-century ranges flanking John Dryden's Tudor staircase tower on Canons Ashby's
south front are hidden behind early eighteenth-century embellishments.

Castle Coole

Co. Fermanagh
1½ miles (2.4 kilometres) south-
east of Enniskillen on the A32
Belfast–Enniskillen road

This austere white palace, James Wyatt's masterpiece, is one of the finest Neo-classical houses in the British Isles. Built between 1789 and 1795 for Armar Lowry Corry, Viscount and later 1st Earl of Belmore, it was designed to provide a suitably grand setting for a newly ennobled member of the peerage and also to surpass Florence Court across Lough Erne to the south, the house that had recently been embellished by Lowry Corry's brother-in-law, Lord Enniskillen.

The shady path up from the car park by the stables suddenly emerges on the grass in front of the house to give an oblique view of the dazzling entrance facade faced in creamy Portland stone. A pedimented portico rising the height of the house is echoed in colonnaded wings linking the main block to pavilions on either side, a rather old-fashioned Palladian design, reminiscent of Robert Adam's Kedleston, which may

ABOVE The massive columned portico which fronts the main block at Castle Coole is echoed in the colonnades which link the house to pavilions on either side.

ABOVE The oval saloon at Castle Coole, where even the mahogany doors are curved, is fitted out with opulent Regency furnishings which act as a foil for the cool Neo-classical decoration.

reflect the fact that Wyatt had to work with the foundations for a scheme of c.1785 by the Irish architect Richard Johnston. This constraint clearly did not dim his enthusiasm. The quality of the interior detailing is superb: fine plaster ceilings by Joseph Rose and carved chimneypieces by Richard Westmacott are matched by similarly superior craftsmanship in the joinery of doors and floors. Unusually, a complete set of building accounts and many drawings have survived and these show that Wyatt even designed furniture and curtains. But he never visited Castle Coole, leaving his plans to be realised, and often altered, by the clerk of the works, Alexander Stewart. Rose and Westmacott too worked from afar, providing decorative features in London that were then shipped to Ireland. The Portland stone cladding of the exterior was brought by boat from Dorset to a special quay built at Ballyshannon and then taken by cart and barge up Lough Erne.

Sadly, Lord Belmore's ambitions far outstripped his purse, exhausting his funds before his new mansion was fully fitted out. Wyatt's chastely elegant interiors were furnished in an opulent Regency style between 1802 and 1825 by Belmore's son, whose relish for the job matched that of his father. The 2nd Earl spent over £26,000, more than it cost to build the house, with the fashionable Dublin upholsterer John Preston, whose fine furnishings include one of the few state beds in Ireland. Extensively restored by the National Trust to reflect its early nineteenth-century appearance, Castle Coole is an intriguing blend of classical and Regency. The dignified entrance hall, with a screen of mock-marble columns and statues in niches, is painted a welcoming pink as it was by the 2nd Earl. In contrast, grey scagliola pilasters ringing the oval saloon beneath Joseph Rose's delicate ceiling echo the original colour scheme, while stoves set in niches and the curved doors following the line of the walls are again strongly reminiscent of designs for Kedleston.

The saloon is the centrepiece of the north front, dividing rooms of very different character. The dining room on one side, still lit only by candles, is pure Wyatt, with fan-like plaster tracery arching over the curtainless windows, slate-green walls hung with family portraits and a delicate classical frieze. There is gleaming gold plate on Wyatt's sideboard, which was produced in 11 weeks by two joiners in 1797. The drawing room at the other end of the house is furnished with gilt couches and chairs upholstered in salmon pink and with a richly patterned nineteenth-century Aubusson carpet. The library across the hall is more comfortable, with a plentiful supply of cushions and bolsters lying casually on the red velvet of the masculine Grecian sofas. The heavy folds of the crimson curtains with their plump tassels are immortalised in white marble on Westmacott's extraordinary chimneypiece, executed while Wyatt was employed on the house but not to the architect's surviving design. Substantial servants' quarters in the basement reflect the number of staff that would have been necessary for a house of this quality.

Castle Coole looks out over a wooded park that was landscaped in the late eighteenth century and slopes gently down to Lough Coole, the site of a previous house. The double oak avenue, along which Castle Coole has been approached since about 1730, has been replanted and will reach maturity some time in the middle of the 21st century.

Castle Drogo

Devon
4 miles (6.4 kilometres) south of
the A30 Exeter–Okehampton road
via Crockernwell; or turn off the
A382 Moretonhampstead–
Whiddon Down road at Sandy Park

When Julius Drewe, the self-made millionaire, retired from his retailing business in 1889 aged only 33, he was determined to set himself up as a country gentleman. Fired with the belief that he was descended from a Norman baron and that the family name had been given to the Dartmoor village of Drewsteignton, he resolved to build a castle on the land that he thought had once belonged to his remote ancestors. Although the initial grandiose plans were massively scaled down, Castle Drogo, set on moorland to the west of the village and built of local granite, looks both suitably medieval and as if it is rooted in the landscape.

As the spectacular views from the roof confirm, the site, on a spur high above the gorge of the River Teign, was well chosen. A road runs along the top of the bluff, but the castle is far more impressive if approached by the steep path leading up from the river far below, when a jumble of granite walls and towers topped by battlements and pierced by mullioned windows suddenly rears up from the bracken-covered hillside ahead. A massive entrance tower with twin octagonal turrets on the west front has a genuine portcullis and the heraldic Drewe lion is proudly displayed over the entrance arch.

This ambitious building was commissioned in 1910 from Sir Edwin Lutyens, then at the height of his powers. The great architect's interiors, with much use of bare stone and unpainted woodwork, initially seem as unwelcoming as the outside. But the use of space is always interesting and carefully designed. The main corridor leading from the entrance hall, for example, is an architectural *tour de force*, with an intriguing interplay of domes and vaults. And, as the plentiful windows suggest, Lutyens in fact created a comfortable country house within the fortress-like exterior. A stately staircase lit by a huge east-facing window links the dining room to the airy, panelled drawing room, where soft green walls and chintz-covered sofas, and windows on three sides, create a restful, luxuriant atmosphere. Similarly, the agreeable bathrooms, one with an elaborate shower arrangement, were designed with pleasure in mind. Exotic Spanish furniture in several of the rooms was acquired as a result of the spectacular bankruptcy of the banker Adrian de Murrieta, friend of the Prince of Wales (the future Edward VII) and extravagant social butterfly, whose vast red-brick Sussex mansion Drewe purchased in 1899.

Lutyens took as much care with the extensive servants' quarters in the bowels of the castle as he did with the rest of the house. A round beechwood table and other fittings in the

LEFT Castle Drogo's entrance tower has a workable portcullis, arrow slits and the heraldic Drewe lion carved in relief above the archway.

ABOVE The long corridor linking the hall with the drawing room at Castle Drogo shows how Lutyens ingeniously combined tunnel vaulting with shallow domes.

lofty kitchen, lit only through a lantern in the roof, were made to his design, as were the oak cupboards, table and teak sinks in the substantial pantry.

Lutyens was also involved in the formal garden to the north of the house, where yew hedges are clipped in geometric shapes and granite steps lead up a flight of terraces, although the layout and planting probably owe more to the garden designer George Dillistone, who had worked for Julius Drewe at Culverden in Kent and was employed at Castle Drogo from 1922.

Sadly, Julius Drewe died only a year after the castle was completed in 1930, but he must have been pleased with his progress in life. Whereas *Burke's Landed Gentry* ignored his similarly wealthy retailing rivals Lipton and Sainsbury, the land Drewe acquired with the fortune amassed from his Home and Colonial Stores gained his inclusion.

During a five-year programme of building works starting in 2013, visitors will be able to see rooms that have not been open before and work in progress.

Castle Ward

Co. Down
7 miles (11.2 kilometres) north-east
of Downpatrick, 1½ miles
(2.4 kilometres) west of Strangford
village on the A25, on the south
shore of Strangford Lough,
entrance by Ballyculter Lodge

Castle Ward, crowning a gentle slope above Strangford Lough, is a very Irish house. Although built at one period, from 1762–70, it is classical on the west side, with a central pediment supported by four columns, and Gothick on the east, with battlements, pinnacles and ogival windows. This architectural curiosity is a result of the opposing tastes of Bernard Ward, later 1st Viscount Bangor, and his wife Lady Anne. Each favouring a particular style, they agreed to differ. The interior also reflects the Wards' eccentric approach, with the rooms on his side of the house, the hall, dining room and library, decorated in a Palladian idiom, while those on the east, the saloon, morning room and boudoir, are in an ornate and opulent Gothick, with pointed doors and plaster vaulting. The versatile architect is

unknown, although tradition has it that, like the stone of which the house is built, he may have come from Bath (the stone was brought from England in Lord Bangor's own ship and unloaded in Castle Bay below the house).

The stylistic division of Castle Ward was followed by the separation of Bernard and Anne, and by her departure for Bath. By the time the 1st Viscount died, their eldest son, Nicholas, was insane and the estate was divided between his two younger brothers, one of whom, after moving Nicholas to Downpatrick, removed most of the contents of the house. But the elaborate decorative schemes have survived almost unaltered. Three-dimensional plaster motifs stand out white against the green walls of the hall: here a festoon of musical instruments, including drums and tambourines, across the room a cluster of agricultural implements, a harrow, axe and billhook. A pedimented door leads into the Gothick saloon, where ogival mirrors between the ecclesiastical traceried windows reflect a cluttered Victorian interior, with photographs on many surfaces, stuffed birds under a glass case, a gossip seat and feathery dried flowers. Lady Bangor's sitting room next door, transformed by the voluptuous curves of the Gothick ceiling into a large pink tent, is even more exuberant. There could hardly be a greater contrast with the restrained treatment of the elegant cantilevered staircase, which has a Venetian window on the half-landing and a frieze of acanthus-leaf scrolls on the walls.

Steps lead down past an impressive array of bells to the kitchens, housekeeper's room and wine cellar in the basement, connected by a long whitewashed tunnel to the Victorian laundry, stables and servants' quarters set round a courtyard apart from the house, as was the fashion in eighteenth-century Ireland. A former billiard room in the basement is devoted to the exceptional Mary Ward (d.1869), scientist, painter and wife of the 5th Viscount Bangor. Her delicate watercolours of wildlife and atmospheric views of the house and estate are on show and cases are filled with her collections of butterflies and insects. Most remarkable are the fruits of her pioneering work with the microscope: magnified images of the eye of a dragonfly, like a blue honeycomb, and of the silvery scales of the jewel beetle.

Castle Ward has one of the most beautiful settings of any house in Ulster, with an eighteenth-century landscape park, in the English style, sloping down to the lough and views over the water framed by mature oaks and beeches. To the north of the house is the Temple Water, a serene artificial lake created in the early eighteenth century which is overlooked by a little classical temple. The formal Victorian garden near the house is different in character, with grassy terraces planted with palms and roses rising from a sunken, brightly flowering parterre to a line of Irish yews and a pinetum beyond.

Corn- and saw-mills, a drying kiln and slaughterhouse set round a yard near the Temple Water were once the centre of a thriving agricultural estate. Here, too, is the early seventeenth-century tower-house which the Wards built soon after they came to Ireland from England. Nearby is a row of slate-roofed late Victorian cottages that were provided for estate workers. Only a few decades before, in 1852, the village of Audleystown had been destroyed and its inhabitants transported to America to improve the view from the house. As the accounts in the estate office reveal, some left still owing rent.

OPPOSITE The boudoir on the Gothick side of Castle Ward has a billowing, tent-like plaster ceiling which was based on drawings of the fan vaulting in Henry VII's chapel in Westminster Abbey.

Charlecote Park

Warwickshire
1 mile (1.6 kilometres) north-west
of Wellesbourne, 5 miles
(8 kilometres) east of Stratford-
upon-Avon, 6 miles (9.6 kilometres)
south of Warwick on the north side
of the B4086

Charlecote has been the home of the Lucy family and their ancestors for some 800 years. The present house, begun by Sir Thomas Lucy in the mid-sixteenth century, stands on the banks of the River Avon at the centre of an extensive wooded deer-park grazed by fallow deer and a herd of rare Jacob sheep. The estate is within easy reach of Stratford and there is a story that Shakespeare was caught poaching here and brought before Sir Thomas Lucy, the resident magistrate, in Charlecote's great hall. Perhaps the young playwright vaulted over the rough oak paling that still surrounds most of the park and has been perpetuated since Elizabethan times. Shakespeare would have been fined, and possibly flogged, and the story goes that he took his revenge some years later by portraying Sir Thomas as the fussy Justice Shallow in *The Merry Wives of Windsor*. Alas, despite a reference to the Lucys' ancient coat of arms, of which Sir Thomas was known to have been very proud, the story is probably just that.

The house is built of red brick to a pleasingly irregular E-shape. With banks of decorative chimneys arrayed across the roofline and octagonal corner turrets crowned with gilded weathervanes, Charlecote seems to sum up the very essence of Elizabethan England, especially when the brickwork is mellowed and burnished by the sun. Queen Elizabeth I spent two nights here in 1572, an occasion that is proudly celebrated in the display of her arms over the two-storeyed porch. With the exception of the porch, however, most of the present building is the result of 'Elizabethan' restoration in the mid-nineteenth century by George Hammond Lucy and his wife Mary Elizabeth, who not only refitted every room but also extended the house to south and west, obscuring much genuine Elizabethan brickwork in the process. The general effect is rich and lush, reflecting advice from the designer and antiquarian Thomas Willement, who, as well as advising on neo-Elizabethan plasterwork ceilings and other period features, even produced convincing Elizabethan versions of such things as fitted bookshelves and pile carpets, unknown in the sixteenth century. The Willement touch is particularly evident in the sunny and comfortable library, where he designed the Elizabethan-style bookcases to house the Lucys' fine collection of books, which includes a late fourteenth-century Book of Hours, and also the carpet, the wallpaper and matching chintz covers on the furniture, and the fire grate and door stops. Apart from the family paintings, which hang in every room, George Hammond Lucy was also responsible for most of the furnishings, many of which came from the 1823 sale of the contents of William Beckford's Fonthill Abbey in Wiltshire. The most expensive purchase was the arresting sixteenth-century Italian marble table in the hall, which came from the Borghese Palace in Rome and is inlaid with brightly

OPPOSITE The great hall at Charlecote Park is hung with portraits of the Lucy family, who have been living on this site since at least the twelfth century and who still inhabit the house.
ABOVE With its finialled turrets and soaring brick chimneys, Charlecote looks like a great Elizabethan mansion, but in fact the house is largely a creation of the nineteenth century.

coloured birds and a slab of onyx like a section through a fossilised tree. Mary Elizabeth, who carried on altering and furnishing the house after George's death in 1845, created the drawing-room wing and purchased the gigantic, ornately carved neo-Elizabethan buffet that dominates the dining room.

Two generations earlier, in the mid-eighteenth century, George Lucy, a cultivated and much travelled bachelor, had employed 'Capability' Brown to redesign the park, sweeping

away the seventeenth-century water gardens (shown in the painting above Shakespeare's bust in the great hall) and altering the course of the River Hele (now the Dene) so that it cascaded into the Avon within sight of the house. George Lucy was also responsible for introducing the Jacob sheep, which he brought back from a trip to Portugal. The balustraded formal garden between house and river, with steps into the Avon, is a nineteenth-century addition.

Chartwell

Kent
2 miles (3.2 kilometres)
south of Westerham

Winston Churchill, whose house this was, once declared that he bought Chartwell 'for that view'. Set on the side of a little Kentish valley, it looks over the garden that falls away steeply below to wooded slopes across the combe and the soft countryside leading onward to the Weald. There are vistas from almost every room and, as the many doors to the garden suggest, a sense of a house linked intimately with its surroundings. This serene setting, still breathtakingly beautiful, was to provide Winston Churchill with inspiration and strength for over 40 years, from 1922 until he left Chartwell for the last time in 1964.

The appeal of this unpretentious red-brick house, with its comfortable airy rooms created by Philip Tilden out of a gloomy Victorian mansion, lies in its powerful reflection of a great and complicated man, whose spirit still seems to linger on here. His bold and colourful paintings hang throughout the house, some, such as the simple study of a magnolia on an upper landing, tranquil still-lifes, others recording landscapes he loved, in France, Italy and Morocco as well as around Chartwell. A half-finished canvas stands on the easel in his garden studio, paints laid ready nearby. Finished pictures hang four and five deep on the walls round about. In the airy, flower-filled drawing room, a card table is set for the bezique he so much enjoyed, and a painting over the fireplace records one of the finest colts from his racing stable. A velvet siren suit, his characteristic wide-brimmed hats and cigar boxes also suggest a man who relished the pleasures of life.

But there are other mementoes too. In the lofty study, with its high roof open to the rafters, is the wide mahogany stand-up desk at which Churchill liked to work. His *A History of the English-Speaking Peoples* and *The Second World War* were mostly composed in this room. Here he reflected on the growing power of Germany during the 1930s, a threat that he felt was perceived by him alone. The study is still essentially as he left it, crowded with family photographs, a dispatch box on the table. A portrait of his father hangs by the fire and a

drawing of his mother confirms her exceptional beauty. Elsewhere, medals, uniforms and other reminders of a life devoted to his country include Churchill's terse directive to Field Marshal Alexander, instructing him to expel the enemy from North Africa, and the field marshal's equally short reply, informing the prime minister that he had done so. Chartwell is also very much a family house. The signatures of Lloyd George, Balfour and Field Marshal Montgomery in the visitors' book are interspersed with the more tentative efforts of the four young Churchills' friends and cousins. And it was the children who decided to mark their parents' 50th wedding anniversary by planting the borders filled with 32 varieties of golden roses that run in a long corridor down the old kitchen garden, close by the wall that Churchill built when he was in the political wilderness before the Second World War.

A loose framework of hedges and walls, with steps from one level to another, divides the spacious garden falling away to the lakes in the depths of the combe. Stretches of trees and grass are complemented by planting schemes reflecting Lady Clementine Churchill's love of cool colours and simple and direct effects. Her walled rose garden lies to the east of the house and there are many butterfly-attracting plants. Most evocative is the secluded pond, where an ample garden chair marks the spot where Churchill came daily to feed his golden orfe and ponder life.

OPPOSITE Chartwell, the home of Winston Churchill from 1922 until 1964, looks out over terraced gardens laid out by the Churchills and the soft wooded countryside of Kent and Sussex beyond.
BELOW Seven round-headed windows looking over the garden light the dining room, where dinner, served at eight, was usually accompanied by champagne.

Chastleton House

Oxfordshire
At Chastleton off the A44, 4 miles
(6.4 kilometres) south-east of
Moreton-in-Marsh

On the fringes of the Cotswolds, eastwards into Oxfordshire, is an unspoilt landscape of well-wooded farmland and limestone villages. Less than a mile (1.6 kilometres) off the main road from Oxford to Evesham, a leafy narrow lane runs steeply up through a straggle of cottages. At the top of the village, set back across a grassy court beside a stump-towered church, is a square, many-gabled Jacobean house. Of mellow local stone, with tall, three-storey ranges set round a tight internal court and mullioned windows, Chastleton is a charming and unaltered example of the kind of manor house which must have adorned a thousand English villages, lived in by families untouched by high office and national events. There are sophisticated touches, such as the arresting south front, with its show of glass and advancing bays, and some fine plaster ceilings, but much else, such as the rough and mossy dry-stone walls lining the entrance court, is rustic and ad hoc.

Until it came to the National Trust in 1991, Chastleton had been in the hands of the same family for almost 400 years. Built c.1610–12 for Walter Jones, a successful wool merchant, who bought the estate in 1602 from Robert Catesby, the future

Gunpowder Plotter, it had been owned by Jones's descendants ever since, with tapestries and furniture identifiable on the inventory taken after his death in 1632. Early prosperity did not last. Although the family was staunchly royalist in the Civil War, when Arthur Jones is said to have evaded a Roundhead search party after the Battle of Worcester by hiding in a secret chamber, there were few rewards at the Restoration, and growing financial difficulties culminated in Henry Jones's imprisonment for bankruptcy in 1755. Chastleton's character comes from the slow accumulation of contents in a house that, like an old coat, was sometimes cut to fit but never drastically altered or updated.

Above a substantial basement, where the smoke-blackened kitchen ceiling, said to ensure the family's luck, remains unwhitewashed, is a sequence of parlours and chambers, some tapestry-hung and the grander with carved chimneypieces of stone or wood and decorative plasterwork. Panelling, now dark with age and dirt, is used like wallpaper, and there are pegged plank doors, undulating floors and deep windowsills. The plan is conservative, centred on a traditional great hall, with an oriel window lighting the high-table end and a carved strapwork screen, and with staircases in crenellated towers to either side of the house. The most ornate interior is the great chamber, where the overmantel, carved with the arms of Jones and his wife, still has much of its rich red, blue and gold colour scheme and the ceiling is an extravaganza of trailing vines and hanging pendants; the most glorious is the bare and airy long gallery on the third floor, with its silvery panelling and plasterwork barrel ceiling. The long refectory table in the hall, leather chests in the gallery, and the blue and red flamestitch hangings lining a little closet are among the furnishings given on the 1633 inventory; a brief burst of refurbishment after 1697, when Walter Jones married the forceful Anne Whitmore, accounts for the James II walnut chairs and exquisite Queen Anne crewel-work; and the family's poverty ensured the survival of some seventeenth-century woollen hangings that were once commonplace and are now very rare. There is also an unbroken run of family portraits, including works by Kneller and Hudson, and a leather-bound bible in the library is said to have been used by Charles I on the scaffold. All is seen in a shadowy half-light, brightened by shafts of sunlight through leaded casements.

It was Anne Whitmore who probably laid out the topiary garden to the east of the house, with a yew circle embracing 24 box figures. Once an impressive display of arboreal sculpture, these are now a collection of intriguingly individual amorphous shapes. To the north is a sequence of grassed terraces where a lawn laid out for croquet recalls the nineteenth-century Walter Jones Whitmore, who first codified the rules of the game. In a field beyond the garden, on a sightline from the house, there is a mature oak, said to have grown from an acorn off the Boscobel tree that sheltered the fugitive Charles II, and a delicious eighteenth-century dovecote stands in the parkland rising to the summit of Chastleton Hill.

OPPOSITE Jacobean Chastleton House, built of mellow local stone, lies on the fringes of the Cotswolds, with only an archway separating it from the straggle of cottages making up the village.
ABOVE Decorative panelling embellishes many of Chastleton's atmospheric interiors.

Chirk Castle

Wrexham
½ mile (0.8 kilometre)
west of Chirk village off
the A5

Chirk Castle is an elegantly appointed house within the carapace of a medieval fortress. The long drive from the baroque entrance gates – a filigree of white ironwork – leads up through the undulating oak-studded park. The castle, appearing suddenly on the brow of the hill, is unexpectedly menacing, with drum towers projecting from battlemented fourteenth-century walls.

A pointed archway marked with the grooves of a portcullis leads into the internal courtyard. Here the west range still has the character of the stronghold Roger Mortimer started in c.1295 as part of Edward I's campaign to subdue the Welsh. Deep underground, reached by a spiral staircase in the thickness of the walls, is a dungeon hollowed out of the rock, only two narrow beams of light reaching those who were incarcerated here. In the courtyard outside a great shaft falls 28.5 metres (93 feet) to the castle well.

These reminders of the turbulent Middle Ages contrast with the later interiors commissioned by the Myddelton family who came to Chirk in 1595, when the castle was sold to the merchant and financier Thomas Myddelton I. In the late eighteenth century, Joseph Turner of Chester created an elegant staircase and a suite of state apartments in the fashionable Neo-classical style within the massive walls of the north range. Gothic touches by A.W.N. Pugin, who was commissioned to redecorate the castle in the 1840s, have been mostly toned down or removed, but some of the strong colour schemes and other details introduced by this exceptional man remain. The sumptuous saloon, with gilded doors and dados and a red and white chimneypiece of Sicilian marble, is graced with an Adam-style coffered ceiling, coloured a brilliant blue by Pugin and his collaborator J.G. Crace and inset with Greek mythological scenes by the Irish painter George Mullins. Mortlake tapestries hang on the walls and the fine contemporary furniture includes pier tables and mirrors by Ince & Mayhew, a pair of stylish serpentine settees and the earliest signed harpsichord, of 1742, by Burkat Shudi, the intricate marquetry of

the interior depicting eagles with outstretched wings. Among the seventeenth- and eighteenth-century family portraits hanging in these rooms are pictures of Richard Myddelton and his wife, who commissioned the state apartments, by Francis Cotes, and two rare portraits by the Flemish landscape painter Peter Tillemanns.

A door from the drawing room leads into the 30-metre (100-foot) long gallery that fills the first floor of the east range. Created in the 1670s, when Sir Thomas Myddelton IV, 2nd Baronet, repaired the extensive damage that Chirk had sustained in the Civil War, the gallery is more than twice the size of the saloon and is little changed, apart from the addition of a ribbed heraldic ceiling and fireplace tiles by Pugin. Dark oak panelling, perhaps by the gentleman-architect William Winde, is grandly conceived, with massive broken pediments crowning the doors and a bold cornice of carved acanthus leaves running above a show of early portraits. Among the few pieces of furniture, all of them probably part of the original contents, is a delicate seventeenth-century Dutch cabinet of ebony inlaid with tortoiseshell and ivory. The silver-encrusted interior is decorated with scenes from the life of Christ that were painted in the Antwerp studio of Frans Francken the Younger, one of which shows Our Lord blessing children against the backdrop of the gabled facades of a Flemish town. Declining a peerage from King Charles II, who had spent two nights at Chirk during the Civil War, Sir Thomas Myddelton II, grandfather of the 2nd Baronet, accepted this cabinet instead.

In 1820, an open colonnade beneath the gallery was transformed by the Chester architect Thomas Harrison into a suite of neo-Gothic family apartments. Subsequently redecorated by Pugin, these still contain Harrison's fan-vaulted ceilings and many features made for Chirk in the 1840s, such as the delightful metalwork door plates and knobs, firebacks and gasoliers supplied by John Hardman & Co. to Pugin's designs and Pugin's stone fireplace in the drawing room. Chirk's exceptional library is also in this range.

These neo-Gothic rooms are fitted out in a 1930s idiom to reflect the life of Thomas, 8th Lord Howard de Walden, the shy and eccentric millionaire and patron of the arts who leased Chirk from the Myddeltons from 1911 to 1946. Specially commissioned furniture reproduces that shown in period photographs and in a portrait of the family by Lavery, a Gothic suit of armour commissioned from Felix Joubert, on loan

ABOVE Chirk Castle, built in the thirteenth century, was later converted into a country house, as its generous windows suggest.
OPPOSITE The guard room in Adam's Tower is still largely medieval in appearance, although both the windows would originally have been arrow slits.

from Dean Castle, reflects the 8th Lord's passion for medieval pursuits, and paintings and other works of art on loan from the family, the Tate and the National Gallery of Wales include a portrait of the 8th Lord by Augustus John, a bust by Rodin, and views of the castle and surrounding countryside by Wilson Steer.

Chirk lies in an oak-studded park, landscaped by William Emes in the late eighteenth century. The garden falls away on the east side of the castle. A show of topiary includes a massive hedge cut to resemble a battlemented wall; a sunken rose garden is centred on a sundial; and a mixed border flanking an expanse of grass was established by Colonel and Lady Margaret Myddelton, who restored the garden after the Second World War. A lime avenue hidden in woodland is the only survival of a seventeenth-century formal layout, and a little pavilion sits at one end of a long terrace, the views from here taking in a great sweep of the Welsh borders.

Clandon Park

Surrey
At West Clandon on the A247,
3 miles (4.8 kilometres) east of
Guildford on the A246

Clandon looks as if it would be more at home on the corner of a piazza in Venice or Florence than set down in the Surrey countryside. A massive four-square block of a house, three storeys high and 11 windows wide on the long garden facade, it is built in the reddest of brick with stone dressings and with a central pedimented section of stone on the entrance front. There is a roofline balustrade, but nothing rises above it to relieve the austere geometry of the building.

This individual Georgian country house, built in about 1731, owes its appearance to the Italian Giacomo Leoni and is one of only five surviving buildings by this Venetian architect in England. The interior is as grand as the exterior, its most impressive feature being the richly decorated formal Marble Hall rising through two storeys. Here, the proportions are Palladian, with an impression of light and space, but some of the decoration is decidedly baroque. Classical statues are set in niches at the level of the first floor, but above them is a freely

modelled theatrical plasterwork ceiling by Artari and Bagutti. Life-like slaves supporting the central relief are perched on the cornice with one leg over the edge, as if they could leap down a any moment. Decorated in shades of white, and with a marble floor and intricately carved marble chimeypieces over the two fireplaces, the hall appears cool and serene, refreshingly so on a hot August afternoon. Leoni even extended the marble floor into the grand saloon next door, as if Clandon were a Mediterranean villa.

Clandon was built for Thomas, 2nd Baron Onslow, to replace the Elizabethan house his great-grandfather had acquired in 1641, and it has remained in the family ever since. The Onslows have traditionally followed political careers; the three who served as Speakers of the House of Commons are commemorated in portraits in the Speaker's Parlour. Here too is the 'vinegar' bible that Arthur Onslow, Speaker from 1728–61 and the most famous of the three, presented to St Margaret's, Westminster, its name deriving from a misprint in the parable of the vineyard. The Maori meeting house in the grounds, its steeply pitched thatched roof reaching almost to the ground, is a memorial to another eminent Onslow, the 4th Earl, who was governor of New Zealand from 1888–92 and who also rescued Clandon from half a century of neglect by his great-uncle.

Most of the original contents have been sold or removed over the years, but Clandon is now filled with magnificent furniture, porcelain, textiles and carpets acquired by the connoisseur Mrs David Gubbay in the 1920s and 1930s. Apart from the English eighteenth-century furniture, which includes fine satinwood and marquetry pieces, the most striking feature of the collection is the array of seventeenth- and eighteenth-century porcelain Chinese birds. About 50 of these vividly plumaged creatures perch on baroque brackets or sit on tables and mantelpieces, the many species represented including a pair of elegant fragile cranes in the Green Drawing Room and brilliantly blue parrots, red and green pheasants and plump ducks in the Hunting Room. A spectacular phoenix presides over the state bedroom, where the four-poster and accompanying chairs were probably made for Sir Richard Onslow, father of the builder of the house. Clandon now also houses the Queen's Royal Surrey Regimental Museum in the basement.

OPPOSITE TOP These enchanting ducks are from a large collection of porcelain Chinese birds which are on display throughout Clandon Park.
OPPOSITE BELOW The Venetian wall lanterns in the Marble Hall were probably introduced in the 1870s, when the hall was furnished as a drawing room.

RIGHT The Palladian-style entrance front, built c.1731, is more typical of Italian piazzas than English country houses, but reflects the fashion of the period.

Clevedon Court

Somerset
1½ miles (2.4 kilometres) east of
Clevedon, on the B3130

During the nineteenth century, the seaside village of Clevedon was transformed into a fashionable resort with Italianate villas, a pier and a Royal Hotel. But the Eltons of Clevedon Court who had done so much to improve the town lived on in the remarkable medieval manor that Abraham Elton I, a Bristol merchant, had acquired in 1709.

Seen from the south, Clevedon is a picturesque assemblage of low, stone-built ranges, mullioned windows, steeply pitched roofs and tall chimneys, all set against the thick woods of Court Hill. Despite some later additions, Sir John de Clevedon's early fourteenth-century house has survived virtually unchanged, its buttressed walls and the portcullis groove on the projecting two-storey porch suggesting that he needed to build with defence in mind. At the north-east corner of the house is a massive four-storey tower, with arrow-slit windows, which may be earlier than the rest of the building but is probably part of Sir John's fourteenth-century work. Carved out of the hillside and rising sharply behind the house are terraced gardens, planted with tender shrubs and adorned with two summerhouses.

Finely crafted fourteenth-century arches on the right of the traditional screens passage bisecting the house were openings to the medieval buttery, kitchen and pantry. To the left is the great hall, now embellished with an eighteenth-century coved ceiling and thickly hung with a mixed bag of Elton family portraits. Sir Abraham, the 1st Baronet, dressed in his scarlet robes as Mayor of Bristol, proudly surveys the descendants who were to enrich Clevedon with literary and artistic associations. A cartoon of William Makepeace Thackeray at the top of the stairs, a shock of white hair standing out from his head and pince-nez on his nose, recalls the novelist's friendship with Sir Charles, the 6th Baronet, a gifted poet whose elegy for his two drowned sons moved his

contemporaries to tears. Sir Charles's youngest daughter Jane, with whom Thackeray fell hopelessly in love, was immortalised as Lady Castlewood in *Henry Esmond*, much of which was written in the house. The poet-baronet's circle also included Lamb and Coleridge, and Tennyson composed his elegy 'In Memoriam' for Sir Charles's nephew Arthur Hallam, who was a close friend of Tennyson and died tragically young.

The family's artistic streak appeared again in Sir Edmund Elton, whose Eltonware pots and vases made of clay from the estate, most of them in rich, dark colours but some pieces of a striking sea-blue with metallic glazes, are displayed in the old kitchen and whose vivid portrait by Emmeline Deane hangs in the hall. This remarkable self-taught man began his career as a potter in about 1880, building up an international reputation for his work. Fragile glass walking sticks, some shot through with spirals and twists of colour, glass rolling pins and improbable pipes tinged rose-pink, crimson and blue are part of the collection of high-quality local Nailsea glass which is also shown in the house.

Another side of Victorian Britain emerges on the stairs, where boldly patterned wallpaper by G.F. Bodley shows off a number of prints and engravings illustrating triumphs of engineering in the late eighteenth and nineteenth centuries, from Abraham Darby's iron bridge at Coalbrookdale, constructed in the 1770s, to the Menai Strait, Severn and Clifton suspension bridges and a host of viaducts and aqueducts that were vital to the achievements of the age. A tall red and green Eltonware candlestick, designed with Sir Edmund's characteristic flair, stands in the tiny first-floor chapel that was part of John de Clevedon's manor and originally consecrated in 1321. A net of stone tracery across the south wall, filled with brilliantly coloured Victorian stained glass by Clayton and Bell, not only recalls the patron saint of fishermen to whom the chapel was originally dedicated but also the Bristol Channel only a mile (1.6 kilometres) or so to the west, where the little islands of Flat Holm and Steep Holm stand out black against the sea in the light of a setting sun.

ABOVE LEFT The window of Clevedon Court's medieval chapel, filled with a net of stone tracery, stands out on the south front of this ancient house.
OPPOSITE The interior of Clevedon Court's chapel, showing the stained glass by Clayton and Bell and the tall candlestick from the pottery set up here by Sir Edmund Elton in the 1880s.

Cliveden

Buckinghamshire
3 miles (4.8 kilometres) upstream
from Maidenhead, 2 miles
(3.2 kilometres) north of Taplow
and the A4

This three-storey Italianate palace floating on a chalk terrace high above the River Thames is a *tour de force* by Sir Charles Barry, who is best known for designing the Houses of Parliament. Built in 1850–1 for the Duke and Duchess of Sutherland, it replaced two earlier houses that had been destroyed by fire, the first a Restoration house by William Winde for the 2nd Duke of Buckingham, which burned down in 1795, the second a Georgian-style house designed in 1827–30 for Sir George Warrender by the Edinburgh architect William Burn, who made use of the foundations and surviving wings of the earlier building. Cliveden had just been sold to the Sutherlands when it was burned down again in 1849. The smoke from the fire alerted Queen Victoria as she came out of chapel at Windsor and she sent fire engines from the castle, which is only 5 miles (8 kilometres) away, but the house was largely gutted. An inscription running below the roofline records the seventeenth-century building, much of whose character and shape Barry preserved, as well as the construction of the present mansion. The two wings surviving from the original house, added on by Thomas Archer for the Earl of Orkney, Cliveden's new owner, in 1706 and linked to the main block by curved corridors, flank a great sweep of gravel on the entrance front, from where the drive, shaded by an avenue of limes, runs straight to an extravagant marble fountain by Thomas Waldo Story. Ornate

stables on the west side of the forecourt, with a top-heavy clock-tower rising high above them, were added in the 1860s.

From the south, Cliveden is more of a piece and more imposing. Here, Barry's main block, with an urn-studded roofline parapet, rises grandly over a long arcaded terrace, 28 arches wide, which extends far beyond it on either side. A legacy of the Restoration house, this magnificent feature was embellished in the eighteenth century by a central double staircase that descends in elegant elbows of stone to a grassy platform. Immediately below the arcade, on a bank above the grass, is the weathered stonework and mellow brick of an early seventeenth-century balustrade, its central opening framed by elaborate pedestals, which was brought here from the Villa Borghese in Rome in 1896.

The Borghese balustrade was introduced by William Waldorf, later 1st Viscount Astor, who bought Cliveden in 1893. Lord Astor also commissioned J.L. Pearson, then in his mid-seventies, and his son Frank to remodel the interior of the house, but some of the painted decoration introduced by the Duchess of Sutherland still survives on the staircase ceiling, where figures by the French émigré artist Auguste Hervieu depict the Sutherlands' four children in the guise of the seasons. Of the three rooms shown (Cliveden is now a hotel), the most seductive is the French dining room, lined with green and gold rococo panelling and with a marble chimneypiece and painted overdoors, all of which came from a mid-eighteenth-century hunting lodge near Paris. Pearson's capacious, low-ceilinged, oak-panelled hall, with a carved stone chimneypiece of c.1525 from a French chateau at one end and early eighteenth-century Brussels tapestries on the walls, is dominated by Sargent's vivacious portrait of Nancy Astor, wife of the 2nd Viscount. Given the house and its contents as a wedding present by William Waldorf in 1906, Nancy and her husband made Cliveden famous as a centre of literary and political society before the First World War, entertaining Henry James, Rudyard Kipling, Curzon and Churchill here. The house parties continued between the wars, when the so-called Cliveden Set, supporting Chamberlain and appeasement, were seen as politically significant, but the guest list, which included Charlie Chaplin, was as eclectic as ever. Only a few years later, during the Second World War, Lord Astor decided to give Cliveden to the

ABOVE Barry's south front is carried on Winde's arcaded terrace.
OPPOSITE The rococo panelling in Cliveden's seductive French dining room came from an eighteenth-century hunting lodge outside Paris.

National Trust, but the family continued to live here until 1966, and it was during these years that Cliveden was caught up in a sensational political scandal. It was here, in 1961, that John Profumo, Secretary of State for War, began his liaison with the call-girl Christine Keeler, a relationship that was to end his political career and seriously undermine the government of the day when it was revealed, two years later, that Keeler was also having an affair with the Soviet naval attaché Evegeny Ivanov.

The rustic cottage where Christine Keeler stayed lies in the extensive wooded grounds that surround the house and stretch down to the river. There are long walks and drives through the trees and magical views over the river and its still pastoral valley. Much of the landscaping dates from the early eighteenth century. The box-hedged parterre on the great grass terrace to the south of the house was also first devised, by Orkney himself, at this time. The 1st Viscount Astor, as well as introducing the Borghese balustrade, was responsible for the informal water garden, with stepping stones leading to a pagoda on an island, and for converting the Octagon Temple, one of two ornamental buildings designed by Giacomo Leoni for Lord Orkney, into a family chapel and mausoleum. The magnificent yew maze which Astor sketched out the year he came to Cliveden has recently been replanted.

Coleton Fishacre

Devon
2 miles (3.2 kilometres) from
Kingswear; take Lower Ferry road,
turn off at the tollhouse

Near the mouth of the Dart estuary, on the headlands east of the river, a deep combe runs steeply down to the wooded cliffs above Pudcombe Cove. At the top of the valley, with its back against the slope, is a long, low house, with mullioned windows, tall chimneys and steep tiled roofs. Below, filling a natural amphitheatre, is a richly planted garden. Architectural near the house, with terraces, steps and walls continuing the lines of the building, the garden becomes wilder and more jungle-like as it nears the sea. Both house and garden were created in the 1920s for Rupert and Lady Dorothy D'Oyly Carte, who had spotted the valley while sailing along the coast and saw its potential for a place in the country. Son of the impresario who promoted Gilbert and Sullivan, Rupert was by then running the company that produced their operettas and

BELOW Set at the head of a small Devon valley running down to the sea, Coleton Fishacre was built in the 1920s as a weekend retreat and includes accommodation for a chauffeur and the family Bentley.

also his father's other enterprise, the Savoy Hotel. While Lady Dorothy lived at Coleton Fishacre, Rupert came down from London for weekends, often bringing distinguished guests such as the conductor Sir Malcolm Sargent. After Rupert's death in 1948, the house was sold and the contents largely dispersed. The present furnishings have mostly been introduced by the National Trust, who have been able to draw on the 1949 inventory and photographic evidence.

The house, its walls now softened by climbers and shrubs, is built of Dartmouth shale quarried from the combe and roofed with Delabole slates. Begun in 1923, it was designed by Oswald Milne, a former protégé of Sir Edwin Lutyens, in an Arts and Crafts idiom, with much attention to craftsmanship and materials and with a flowing roofline that unites the rather rambling layout. While his treatment of the exterior looks back to the late nineteenth century, Milne's Art Deco interiors are very much of their time. The impression is of a comfortable, unpretentious family house but also of a kind of spare modernism, relieved by strong splashes of colour, original honeycomb ceiling lights and other details. Rooms are low ceilinged, walls are often roughly plastered, with smooth coves marking junction points, and there are deep windowsills lined with black Staffordshire tiles and much use of limed oak and pine. Long passages on both floors are bland and impersonal, but the main rooms have individuality and character.

At the west end of the house, angled out from the main building so as to give clear views over the garden, is the saloon. Entered down a theatrical flight of steps, and almost 12 metres (40 feet) long, the room is dramatically furnished in yellow and green, including original carpets made in the 1930s by the designer Marion Dorn. A little library filling the bay on the garden front is fitted out with pine shelves and is dominated by George Spencer Hoffman's delightfully rose-tinted bird's-eye view of Coleton Fishacre, setting the house and combe in an enchanting blue-green patchwork of fields and lanes bounded by the sea. The original ultramarine scagliola table top and lapis lazuli bell-push in the dining room at the east end of the house bring the sea indoors and, whenever the weather was clement enough, meals were taken in the airy vine-hung loggia, with views deep into the valley, which lies beyond.

Upstairs, where almost none of the D'Oyly Cartes' furniture survives, the rooms have been fitted out with 1930s-style oak

pieces from Heal's. Lady Dorothy's bedroom has been re-created from photographs and the black-and-white floral fabric designed by Raoul Dufy that was used for the curtains, cushions and seat-covers, and the near-black carpet, have been reproduced. Original features include splashes of colour from blue-green glass tiles round the basins in every room and period bathrooms with sunken baths and pictorial tiles by the young Edward Bawden. A glitter of gold on the stairs comes from the gleaming cupolas and crosses in a painting of St Mark's, Venice by W.R. Sickert, which had belonged to Bridget D'Oyly Carte and has been loaned back by the British Council. In the substantial servants' quarters at the east end of the house, a double sink in the kitchen is supported on sections of the railway track that was used to bring stone from the garden quarry.

Even before the house was completed, Rupert and Lady Dorothy were planting shelter belts to protect the valley from the prevailing wind and together they planned every detail of the garden, capitalising on the drama of the site, with its panoramic views, and on the presence of a little stream rushing headlong to the sea. Paths contour round the sides of the combe, follow the stream, or zigzag steeply up and down, with steps linking different levels. An upper path from the lawn by the loggia leads along the north side of the valley to the vine-hung gazebo, perched high above the quarry. The lower garden is spread out below, filled with colour in spring from a display of rhododendrons, azaleas, magnolias, dogwoods, camellias and Chilean fire trees.

BELOW Art Deco alabaster light fittings, a cool green 1930s carpet by Marion Dorn, and the strong yellow cushions in the Saloon at Coleton Fishacre offset the spare modernism of walls and ceiling.

Corfe Castle

Dorset
On the A351 Wareham–Swanage road

The ruins of Corfe Castle rise like jagged teeth from the summit of a steep chalk hill that guards the only natural route through the Purbeck Hills. Although now reduced to broken walls and towers, this monument to the power of medieval kings is still architecturally striking and still dominates the little village huddled below. Strategically placed and the most defensible of all English castles, Corfe was eventually undone by treachery, not by the might of a besieging army.

Although there may have been a royal hunting lodge at Corfe in Saxon times and there is a tradition that the child-king Edward the Martyr was murdered here in 978, the castle was begun by William the Conqueror, whose fortifications formed part of the network of carefully placed strongholds with which he consolidated his hold on his new kingdom after 1066. These early Norman defences were gradually strengthened, with wooden features such as the original timber palisade being slowly replaced in stone. The massive keep crowning the hilltop, still rising some 22 metres (70 feet) in dramatic fingers of stone, was completed during the reign of Henry I, who imprisoned his elder brother Robert, Duke of Normandy here in 1106. The tower-studded curtain wall looping round the crest of the hill was a later addition, dating from the early years of the reign of King John (1199–1216), when Corfe's position so close to the south coast became of considerable importance in the renewed war with France. After the loss of Normandy in 1204, the castle was in the first line of the king's defences against a French invasion.

In a time when monarchs would travel round their kingdoms administering justice and enforcing loyalty by their presence, Corfe was a centre for government and administration as well as a stronghold. Part of the huge sum of £1,400 spent on building operations at Corfe during John's reign went to construct the king's 'Gloriette', a tower-house arranged round a courtyard in the topmost inner ward. The quality of the surviving masonry shows that this was a building of distinction, a compactly planned domestic residence fit for a monarch, with a great hall, chapel and parlour, and chambers for the queen overlooking a garden.

Apart from a brief period in the mid-sixteenth century, Corfe remained in royal hands until Elizabeth I sold it to Sir Christopher Hatton. About 50 years later the castle and estate were bought by Sir John Bankes, a staunch Royalist, who also purchased the neighbouring property of Kingston Lacy. Of major strategic importance to both sides in the Civil War, Corfe was twice besieged. In 1643 Lady Bankes, who must have been a woman of strong character, held the castle against a force of local Parliamentarians in her husband's absence, but in the winter of 1645–6 Corfe was again attacked and fell through the treachery of one of the defenders, who arranged for enemy troops, disguised as reinforcements, to enter the castle. The victorious Roundhead colonel, impressed by Lady Bankes's courage, not only allowed the garrison to depart but also permitted his spirited opponent to take the keys of the castle with her; they now hang in the library at Kingston Lacy. Corfe was deliberately ruined, leaving only the romantic remains that inspired one of Turner's evocative watercolours.

BELOW A great ditch dug in 1207 and a formidable towered gatehouse guarded the approaches to Corfe's massive keep in the innermost part of the castle.
OPPOSITE The ruins of Corfe Castle, standing high on the chalk ridge crossing the Isle of Purbeck, are dominated by the remains of the great twelfth-century keep at its heart.

Cotehele

Cornwall
On the west bank of the Tamar,
1 mile (1.6 kilometres) west of
Calstock by footpath (6 miles/
9.6 kilometres by road), 8 miles
(12.8 kilometres) south-west of
Tavistock

The River Tamar, dividing Devon from Cornwall, has proved one of the most effective natural boundaries in England. Until 1962, when a suspension bridge was opened at the mouth of the river to link Plymouth and Saltash, the first road crossing was 15 miles (24 kilometres) upstream as the crow flies, but almost double that distance following the twists and turns of the river. For the villages and hamlets along its banks, the Tamar was for centuries the only effective route to the outside world. So it was for this Tudor courtyard house built by Sir Richard Edgcumbe and his son Sir Piers between 1485 and c.1540.

Low granite ranges set round three courtyards lie at the head of a steep valley running down to the river. The approach, past Sir Richard's massively buttressed barn and through a battlemented gateway tower, the arch of which is just wide enough to admit a loaded packhorse, signals the ancient character of the place. The rooms are small and mostly dark, reached by flights of worn stone steps and through massive wooden doors in granite archways. Three Tudor windows light the dais end of Sir Richard's medieval great hall, where an oak refectory table is set in the middle of the rough lime-ash floor and whitewashed walls rise the height of the house to a decorative timber roof. Adam and Eve are carved on one of the early seventeenth-century chairs at either end of the table, and the walls are hung with a collection of arms and armour that includes Elizabethan matchlocks, Civil War breastplates and lobster-tail helmets as well as some exotic pieces, such as long Indian swords.

The family chambers, with their large Tudor fireplaces and richly coloured hangings used like wallpaper, seem more inviting. On the late seventeenth-century bacchic tapestries adorning the little Punch Room, naked figures treading huge vats of grapes as if indulging in a communal bubble bath are clearly preparing a vintage to fill the arched niches in the cupboard-like wine cellar in one corner. In the Red Room upstairs, rich crimson drapery on the huge four-poster is set off by faded seventeenth-century arras on the walls, children at play with marbles and hoops on three of the panels contrasting with the scene of nightmarish violence by the bed illustrating the death of Remus. Across the landing, steps lead up to the rooms in the three-storey battlemented tower that was added on in 1627. At the top of the tower, reached by a steeply winding stair, are two bedrooms, one of them reputedly slept in by Charles I in 1644 on his march from Liskeard to Exeter, while some intriguing and exotic ebony furniture in the old drawing room that fills the floor below, once thought to be Tudor, is now regarded as having come from southern India, and to have been made, in some cases, as long ago as the early 1600s. Only a few decades after the addition of the tower, at the end of the seventeenth century, the family deserted Cotehele for Mount Edgcumbe, their much grander seat overlooking Plymouth Sound, and the old house was left largely undisturbed for 200 years, although the antiquarian interest of the place was already being recognised in the eighteenth century, when various royal parties were taken up the Tamar to visit the house. Even when the widow of the 3rd Earl of Mount Edgcumbe returned here in 1862, thus initiating another period of family occupation, much of the house remained unchanged. The east wing was improved and updated to provide modern comforts, such as central heating, but the new work was carefully designed to blend with the old.

This nineteenth-century wing looks over a luxuriant garden, sheltered by woodland, laid out in a valley leading down to the Tamar. At the head of the valley, just below some stone-walled terraces, are a medieval stew pond and a domed dovecote that once provided meat and fish for the community here, and hidden in the woods and set along the river are further reminders of the way the Cotehele estate once operated and of the one-time importance of river traffic.

Cotehele Quay, described in 1819 as 'a very large and commodious quay with a most desirable situation on the river', lies a quarter of a mile (0.4 kilometre) downstream. Clustered round the quay is a group of impressive old grey

stone buildings, one of which houses an exhibition telling the story of the local shipping industry. At the end of the nineteenth century, when strawberries and other soft fruit from growers in the valley were taken over the river to Bere Alston station on the new Plymouth–Tavistock line, the quays would have been regularly visited by the sailing barges that plied the river, one of the last of which, *Shamrock*, is berthed here. Earlier in the century there had been shipments of ore from mines in the wooded Danescombe Valley upstream, the sites of which are now marked by grassy humps and some old mine buildings. These mines, at their peak in 1844–70, were just some of the many which exploited rich sources of copper and arsenic along the Tamar Valley.

The buildings of Cotehele Quay seem too tranquil for this industrial past, but hidden in the woodland across a reedy inlet to one side are the remains of a row of huge lime kilns, now romantically shrouded in greenery but once a source of lethal fumes. A path from here leads through woodland up the tributary valley of the River Morden to another picturesque group of estate buildings, including a three-storey eighteenth-century mill powered by an overshot wheel. This is now in working order and produces stoneground wholemeal flour

OPPOSITE Cotehele is an atmospheric place of small dark rooms, worn stone steps and massive wooden doors, with glimpses of the lushly planted garden from casement windows.
ABOVE The east wing of Cotehele has beautiful views over the valley garden to the River Tamar.

that is sold in the National Trust shop. Here, too, are a wheelwright's shop, with a lathe driven by a huge flywheel, a forge where charcoal smoulders gently in the hearth, a saddler's shop filled with harness, lengths of chain and stirrups, and a sawpit and carpenter's shop.

Above the house, beyond a sloping daffodil meadow, is a building of a different kind. Set in a field is a triangular tower with granite pinnacles and dummy Gothic windows that gives the illusion, from only a short distance away, of being much more substantial than it is and was perhaps built to celebrate the visit of King George III and Queen Charlotte in August 1789. Panoramic views from the top look west to Kit Hill and east to Dartmoor, and in the valley below are the graceful arches of the Calstock Viaduct. This beautiful structure was built to carry the new railway opened in 1908, whose advent killed the river traffic.

Coughton Court

Warwickshire
2 miles (3.2 kilometres) north of
Alcester on the east side of the A435

Only an expanse of grass separates Coughton Court from the main Studley to Alcester road, giving passing motorists a memorable view of the great Tudor gatehouse dominating the entrance facade. Dating from the early years of Henry VIII's reign, when even

in remote countryside on the southern fringes of the Forest of Arden men could at last build to please themselves rather than to protect their property, the gatehouse is a glittering glass lantern, with the stone tracery and gleaming panes of a two-storeyed oriel window stretching the width of the two upper floors. Though Sir George Throckmorton thought it prudent to surround his new house with a moat, this may also have been regarded as a status symbol rather than purely as a means of defence. Less showy Tudor ranges flank two sides of the courtyard beyond the gatehouse, their domestic gabled facades and half-timbered upper storeys a direct contrast to the stone splendour of the gatehouse and a foil for a formal garden planted with white roses in box-edged beds. Lawns framed by avenues of pollarded limes stretch away from the open east side of the court, past two sunken gardens, towards the little River Arrow and peaceful wooded countryside beyond.

The Throckmortons, whose descendants live here still, first came to Coughton Court in 1409 and much of the fascination of the house derives from its continued association with this prominent Roman Catholic family. Increasingly prosperous during the fifteenth and sixteenth centuries, they were to pay a high price for their faith during the reign of Elizabeth I and the years that followed, when Roman Catholicism was associated with treason. In 1584 Francis Throckmorton was executed for his part in a plot to depose Elizabeth and replace her with Mary Queen of Scots. Francis's cousin, Thomas, was more circumspect. Although he lent Coughton to the conspirators in the Gunpowder Plot, he took care to be absent on the night of 5 November 1605 when a small group waited anxiously for news in one of the gatehouse rooms.

Like Baddesley Clinton only a few miles to the north-east, Coughton was a refuge for recusants. Mass continued to be celebrated here and priests were concealed in ingenious hiding places, among them a compartment above the newel stair in the north-east turret, discovered only in 1858, that was furnished with a bed and a folding leather altar. Another reminder of these times is the painted canvas hanging in the room above the hide that displays the arms of all the Catholic

LEFT The magnificent Tudor gatehouse at Coughton Court, with a beautiful double-storeyed oriel window lighting the upper floors, is one of the finest of its kind in England.

gentry who were imprisoned for recusancy during Elizabeth's reign. Other religious memorabilia include a magnificent early sixteenth-century cope of purple velvet embroidered in gold.

Staunchly Royalist during the Civil War, the Throckmortons' loyalty was tested when the house was besieged and occupied by Parliamentary troops in 1643, the rising ground where the Roundhead army placed their guns only too visible in the view west from the top of the gatehouse tower. Two generations later the entire east side of the courtyard was destroyed when Coughton was sacked by a Protestant mob running wild after the flight of James II and it was never subsequently rebuilt. A number of mementoes in the house, including a linen shift that belonged to Mary Queen of Scots in the year she was beheaded and locks of hair from the Old and Young Pretenders, reflect the Throckmortons' allegiance to the Stuart cause.

In later years, partly as a result of prudent marriages, the family fortunes revived. The stone-built Gothick wings on either side of the gatehouse were added in the 1780s by Sir Robert, 4th Baronet, who embarked on an extensive refurbishment of the house when already an old man and who probably also filled in the moat. Sir Robert, whose portrait by Largillière presides over the drawing room, was responsible for the delicate Gothick entrance hall, which he created out of the ground floor of the gatehouse, and for the elegant classical staircase, which is now hung with a magnificent array of early family portraits. Like the Catholic memorabilia and other contents, many of these paintings were brought to Coughton when grander family properties elsewhere were disposed of. There is some fine furniture, including a set of late seventeenth-century walnut-veneered Dutch chairs and a cabinet of the same date with a mirrored recess that was used to hold the Host, while the tapestry bedroom is hung with eighteenth-century pastels of the family, most of them by William Hoare of Bath.

A mid-Victorian Roman Catholic chapel close to the house is one of the family's last building ventures. House and chapel stand cheek by jowl with the ancient parish church just to the south in a group that is an enduring reminder of the divisions bred by religion.

ABOVE Detail of the lattice-paned stained windows, commemorating the marriages of the Throckmorton family with other Catholic families, in the Drawing Room at Coughton Court.

Cragside

Northumberland
13 miles (20.9 kilometres) south-west of Alnwick on the B6341 and 16 miles (26 kilometres) north of Morpeth via the A697

When the inventor and industrialist William Armstrong visited Rothbury in 1863 as a break from the unrelenting pressures of his factory on the River Tyne, he decided to purchase what he could of the secluded Debdon Valley where he had so often wandered as a boy during family holidays. Four years earlier he had seen the army adopt the new gun he had developed after the poor British performance in the Crimean War and, as a result, his prosperous engineering firm was being gradually transformed into a vast industrial concern. Once primarily concerned with hydraulic machines, by the late nineteenth century Armstrong's was an international arms manufacture, rivalled only by Krupps of Germany.

A couple of watercolours showing tall chimneys belching smoke over factory buildings ranged along the Tyne are the only direct reminders of the works that financed the rambling house set high above a ravine on the Debdon burn, with a jumble of gables, soaring chimneys, mullioned windows and half-timbering framed against a wooded hillside. But there are other pointers to the inventive mind of the man who built it. This was the earliest house in the world to be lit by hydroelectricity and water was also used to power a saw-mill, a revolutionary hydraulic lift and even a kitchen spit.

Armstrong's activities are reflected too in the gradual transformation of Cragside, which was originally built, in 1864–6, as a modest weekend retreat. Shortly after the completion of this first building, Armstrong engaged the distinguished architect Richard Norman Shaw, who over the next 15 years turned the house into a country mansion and enriched it with some of his most original work. Shaw's grandest rooms were designed for important overseas clients. The King of Siam, the Shah of Persia and the Crown Prince of Afghanistan all slept in the monumental black walnut bed, with solemn owls carved on the end posts and a massive half-tester which Shaw created for the guest chambers. No doubt they appreciated the plumbed-in washstand and the sunken bath in an alcove in the dressing room next door. A long top-lit gallery with a wooden barrel ceiling leading from the Owl Suite was once hung with the best of Armstrong's Victorian paintings. These were mostly sold after his death, but pictures and sculpture are still set against the deep-red walls, and at the far end is Shaw's *tour de force*, the drawing room completed for a royal visit in 1884. The top-lit cavernous interior is dominated by W.R. Lethaby's Renaissance-style carved marble chimney-piece, with veining in the stone round the fireplace suggesting running water. Inglenooks with red leather settees

LEFT Cragside, dramatically set on a steep wooded hillside, was designed as a romantic assemblage of stone-mullioned windows, gables, half-timbering and soaring chimneystacks.
OPPOSITE James Ramsay's portrait of William Armstrong, painted when he was studying law, as his father wanted, hangs over the fireplace in the study.

are set on either side and white lamps hang in clusters from the ceiling like bunches of snowdrops.

The little rooms of the original lodge and Shaw's early additions for the family are quite different in character. His beautiful and unusual library with magnificent views of the glen is perhaps the most harmonious room in the house, the warm reds and browns of the furnishings setting off brilliant-blue tiles and onyx panels framing the fireplace and glowing enamelled electric lamps along the low bookcases.

Armstrong alone seems to have been responsible for Cragside's wildly romantic setting, for which the hillside was blasted to expose craggy rock formations and over 688 hectares (1,700 acres) of pleasure grounds created by planting millions of conifers, rhododendrons and alpines on what were originally bare slopes. A pinetum was established in the valley and on the steep slope below the house, like an expanse of scree above the burn, is a huge rock garden, planted with heathers, alpines and shrubs. On a south-facing slope on the other side of the valley, reached across Armstrong's steel footbridge and up a steep path from the stream, is a formal terraced garden with ferneries, a fruit house and a display of Victorian carpet bedding. An intricate network of paths snakes across the estate, with dramatic views to the Cheviots from the higher routes, and a scenic drive takes in the lakes over 100 metres (340 feet) above the house which were used to feed the hydroelectric turbine.

Croft Castle and Parkland

Herefordshire
5 miles (8 kilometres) north-west of Leominster, 9 miles (14.4 kilometres) south-west of Ludlow

This engaging house, with slender corner towers and rough stone walls, has a long history. Dating back to a time when this glorious country on the Welsh borders was insecure and torn by rebellion, the shell of the house is the four-square castle round a central courtyard which the Croft family, who came here from Normandy some years before the Conquest, built to defend their property. Much modified since, Croft was massively remodelled in the eighteenth century and features from various periods contribute to its present picturesque appearance. In the centre of the entrance front, Georgian bays with playful Gothick sash windows frame a mock-Jacobean castellated porch, added in 1913. The approach is through what appears to be a medieval archway, but this too was a more recent addition, probably built in the 1790s.

The country house takes over inside. Thomas Farnolls Pritchard, the Shrewsbury architect who designed the world's first iron bridge at Coalbrookdale, was responsible for the light-hearted Gothick interiors introduced in 1765, his pointed arches in white plaster on a coffee background on the stairs strongly reminiscent of a row of church windows. Even the stair balustrade looks ecclesiastical: column clusters forming the newel posts are miniature versions of those that might support the vaulting of a nave. Rare and valuable furniture in the same style includes a set of Gothick chairs in dark oak in the long gallery that would be suitable props for a dramatisation of Mary Shelley's *Frankenstein* or Horace Walpole's *The Castle of Otranto*. T.F. Pritchard also had a hand in the similarly striking but quite different decoration of the Blue Room, where *trompe-l'oeil* gold rosettes stud blue Jacobean panelling. Family portraits hang in almost every room, including a beautiful study by Gainsborough of Elizabeth Cowper, wife of Sir Archer Croft, the colouring all brown and red, and works by Lawrence and Philip de Laszlo. Crofts also dominate the little church of rough local stone set just east of the house. The most memorable of the many family memorials here is an early sixteenth-century altar tomb to Sir Richard and Dame Eleanor Croft, with realistic effigies showing the couple in extreme old age.

Thickly wooded parkland surrounds the castle, as it has done for centuries, the great avenues for which Croft is famous including a line of Spanish chestnuts, in which some of the trees may be 350 years old, stretching about half a mile (0.8 kilometre) to the west, and oaks and beeches flanking the long entrance drive. An ancient lime avenue that once shadowed the chestnuts has now been replanted. While most of the park escaped the attentions of an improver of the 'Capability' Brown school, the late eighteenth-century landscaping of Fish Pool Valley in the Picturesque mode was a direct reaction to his ideas. This little steep-sided glen planted with mixed deciduous and evergreen trees has a dramatic wilderness quality, which is in perfect accord with the castle's Gothick interiors. Another notable feature of the estate is the Iron Age hill-fort of Croft Ambrey, set on a ridge a mile (1.6 kilometres) north of the house.

RIGHT The elegant staircase hall at Croft Castle, with its delicate Gothick plasterwork, was created by T.F. Pritchard in the 1760s when he remodelled the interior of the house.

ABOVE Many members of the Croft family, who came to this beautiful place before the Conquest, are commemorated in the tiny medieval and Tudor church that lies close by the castle.

Dudmaston Estate

Shropshire
At Quatt, 4 miles (6.4 kilometres)
south-east of Bridgnorth on the
A442

Looking west over the River Severn to the Clee Hills, Dudmaston lies close to some of the most beautiful countryside in Britain. Built for Sir Thomas Wolryche in the late seventeenth century, it is an unpretentious four-square house attributed to Francis Smith of Warwick, with some later alterations. Sir Thomas's line died out in the eighteenth century, but descendants of his sister Anne, who took the name Wolryche-Whitmore, continued to live here. Today, the small-scale intimate family rooms display the collections and decorative taste of Sir George Labouchere and his wife, Rachel Hamilton-Russell, who inherited the property from her uncle, Geoffrey Wolryche-Whitmore, in 1966. Sir George was responsible for the unusual assemblage of twentieth-century painting and sculpture, while Lady Labouchere introduced historic art and furniture.

Lady Labouchere's interest in botanical art, continuing a long family tradition, is shown in the collection of works by

such great exponents as Pierre-Joseph Redouté (1759–1840), P. Reinagle (1749–1833), G.D. Ehret (1708–70) and W.H. Fitch (1817–92). Formal studies by these masters and glowing flower canvases by the eighteenth-century Dutch painter Jan Van Os in the library contrast with the fresh, fluid approach adopted by Mary Grierson (1912–2012), who was the official botanical artist at Kew for 12 years. A similar love of nature is revealed in the displays of photographs and drawings by the naturalist Frances Pitt (1888–1964), who lived in this area all her life and was a close friend of the Wolryche-Whitmore family. A notebook in her neat writing meticulously records her finds.

Two rooms devoted to twentieth-century painting and sculpture, including abstracts by Ben Nicholson, sculptures by Henry Moore and Barbara Hepworth, and some rather forbidding Spanish paintings acquired by Sir George while he was Ambassador in Madrid, set a more sombre tone. Apart from flashes of red and yellow from two Poliakoffs and Alan Davie's still-life in red, green and orange, colours are muted: grey and black, green and brown. Chinese porcelain and French furniture are also fruits of years in the diplomatic service, as are some of Lady Labouchere's delightful topographic watercolours, which include pictures of Barcelona, Bruges, India and China, among them Edward Lear's tiny study of the gardens of Government House, Calcutta, and William Alexander's cameo of a smoking Chinaman, as well as atmospheric English landscapes and local views of Bridgnorth and Shrewsbury.

Associations of a different kind are reflected in the gallery devoted to the connection between Lady Labouchere and the Darbys of Coalbrookdale, cradle of the Industrial Revolution. By a strange coincidence, Dudmaston is also linked with the modern microchip revolution, as Charles Babbage, the father of the computer, married a daughter of the house in 1814 and spent much time here.

The great oaks and cedars on the terraced lawns stretching down to the lake known as the Big Pool on the garden side of the house are reminders of another pioneer, Geoffrey Wolryche-Whitmore, whose enlightened approach to forestry on the estate in the first half of the twentieth century earned him a national reputation.

OPPOSITE A room at Dudmaston displays the Laboucheres' collection of twentieth-century British and French art, including Barry Flanagan's 'Boxing Hares' and works by Henry Moore and Jean Dubuffet.
ABOVE These decorative gates, commissioned by Sir George and Rachel Labouchere in 1993 to mark their golden wedding, echo the display of modern art and sculpture at Dudmaston.

Dunham Massey

Cheshire
3 miles (4.8 kilometres) south-west
of Altrincham, off the A56

Dunham Massey reflects long occupation by the Booth and Grey families and the gradual enlargement and rebuilding of the Elizabethan and Jacobean core. A finely crafted mechanical model of the solar system, showing how the six known planets moved round the Sun (Uranus and Neptune were yet to be discovered), is the centrepiece of the library that was created for George Booth, 2nd Earl of Warrington, as part of extensive remodelling of the house by the obscure John Norris in the early eighteenth century. The earl's cipher appears on many of the faded bindings in the oak bookcases and over the fireplace is a dramatic, in-depth carving of the Crucifixion by the young Grinling Gibbons, who based it on a painting by Tintoretto and set his agonised figures in a tranquil floral border.

Apart from the south front, with its sash windows and Edwardian dormers, the exterior of Dunham Massey is much as George Booth left it, an attractive red-brick building, long and low, set round two courtyards and still protected by the medieval moat that embraced the earlier house. The sombre, low-ceilinged, oak-lined chapel and the magnificent collection of Huguenot silver are both reflections of the Booth family's ardent Protestantism. The glittering display now set out in the Rose Room includes a wine cistern made in 1701 by Philip Rollos, who created handles in the form of the wild boars of the Booth crest.

Dunham Massey's exceptional Edwardian interiors were commissioned by William Grey, 9th Earl of Stamford, whose family acquired the estate through the marriage of George Booth's daughter, Mary, to the 4th Earl. With advice from the connoisseur and furniture historian Percy Macquoid, and the outstanding firm of Morant & Co., decorators to Edward VII, the 9th Earl and his wife created rooms that rival the appeal of those from 200 years earlier. In their long saloon with a bay window arching out into the garden, Grey family portraits hang against deep-green walls suggested by Macquoid, who also advised dyeing the two mossy Donegal carpets and reupholstering the fine early eighteenth-century walnut chairs, from the same period as the magnificent walnut chests on show elsewhere in the house, to match the room. Yellow damask curtains hanging at the long sash windows give the

ABOVE The early eighteenth-century brick south front of Dunham Massey was substantially remodelled in 1905, when the elaborate stone centrepiece and dormer windows were added.

OPPOSITE The great hall is a survival of the Tudor house, but its decoration, including the deep yellow of the walls and the plaster frieze, is largely Edwardian, as is the upholstery. The large Kangxi vases framing the fireplace were probably bought specially for the room in the early eighteenth century.

final touch in a colour scheme that could well have been created for Bunthorne in Gilbert and Sullivan's *Patience*. The 9th Earl also commissioned J. Compton Hall to create an elaborate neo-Jacobean entrance front loosely based on the one at Sudbury Hall.

A remarkable series of early views of Dunham Massey, recording its gradual transformation from 1696 to c.1750, hang in the great gallery and here, too, is Guercino's early seventeenth-century *Mars, Venus and Cupid, with Saturn as Time*, possibly purchased by the 2nd Earl of Warrington. The young 5th Earl of Stamford, when on his Grand Tour, arranged for the two huge caricatures of his travels by Thomas

Patch which hang in the early eighteenth-century tearoom. Commissioned as light relief from the serious study of Italian art and culture, they are an irreverent look at the earl and his friends.

A courtyard beside the house contains the kitchens and other domestic offices and there is an Elizabethan watermill beyond the eighteenth-century stables. A delightful gabled building of warm red brick with mullioned windows, the mill is the only visible survival from the time of Sir George Booth, 1st Baronet. Originally used for grinding corn, in c.1860 it was refitted as a saw-mill and estate workshop. The overshot waterwheel is fed from a continuation of the lake in front of the house and the Victorian machinery, including a big frame saw for cutting up trees known as the Dunham Ripper, is all in working order.

An ancient deer-park surrounding the house is enclosed by the 2nd Earl's high brick wall and still shaded by trees he established, some of which form a series of radiating avenues. Yews and oaks on the lawns to the east of the house were part of an informal Victorian and Edwardian layout, which has now been re-established and enhanced, with beds of rhododendrons and azaleas and a water garden along the stream feeding the moat. A curious mound just north-west of the house may be the remains of a Norman motte.

Dunster Castle

Somerset
In Dunster, 3 miles (4.8 kilometres)
south-east of Minehead on the
A396, just off the A39

A few miles east of Minehead, a ridge of the Brendon Hills reaches almost to the Bristol Channel, ending in a steep-sided outlier. This natural defensive site was chosen by the Norman William de Mohun for his castle. Besieged for 160 days by Cromwell's troops in the Civil War, Dunster was considered a major threat to the Commonwealth and the regime ordered its complete destruction, sparing only the Jacobean mansion, by the local stonemason William Arnold, which had been built within the walls. Although little trace of the medieval defences survives, Dunster still looks like a castle, with a tangle of towers and battlements rising romantically from the thickly wooded hill. Largely a nineteenth-century vision of what a castle should be, this is a house masquerading as a stronghold, created by Anthony Salvin in 1868–72 for George Fownes Luttrell, whose family had lived here since 1405. Salvin kept the Jacobean mansion, grafting on towers and battlements and remodelling much of the interior.

A steep approach from the village clustered below the tor leads to the fifteenth-century gatehouse. Beyond, a thirteenth-century gateway, the oldest surviving feature of the castle, gives access to what was once the lower ward. Across it, the north facade of the house is dominated by Salvin's great four storey tower, with an octagonal staircase turret, complete with authentic medieval arrow loops, rising above it. The nineteenth-century work blends so well with the Jacobean walls to the right that only details in the New Red sandstone masonry show where one ends and the other begins. Two of the finest features of the interior were commissioned by Colonel Francis Luttrell in the late seventeenth century. He was responsible for the fine oak staircase with naked cherubs and dogs racing through a thick acanthus undergrowth carved on the panels of the balustrade. The work is cunningly dated by the fact that one of the beasts leaps over a clutch of Charles II silver shillings from the 1683–4 issue. The carving is of a very high standard, comparable with that on the staircase at Sudbury Hall, and it may be that the distinguished Edward Pierce, who was engaged at Sudbury, also worked here. Craftsmanship of similar quality is displayed in the plasterwork ceiling in the dining room, also dating from the

BELOW The row of bells in the servants' corridor at Dunster includes one for a room named after Charles II, who is said to have slept at the castle when he came to the West Country as Prince of Wales in 1645.

ABOVE The north front of Dunster Castle, built of red sandstone, owes much to romantic remodelling in 1868–72 by Anthony Salvin, who added towers and battlements to the existing house.

1680s, where a thick encrustation of flowers and foliage almost conceals the creatures hidden in the design. Here a cherub shoots a deer with a bow and arrow; there a winged horse bursts from a blossom. A spider's web of plaster in the hall, the only original Jacobean ceiling to escape remodelling, looks down on an allegorical portrait of Sir John Luttrell, dated 1550, in which he is shown emerging half naked from a stormy sea while sailors abandon a foundering ship behind him. Less enigmatic but equally striking is the set of seventeenth-century painted leather hangings illustrating the story of Antony and Cleopatra which fills Salvin's gallery, the curiously expressionless faces and wooden horses redeemed by the brilliant, glittering colours produced by painting on silver foil.

A deliciously cool Victorian conservatory, a leafy extension of the airy, pale-green drawing room, leads out onto a sheltered south-facing terrace. Although the tor is exposed to westerly winds, the mild maritime climate allows tender plants and shrubs to grow here. Steep paths curling round the hill below the castle are lined with fuchsias and hydrangeas, there is a grove of strawberry trees and huge conifers tower above willows, camellias, rhododendrons and moisture-loving plants along the River Avril in the depths of the valley. A path following the river round the base of the tor leads to Dunster water-mill and an eighteenth-century bridge over the water. There has been a mill on this site since medieval times, but the present building, which has been restored to working order, dates largely from 1779–82.

The grassy platform which was the site of the Norman keep and many rooms in the castle has magnificent views over the surrounding countryside, where a patchwork of small hedged fields rolling away to the hills of Exmoor still looks very much as it is depicted in a set of early eighteenth-century scenes. To the north, the tower of the village church is echoed in the folly on Conygar Hill, with the blue of the Bristol Channel beyond.

Dyrham Park

Gloucestershire
8 miles (12.8 kilometres) north
of Bath, 12 miles (19.3 kilometres)
east of Bristol

After recording the burial of John Wynter in 1688, the local rector drew a thick line across the page. He knew it was the end of an era. Two years previously John's only surviving child, his 36-year-old daughter Mary, had married William Blathwayt, a rising civil servant, and by the end of the century this energetic self-made man had totally transformed the Tudor manor his wife inherited, creating this great mansion set beneath a spur of the Cotswolds. Despite his loyalty to James II in the Glorious Revolution, a rare fluency in Dutch coupled with an unusual gift for administration recommended Blathwayt to William III, for whom he acted as Secretary of State from 1692–1702.

Rebuilt in stages between 1692 and 1705, as and when money was available, Dyrham's contrasting facades reflect Blathwayt's rising fortunes. The earlier west front, with glorious views over the countryside towards Bristol, is an attractive building crowned with a balustrade. Low, one-storey wings, one of which forms a covered passage to the medieval village church, embrace a courtyard terrace. An Italianate double stairway descends from the terrace to a great sweep of grass, and the facade as a whole has continental overtones, as if its architect, the shadowy Frenchman S. Hauduroy, was planning a grand Parisian town house.

By the time Blathwayt constructed the east front with its state apartments, he was important enough to obtain the services of William Talman, Wren's deputy and rival, whose grand baroque facade is proudly surmounted by the Blathwayt eagle. The monumental orangery that extends the range to the south, successfully obscuring the service quarters in the view from the hill above the house, is also Talman's.

The elaborate formal Dutch water garden that once surrounded this palatial mansion has long disappeared. In its place is Charles Harcourt-Masters's beautiful late eighteenth-century park, with groves and clumps of beeches, chestnuts and cedars spilling down the hillsides. But the interior still reflects the taste for Dutch fashions inspired by the new king, which Blathwayt would have had ample opportunity to see at first hand. In Talman's entrance hall bird paintings by Melchior d'Hondecoeter hang against embossed leather

bought in The Hague. Door locks and hinges in the Balcony Room, where the carved panelling was originally painted to resemble marble, are engraved with tulips and daffodils, and characteristic blue and white Delftware, including two impressive pyramidal flower vases intended for the display of prize blooms, is seen throughout the house. Sumptuous crimson and yellow velvet hangings adorning the state bed in the Damask Bedchamber are typical of the rich fabrics and textiles with which Dyrham was once furnished. And then there are the paintings. Cool Dutch interiors, soft land- and seascapes and serene still lifes, including works by Abraham Storck, David Teniers the Younger and Samuel van

Hoogstraeten, feature throughout the house. One of Hoogstraeten's perspective paintings shows a view through an unmistakably Dutch interior, with tiled floors leading to a distant room, where a chair is set by a glowing fire. This painting, like others at Dyrham, came from the London home of Thomas Povey, Blathwayt's uncle, where Pepys, who was a frequent guest, much admired it, and the glazed bookcases in the hall, one of which also came from Povey's home (the other is a copy), are almost identical to those made for Pepys in 1666.

The Hoogstraeten painting was bought back, together with the furniture and other pictures, by Colonel George William Blathwayt, who inherited Dyrham in 1844 after the contents had been dispersed. As part of his scheme to save the house, for which he took out a huge loan, he modernised the servants' quarters set round two courtyards behind the orangery, creating a suite of early Victorian rooms arranged either side of a long passage. Here are the bakehouse, kitchen, wet and dry larders and tenants' hall, where the most important estate tenants dined on rent days. A delicious dairy, with marble shelves and a stone fountain to keep it cool, is lined with blue and brown Delft tiles that were probably re-used from the 1698 domestic offices.

OPPOSITE This vast state bed was made in *c.*1704 in the fashionable Anglo-Dutch style for Blathwayt's new apartments along Dyrham's east front.
BELOW By the time William Blathwayt built Dyrham's east front, he was in a position to engage William Talman, the king's architect, who designed a grand baroque facade crowned by the Blathwayt eagle.

East Riddlesden Hall

West Yorkshire
1 mile (1.6 kilometres) north-east of Keighley on the south side of the B6265, on the north bank of the River Aire and close to the Leeds and Liverpool Canal

Although W.S. Gilbert is said to have based the Bad Baronets in *Ruddigore* on the Murgatroyds of East Riddlesden, it seems the family does not entirely deserve its dubious reputation. Certainly the rich clothier James Murgatroyd, who bought the estate in 1638, was a respected local figure, and it is he who was largely responsible for the present house, set on a bluff above the River Aire. The unusual entrance front is dominated by a striking castellated and pinnacled two-storey porch, with classical columns framing the doorway and with an ecclesiastical rose window at the level of the first floor. To the left stretch the mullioned windows and gabled facades of the square main block of the house, while to the right a great hall that was probably also built by Murgatroyd forms a link to the remains of another substantial wing. Pedimented windows and other classical details on the one surviving facade of this part of the house are the work of Edmund Starkie, James Murgatroyd's great-grandson, who seems to have remodelled the original medieval hall in the 1690s.

Absentee owners from the beginning of the nineteenth century ensured that this fine example of a seventeenth-century Yorkshire manor survived unaltered, although most of the 'Starkie' wing was demolished in 1905 and none of the original contents remains. Virtually empty when it was saved from dereliction by the Briggs brothers of Keighley in 1934 and given to the National Trust, East Riddlesden has been completely refurnished. The panelled family rooms are now filled with locally made period oak pieces, among them a carved and canopied early seventeenth-century cupboard in the dining room, said to be the one described by Emily Brontë in the opening pages of *Wuthering Heights*, and a magnificent oak settle in the drawing room. A late sixteenth-century copper curfew for keeping in the embers of a fire overnight, a grain chest and a shepherd's chair designed with a hutch for a lamb or a dog under the seat are among a number of rare and intriguing objects in the house, and there are also displays of pewter, Dutch and oriental porcelain and some seventeenth-century stumpwork.

The great stone barn in front of the house, one of two shielding the hall from the sprawl of Keighley, is said to be the finest in the north of England. Tradition has it that this is a medieval barn incorporating later masonry from either nearby Kirkstall Abbey or Dalton Priory, and that the present external stone cladding was added by James Murgatroyd, but it is more likely that the whole building was constructed in the seventeenth century. The fish-pond, across which visitors get their first view of the hall, is associated with the ghost of a woman in white, a lady of the manor who drowned here when she was thrown from her horse. Among several other apparitions said to be connected with East Riddlesden is the shadowy figure known as the Grey Lady, reputed to have been shut up in her room to starve to death by her sadistic husband after she had been discovered with her lover.

OPPOSITE The striking two-storey porch on the garden front of East Riddlesden Hall has a doorway flanked by Doric columns and a fine rose window lighting the little room above.
ABOVE The impressive great hall at East Riddlesden Hall, with its carved stone fireplace and period oak furniture, would have been used for receiving visitors in the seventeenth century.

Erddig

Wrexham
2 miles (3.2 kilometres) south
of Wrexham

Visitors to Erddig are given a sense of the country house as a functioning community. Instead of being welcomed at the front door, they are taken through the extensive and atmospheric complex of eighteenth- and nineteenth-century brick outbuildings that formed the estate yards. Here, tools and equipment give a unique picture of how these households and their lands were nurtured day by day. Saws hang on the walls of the pit where timber was cut into manageable widths, the tools in the blacksmith's shop are the very ones that were used to repair the fine eighteenth-century ironwork screen in the formal garden, and the dry laundry sports a mangle in which clothes were pressed using the weight of a box of stones. Similarly, the tour of the house includes the spacious, airy rooms on the attic floor where the servants slept.

Judging by the staff portraits in the servants' hall, which go back to the 1790s, life was agreeable here. One of the housemaids is depicted at the age of 87 and the 75-year-old estate carpenter looks spry enough to wield the axe he carries over his shoulder. Sadly, what was thought to be a portrait of the black coachboy who was at Erddig in the early eighteenth century now appears to be a later fabrication.

The tradition of recording the servants seems to have been started by Philip Yorke I, who inherited the house in 1767 from his great-uncle, the successful London lawyer John Meller. Philip I was also responsible for commissioning James Wyatt to re-face the west front, which had been badly damaged by the westerly gales and driving rain which are a regular feature of the weather here. The rather severe Neo-classical composition of the 1770s on this side of the house contrasts with the warm brickwork of the garden front, where the original late seventeenth-century central block is flanked by wings added by Meller in 1721–4. The length of the facade and the uniform sash windows give this front the look of a row of town houses.

After the architecturally modest exterior, Meller's superb furniture and rich textiles are a surprise, his sets of silvered and walnut chairs and ornate looking-glasses all having been obtained from leading London cabinet-makers. Goblin-like masks smiling wickedly at each other across the head of the

ABOVE The painted seventeenth-century panelling in the white bedroom came from a manor on the estate that was partly burnt down in 1886.

pier glass in the saloon are by the same hand as the carved and gilded birds on the tester of the sumptuous state bed, their exotic plumage echoed by a flock of diminutive painted companions, flashes of brilliant peacock-blue suggesting kingfishers on the wing. More birds perch in the borders of the summery Soho tapestries made for the principal bedroom.

Philip I created the library that now displays his passionate antiquarianism as well as his great-uncle's legal tomes, and he was also responsible for the delightful Chinese wallpaper in the room next to the chapel, with handpainted cameos showing oriental labourers at work. Betty Ratcliffe, companion and maid to Philip I's mother, made the extraordinary Chinese pagoda decorated with mother-of-pearl and the other model buildings in the oak-panelled gallery.

Philip I's concern for the past also led him to preserve the then old-fashioned garden. Although William Emes was employed to landscape the park between 1766 and 1781, contributing the unusual circular waterfall known as the Cup and Saucer, the hanging beech woods and picturesque walks, Philip deliberately retained the formal layout near the house, the essential features of which, such as the enclosing walls, date from 1718–32. With the aid of a bird's-eye view engraved by Thomas Badeslade in 1740, the garden has been reconstructed as it was in the early eighteenth century and is a rare example of a design of the period.

A long gravel path stretching away from the east front, its line emphasised by a double avenue of pleached limes, provides a strong central focus, which is continued by a canal. A decorative wrought-iron screen closes the vista at the far end and magnificent mature limes shade the water. To the north,

apple trees planted in blocks mirror the orderly rows shown on the engraving. Plums, pears, peaches and apricots, most of them varieties listed as growing here in 1718, are trained on the walls, and there are old varieties of daffodils and narcissus in the borders below. A Victorian parterre immediately in front of the house is perfectly in tune with the formal eighteenth-century layout.

BELOW Erddig's rather severe, stone-faced west front, the result of remodelling in the late eighteenth century. is a complete contrast to the warm brickwork on the other side of the house.

Farnborough Hall

Oxfordshire
6 miles (9.6 kilometres) north of Banbury, ½ mile (0.8 kilometre) west of the A423

This honey-coloured stone house, home of the Holbech family for over 300 years, looks out over a well-wooded patchwork of fields and hedgerows to the scarp of Edgehill and the Malvern Hills beyond. It is still largely as created between 1745 and 1750 by William Holbech, who needed a setting for the sculpture and art he had collected on a protracted Grand Tour. Probably with help from his close friend, the gentleman-architect Sanderson Miller, who lived only a few miles away, Holbech remodelled the old manor house acquired by his grandfather, adding long facades with sash windows, pedimented doorways and a roofline balustrade to the earlier classical west front commissioned by his father. The result is harmonious, but there are some amateur touches too, such as floor-level bedroom windows.

The front door opens straight into the Italianate hall. Busts of Roman emperors and of goddesses from classical mythology look down on visitors from their niches high in the walls, there is magnificent rococo plasterwork on the ceiling by the Yorkshireman William Perritt and a copy of a view of Rome by Panini over the fireplace. This fine interior is a prelude to the outstanding decoration in the sunny former saloon, now a family-sized dining room, which was designed specially to house four large canvases of Venice by Canaletto and two of Rome by Panini (now replaced by copies). Here, sinuous, three-dimensional rococo plasterwork, standing out white against the blue walls, clamours for attention. A cornucopia bursts with fruit and flowers over the wall mirror between the windows, a fully strung violin and guns, bows and arrows reflect William's musical and sporting interests, and little dogs with upturned noses are profiled on the plasterwork picture frames set into the walls. The ceiling decoration, white on white, is similarly arresting. Although also by Perritt, whose bill for the room survives, some of the plaster detailing, such as the foliage curling over the mirror as

LEFT The pedimented classical doorway in the 1740s entrance front.
ABOVE The south and west fronts of Farnborough Hall look over the eighteenth-century park.
BELOW One of the two pavilions at Farnborough Hall is ornamented with rich rococo plasterwork.

if embracing it, suggests the work of Roberts of Oxford, or even the hand of the Italian Francesco Vassali. The late seventeenth-century garland of fruit and flowers ringing the domed skylight above the stairs is also very fine, each plaster blossom, grape and pomegranate fashioned individually.

The south front surveys a stretch of grass and trees bordering a long ornamental lake, one of two in the eighteenth-century landscape park. To the south-east William's striking grass terrace stretches along a ridge high above the valley, its smooth sward, hedged with bushy laurel, wide enough for two carriages to pass with ease and adorned with what are probably Sanderson Miller's eye-catchers. A little

pedimented temple, its Ionic columns pleasingly weathered, is almost hidden by trees. Further along the terrace, a curving stone staircase gives access to the upper room in a two-storey domed pavilion, where rococo plasterwork picked out in white against blue echoes the craftsmanship in the house. Perhaps the Italian prisoners treated at the military hospital set up here during the Second World War, who inscribed their names on the obelisk at the end of the terrace, appreciated the panoramic view, now, alas, spoiled by the routing of the M40 through the Warmington Valley below the house.

BELOW Farnborough's entrance hall has a fine rococo plasterwork ceiling and classical busts in niches set round the room.

Felbrigg Hall, Gardens and Estate

Norfolk
Near Felbrigg village, 2 miles (3.2 kilometres) south-west of Cromer, off the A148 Holt Road

In 1738 William Windham II, accompanied by his multi-talented tutor Benjamin Stillingfleet, whose sartorial habits are the origin of the term 'bluestocking', set off on a protracted five-year Grand Tour. As soon as William succeeded to Felbrigg in 1749, he asked James Paine to remodel part of the interior to provide a suitable setting for the paintings he had acquired, some of the best of which now hang in the intimate Cabinet Room in the west wing. Here small Dutch and Italian canvases, including 26 delightful gouaches by Giovanni Battista Busiri, are set three deep on crimson damask, displayed in frames that William commissioned and in a carefully balanced arrangement which he worked out. The young William also acquired Samuel Scott's panoramic *Old London Bridge* and the companion piece of the Tower of London, both of which may have been painted for their present positions in the drawing room, and the huge canvas by William van der Velde showing a battle at sea in 1673.

Paine's sumptuous and beautiful eighteenth-century interiors, with some flowing rococo plasterwork by Joseph Rose the Elder, lie within a largely seventeenth-century building that was the work of William's great-grandfather, Thomas Windham, a descendant of the wealthy merchant who had purchased the estate in 1459, and his son William Windham I. Thomas was responsible for Felbrigg's haunting Jacobean entrance front, the plaster-covered brick and flint with stone dressings of which it is built now attractively weathered and lichened. A projecting central porch, with classical columns supporting nothing framing the front door, rises the height of the house; a huge mullioned window incorporating fragments of English and continental stained glass lights the great hall to the left of the porch; and banks of octagonal brick chimneys rise from the roof. Most striking are the huge stone letters carved into the parapet crowning the façade, which spell out the inscription GLORIA DEO IN EXCELSIS. This balanced composition is almost certainly the work of Robert Lyminge of Blickling.

Paine's Gothick library was intended to complement this Jacobean work. The exceptional collection now housed here,

ABOVE James Paine's eighteenth-century interiors at Felbrigg include the drawing room, where he complemented the existing plasterwork ceiling with finely carved swags of fruit above the doors.

which was started by William Windham II, owes much to his politician son, whose friendship with Dr Johnson is commemorated in books once owned by the learned lexicographer.

Although William Windham I was building only 50 years later than his father, a mid-century revolution in architectural styles resulted in an extraordinary contrast between the two phases of work. Walking round the house, there is an abrupt transition from the romantic Jacobean front to the ordered classicism of the late seventeenth-century west wing designed by William Samwell, with its sash windows and hipped roof. This austere exterior hides ornate plasterwork that is probably by the celebrated Edward Goudge, who is best known for his work at Belton House. Peaches, pears, grapes, apricots, lemons and other fruits moulded in sharp relief on the drawing-room ceiling are accompanied by lovingly detailed depictions of pheasants, partridges, woodcock and plover.

More birds dart and perch amidst lotuses and peonies on the eighteenth-century Chinese wallpaper in one of the bedrooms, the relatively sombre plumage of a couple of ducks floating companionably on a pond contrasting with the brilliant-red tail feathers of a bird of paradise.

Birds also feature in the walled garden set on a gentle south-facing slope to the north of the drive, where a peacock weathervane crowns the octagonal brick dovecote at one end. Undulating parkland, studded with stands of mature woodland, comes right up to the front of the house. Thousands of trees – beeches, sycamores, oaks and maples – date from the time of William Windham I, who laid the foundations of the Great Wood which shelters the house from biting winds off the North Sea only 2 miles (3.2 kilometres) away. His work was continued by his son with advice from the improver Nathaniel Kent and possibly also from Humphry Repton, and was taken up again by the last squire of Felbrigg, who planted some 200,000 trees and formed the V-shaped rides commemorating VE day in Victory Wood. Memorials of a different kind, monuments to generations of Windhams, including some fine brasses, fill the little flint church in the park, all that remains of the village that once stood here.

ABOVE Weathering has enhanced the appeal of Felbrigg Hall's glorious Jacobean entrance front.

Fountains Abbey and Studley Royal

North Yorkshire
2 miles (3.2 kilometres) west of Ripon, off the B6265 to Pateley Bridge

The ruins of Fountains Abbey lie hidden in the valley of the River Skell, framed by steep wooded slopes. The approach from the west follows a narrow lane past the mellow stonework of the late Elizabethan Fountains Hall, which was partly built with material from the abbey ruins. The hall's symmetrical, many-windowed facade, with a deeply recessed central bay and projecting towers at both ends, has echoes of Hardwick Hall, and Robert Smythson, who designed Hardwick, may also have been involved here. Classical columns and delightful carved figures flank the porch and there is an impressive carved chimneypiece in the Great Chamber, with a panel depicting the Judgement of Solomon.

Beyond the hall, and the monastic water-mill, the lane suddenly opens out into a grassy court in front of the monastery. Ahead, the west end of the abbey church, with the outline of a huge window above the west door, is dwarfed by Abbot Marmaduke Huby's great tower projecting from the north side of the nave. Almost 53 metres (172 feet) high, the tower is so tall that it can be seen from far away peering over the rim of the valley. To the right stretches the west range, as impressively long as Huby's tower is tall and extending over the Skell at one end. All is built of the greyish sandstone that outcrops just beside the abbey.

Fountains is the largest abbey in England and has survived remarkably complete, probably because it was too remote to be turned into a country house or extensively plundered for building stone after its dissolution in 1539. The impressive remains, centred on the cloister at the heart of the abbey, contain many telling reminders of the daily life and routines of the community that lived here for 400 years. Worn stone steps on the south side of the cloister once led up to the long dormitory where the monks slept and the room beside the stair still has the two great fireplaces where a wood fire was kept burning from November to Easter, so the monks had

somewhere they could warm themselves. Stone benches by the refectory door once held the basins where the community could wash their hands before meals, drying them on towels from a cupboard built into the arched recess that can still be seen on the wall of the warming room. The stone supports for the tables in the refectory itself still protrude from the grassy floor, and a flight of steps built into the thickness of the wall leads up to the pulpit where devotional works were read to the brothers while they ate.

A group of idealistic monks who had rebelled against the relaxed atmosphere of their parent Benedictine house founded St Mary of Fountains in 1132 as a pioneering Cistercian community. The austere and simple lifestyle of the early days is reflected in the unadorned architecture of the oldest parts of the abbey, such as the huge tree-trunk pillars supporting the cathedral-like nave. But the very success of the community was to lead to the relaxation of the principles that had made it great. With the aid of lay brothers, who vastly outnumbered the monks themselves, the abbey eventually controlled huge

ABOVE LEFT The Gothic church of St Mary the Virgin, built in the 1870s, was the last addition to the rich variety of buildings on the Fountains Abbey estate.
BELOW The rhythmic stone vaulting of the west range of the abbey.
OPPOSITE The west front of Fountains Abbey dates from about 1160, but the great window above the west door is fifteenth-century and Abbot Huby's tower was added only in the monastery's last decades.

estates stretching west into the Lake District and north to Teesside, the source of the wealth that made it one of the richest religious houses in Britain by the mid-thirteenth century. Wool merchants who came to Yorkshire from Flanders and Italy were accommodated in self-contained suites in the guest houses that can still be seen on Abbey Green.

This prosperity financed later building, such as the early thirteenth-century Chapel of the Nine Altars at the east end of the church, with its soaring Perpendicular window. But the greatest monument to earthly concerns, Marmaduke Huby's tower, was added in the community's final decades. A prodigy tower in the spirit of Sissinghurst or Tattershall Castle, Huby's creation, erected to his personal glory, was in direct contravention of early Cistercian practice. A magnificent example of the strength of religious faith, Fountains is also a monument to lost ideals.

Downstream from the abbey is the eighteenth-century water garden of Studley Royal whose creator, John Aislabie, retired here in 1720 after involvement in the South Sea Bubble brought his political career to an abrupt end. Mirror-like ponds on the valley floor reflect classical statues and a Tuscan temple and walks threading the wooded slopes on either side give vistas to a Gothic tower and other eye-catchers. Most memorably, from a high-level path through the trees there is a sudden view up a sweep of grass-framed water to the abbey ruins. The serenity of this part of the garden contrasts with a wilder landscape downstream, beyond a lake fed by the Skell. Here Aislabie's son William enhanced the natural drama of a gorge-like section of the river and planted beech woods to create an early example of a Picturesque landscape.

Running down to the valley of the Skell is an extensive deer park where another spectacular building was an addition of the late nineteenth century. Silhouetted on the skyline at the end of a lime avenue which climbs slowly from gates on the eastern side of the park is the Gothic church of St Mary the Virgin, with a spire soaring above the trees. Built for the 1st Marquess and Marchioness of Ripon from 1871–8, this is a *tour de force* by William Burges. The exterior is relatively restrained but the interior is a riot of colour and rich carving in wood and stone. Angelic musicians set against a gilded background throng the sanctuary, the choir-stalls are carved with multi-coloured parrots, the organ case masquerades as a medieval house, complete with spiral staircase, and there is stained glass illustrating the Book of Revelation.

This sumptuous example of High Victorian taste adds to the richness and variety of what is overall an exceptional property, now designated a World Heritage site.

Godolphin

Cornwall
Between Hayle and Helston, off
a zigzag road from Godolphin
Cross to Townshend

The Godolphin estate lies deep in Cornwall, in a well-wooded landscape of small fields, scattered settlements and twisting lanes, and with a sense of the sea near at hand. At its heart, beneath the cone of Godolphin Hill and shielded by woodland along the Hayle River, is this magical Tudor and Jacobean house. Low, two-storey ranges, lit by stone-mullioned windows and built of local granite like the field walls and stiles on the estate, are set round three sides of a grassy courtyard. What was the great hall range on the south side, with an arched porch giving onto the court, is now a romantic ruin and a second courtyard that once lay beyond it was demolished in the early nineteenth century.

The Godolphin family, who were living on this site from the twelfth century, grew rich on the mining of rich seams of tin and copper on the estate and, through judicious marriages and loyal service to the Crown, gradually secured their position as one of the leading families of Cornwall, emerging as players on the national stage from the reign of Henry VIII. The old king, diseased and failing, knighted William Godolphin after the successful siege of Boulogne in 1544 and Francis Godolphin, who inherited in 1575, was the first of a line of Godolphins to be governor of the Scilly Isles, which were held for the king in the Civil War. As the family's status grew, so the house was enlarged, becoming the largest and grandest in Cornwall in the seventeenth century. This was the high point. By the time Sidney Godolphin, the 1st Earl, became Queen Anne's First Lord of the Treasury in the early eighteenth century, the family had a London house and their old Cornish seat, increasingly neglected, slowly decayed, becoming a run-down farmhouse. Godolphin was lovingly restored by Sydney Schofield, son of the American landscape painter Elmer

LEFT A Tudor archway closed by oak doors leads into Godolphin's inner court.

Schofield, and his wife Mary, who came here in 1937. The National Trust bought the estate from the Schofields in 2000, and in 2007 the house and garden were also acquired.

Weathered, lichen-spotted stone and mossy cobbles add to the appeal of this exceptional place. Across what was once a walled forecourt, eight stocky Tuscan columns of carved granite form a long colonnade in the centre of the north-facing entrance front. This Italianate loggia, an exceptionally sophisticated feature for its date in this part of the country and separated only by a screen wall from an identical colonnade looking onto the courtyard, was added in the 1630s, together with the rooms above, when the house was remodelled for the last time by Sir Francis Godolphin II. A cultured and sophisticated man, whose brother was the poet Sidney Godolphin, Sir Francis would have moved in court circles and been aware of the new Italianate architecture, typified by Inigo Jones's Banqueting House, appearing in London. The lead drainwater heads on this front carry the double-headed eagle of the Godolphin arms and the leaping dolphin of the family crest, and a Tudor arch closed with original massive oak doors that was incorporated in the seventeenth-century work leads through into the courtyard.

The interior is a succession of light, airy rooms, the most glorious being the long chamber with windows on both sides that runs above the colonnade. A room that was used by William Godolphin IV, friend of the diarists Pepys and Evelyn, still has its 1630s decorative frieze, original pine floorboards, and enchanting blue and white seventeenth-century Delft tiles featuring mythical beasts round the fireplace. The closet off, now a bathroom, was probably William's library and study. Seventeenth-century improvement also accounts for the lofty chamber in the west range with large mullioned windows looking onto the courtyard. Known as the King's Room, this is where the future Charles II is said to have rested when he was fleeing to the Scilly Isles and France in 1646 after his crushing defeat at the Battle of Naseby in 1645. The high coved ceiling has pendants of what may be Jacobean plasterwork and a richly carved oak overmantel on the south wall is thought to commemorate the wedding of William Godolphin III and Thomasine Sydney in 1604. Once in the hall, it was moved to this room in the nineteenth century when the hall was demolished. The earliest parts of the house, dating from the 1470s, are in the east wing, where rich linenfold panelling and carved ceiling beams in one of the intimate rooms are embellishments of 1537.

Godolphin came to the Trust without any contents and, although now a holiday let, has been sympathetically furnished with pieces that, like the refectory table in the dining room, of 1750–1830, suit the spirit of the house. There are a couple of Godolphin family portraits and striking paintings of Cornish fishermen by Walter Schofield, who used one of the rooms in the west range as his studio. A squint big enough to take a musket covering the entrance is a reminder of Cornwall's former lawlessness and of the Godolphins' support for Charles I in the Civil War, the expense of which probably prevented Sir Francis from completing the updating of his house.

A sixteenth-century stable block with a rough cobbled floor sits beside the house, while to the east are the skeletal remains of a compartmental fourteenth-century garden, with raised walks and the depressions of former fishponds. In the woodland along the river and up on the hill are the pits, gullies, spoil heaps and other remains of mining in the nineteenth century, now romantically deserted and overgrown.

OPPOSITE Godolphin's Elizabethan stables frame one side of the King's garden.

Greenway

Devon
Greenway Road, Galmpton, on the
east bank of the River Dart off the
A379.

One of the most successful and prolific authors of all time, outsold only by Shakespeare, is Agatha Christie (1890–1976). As well as producing a library of ingenious detective stories and a number of other books, she also wrote several plays, one of which, *The Mousetrap*, has been running continuously on the London stage for over 60 years. It seems appropriate that this exceptional woman, who knew how to conjure up suspense and mystery, should have fallen for this romantic and atmospheric place overlooking the magical Dart estuary. A luxuriant woodland garden, developed over the last 200 years and filled with many rare and tender plants and specimen trees, surrounds the house and plunges steeply to the water, adding greatly to Greenway's individual charm. On the other side of the river is the little village of Dittisham, from which ferries cross to the quay below the property, and there are spectacular views over the water and down the estuary to Dartmouth.

Although there was a late sixteenth-century Tudor mansion here, home to several generations of the adventuring Gilberts of Compton Castle, the central block of the present white Georgian house was built, by an unknown architect, for the merchant adventurer Roope Harris Roope in 1771 on a site in front of the old Greenway Court. A tall stuccoed building, with an array of sash windows looking west over the river and a hipped roof, the house is tucked into the slope at the top of the garden. One-storey wings fronted by colonnaded porticoes on either side of the main block were added in 1815 by James Marwood Elton, whose father, another merchant adventurer, had bought the property in 1791.

Dame Agatha, whose childhood home in Torquay lies just a few miles away, bought Greenway with her second husband, the archaeologist Max Mallowan, as a holiday home in 1938, employing the young Guilford Bell to demolish a billiard-

room wing that had been added in the later nineteenth century and make other alterations. Their daughter Rosalind Hicks and her husband Anthony lived here from 1978 and in 2000 Rosalind and Anthony, together with Rosalind's son Matthew Prichard, gifted the property, with its shield of surrounding woodland and farmland, to the National Trust. The garden has been open since 2003 and the house, which came to the Trust with all its contents, opened in 2009.

Shown as it was when a holiday home in the 1950s and '60s, Greenway is a most attractive house, with light, well-proportioned rooms, their cream decoration being one of Guilford Bell's improvements, and a sense of comfort and serenity. Apart from some de-cluttering by the Trust, the furnishings are largely as recorded in the 1942 inventory and there are displays of family portraits and photographs and the kind of belongings that make a house feel lived in, from Anthony Hicks's hats to golf clubs, walking sticks and soft toys. All the family were great collectors and every table, chest and mantelpiece and every glass-fronted cabinet is used to display their rather individual treasures, among them ceramics, pocket watches, boxes made of scrolled paper and Tunbridgeware. Large built-in cupboards in what was originally the housekeeper's sitting room are stuffed full of further items, including modern studio glass and the Mallowans' collection of silver.

In the drawing room filling the west wing, a sofa and deep armchairs are set invitingly round the fire, as the family had it. This is where Agatha Christie used to read the manuscript of her latest thriller to family and friends, asking them to guess who the murderer in the story might be; she wrote letters at the mahogany bureau and played the boudoir grand that sits in a corner of the room. A portrait of Agatha aged 4, painted by Douglas Connah in 1894, hangs in the room next door, and the doll she is shown clutching sits on the chair below. Upstairs, the writer's bedroom, with its large walk-in closet and display of *papier-mâché* furniture, is largely unchanged, and a striking black and gold kimono here is the one being worn by her mother in a photograph downstairs. An adjoining room is now devoted to Max Mallowan's excavations in Mesopotamia, with a display of miniature pottery heads and other finds. A haughty ceramic camel dating from the Tang dynasty (AD618–906) was a present from Max to Agatha and other pieces in the house came from her childhood home.

Another aspect of Greeenway's history comes through in the library, where an unusual frieze dates from the Second World War when the 10th Flotilla of the US Coastguard was based in the house and Greenway was caught up in the preparations for D-Day. Painted by Lt Marshall Lee in 1943 in what was the officers' bar, the frieze depicts incidents in the flotilla's war, such as the hard-fought invasion of Sicily; a final tableau shows the house half-hidden in trees high above the Dart, with a naval vessel in the deep-water anchorage below.

A stable block tucked away to the north-west of the house, still with some original stalls and loose-boxes, also dates from the eighteenth century, but a bell tower and clock were additions of the 1850s. Down on the river, in leafy seclusion, is a substantial two-storey late Georgian boathouse. The lower level is a bathing room, which fills with salt water at high tide, while above, with a balcony overlooking the Dart, is a roomy saloon, complete with fireplace. This is where Agatha Christie set the murder of Marlene Tucker in *Dead Man's Folly*, thus bringing the place she loved into her writing.

In keeping with Greenway's history as a much-loved retreat for Agatha and her family, the top of the house has been turned into a spacious holiday apartment.

OPPOSITE Agatha hung French ivory-framed mirrors above the bookcases in her bedroom.
ABOVE Greenway is an attractive Georgian house set high above the Dart estuary, with magical views over the river and downstream towards Dartmouth.

Ham House

Surrey
On the south bank of the
River Thames, west of the
A307, at Petersham

Ruthless ambition created this red-brick palace beside the River Thames, with its principal rooms still furnished in the style of Charles II's court. Elizabeth, Countess of Dysart, was not content with the Jacobean house she inherited from her father, William Murray, 1st Earl of Dysart, despite the improvements he made in 1637–9. A second marriage gave her the opportunity to spend lavishly on remodelling. Even before the death of her first husband, the countess's name was being linked to the high-flying Earl of Lauderdale, a member of Charles II's cabal ministry. When his wife conveniently died, the two were married. In the same year, 1672, the earl received a dukedom, and the couple set out to mark their position with new building. He was at the height of his power; she, it was said, with complete ascendancy over him. The haughty, rather unattractive couple confidently surveying the world from Lely's portrait in the round gallery clearly deserved each other and together they produced one of the most lavishly appointed houses of their day.

Externally, Ham is sober enough. A long three-storey block of a house with tall chimneys, it is enlivened on the entrance front with two projecting wings, each of which incorporates a short colonnade, and with sixteen busts set in niches at the level of the first floor. More busts are set round the brick wall enclosing the forecourt. There were once wings on the south front too, but these were engulfed when the Lauderdales doubled the size of Ham by building new apartments along this side of the house. The new rooms were given sash windows, which had only recently been invented, but these were designed to blend with the Jacobean casements.

Inside, there are few traces of the interiors created in 1610 for Sir Thomas Vavasour, Knight Marshal to James I, for whom Ham was built, but several rooms still display the taste of Elizabeth's father, which reflects the period love of rich effect. Bronzing picks out martial details – a drum, armour, a cannon with a pile of shot – on the carved and pierced panels of his great staircase and on the baskets of fruit crowning the newel posts. The stairs lead to the sequence of first-floor state rooms created by William Murray along the north front. His great dining room is now the gallery above the hall. Beyond lie his tapestry-hung drawing room and his refurbished long gallery, the first with original plasterwork, woodwork and marble chimneypiece, the second lined with gilded panelling divided by Ionic pilasters which the earl added to the Jacobean room.

Portraits in sumptuous gold frames line the gallery, among them several works by Lely and the portrait that Charles I gave to William Murray, who was one of his most loyal supporters. A rare survival is the intimate Green Closet off the gallery, where some 60 miniatures and small paintings framed in ebony and gilt are hung closely on brilliant green damask. Many of the pictures, which include miniatures by Nicholas Hilliard and Isaac Oliver, were hanging here in the seventeenth century. The ceiling paintings of cupids, nymphs and satyrs, in tempera, are by Franz Cleyn, who was principal designer for the Mortlake tapestry works.

RIGHT Originally fitted out in 1673 for a visit by Catherine of Braganza, Charles II's consort, the Queen's Bedchamber is now furnished with mostly eighteenth-century pieces, but the table with legs carved as caryatids was in the house when the queen came to Ham.

RIGHT The north front of Ham House.

Along the south front, arranged over two floors, are the apartments created by the Lauderdales. On the first floor, the long gallery leads into a suite of three rooms fitted out for Charles II's queen, Catherine of Braganza, in 1673. Although partly refurnished in the eighteenth century by the duchess's great-great-grandson, the 4th Earl of Dysart, many of the extravagant original fittings remain. There are hangings of silk damask and velvet, fire-irons ornamented with silver, intricate parquet floors and a carved wooden garland of subtle craftsmanship. Most of the seventeenth-century decor survives in the intimate closet at the end of the suite, which is still hung with winter hangings of 'crimson and gould stuff bordered with green and gould stuff' and has a baroque ceiling painting by Antonio Verrio, who had worked extensively for Charles II. More paintings by Verrio in the overblown style favoured at the time, such as a group of maidens representing the arts, also adorn the private closets in the two suites of rooms that the Lauderdales created for themselves on the ground floor of the south front. Here the flavour is more mixed. The Duchess's closet, where she would have retired for privacy, or to talk to her closest friends, shows the white crackled teapot that brewed her precious tea; and survivals of the original decorative scheme include inset sea paintings by William van der Velde (in his rooms) and bird paintings by Francis Barlow (in hers). But her bedroom has had to be re-created as it might have appeared, and what was the duke's bedchamber has the 1740s furnishing scheme of the 4th Earl, who turned it into a drawing room. Flemish tapestries have an elegant French flavour, gilded chairs and sofas upholstered in gold silk have X-frames in the style of William Kent, and a new carpet woven for the room, based on archive material, has been designed to pick up the strong blues and pinks in the tapestries.

The spirit of the house extends into the garden, where the formal seventeenth-century layout, in which the garden was devised as a series of contrasting compartments, has been re-created. The south front looks over a broad terrace to a lawn divided into eight uniform square plats and beyond to the wilderness. Looking from a distance like a well-ordered wood, this too has an architectural plan. Grassy walks lined by hornbeam hedges radiate from a central clearing, dividing the wilderness into a series of small enclosures, four of which contain little summerhouses. East of the house, a secluded knot garden is flanked by the cool green tunnels of hornbeam alleys and a period kitchen garden has been restored in front of the wisteria-hung seventeenth-century orangery to the west. Outhouses include the eighteenth-century dairy, with marble shelves carried on cast-iron cow's legs, and the late seventeenth-century slate-floored still house, where soaps, sweet-scented waters and ointments were prepared. Close by, down one of the avenues that lead the eye beyond the garden, is the Thames and the little ferry from Twickenham, which has for centuries brought visitors across the water.

Hanbury Hall

Worcestershire
4½ miles (7.2 kilometres) east of
Droitwich, 1 mile (1.6 kilometres)
north of the B4090; 6 miles
(9.6 kilometres) south of
Bromsgrove, east of the M5

James Thornhill was at the height of his career when Thomas Vernon, a successful barrister, commissioned him to decorate the staircase of his new house in 1710. Although his work for St Paul's Cathedral was still in the future, Thornhill had completed the Sabine Room at Chatsworth in Derbyshire and was halfway through his magnificent Painted Hall at Greenwich. Like this masterpiece, the Hanbury staircase is exuberantly baroque, with mythological scenes, most of them taken from Homer's *Iliad*, framed between classical columns on the walls and a host of deities set among clouds looking down from above. In the long hall below, where a bust of

Vernon stands over the fireplace, the subtle monochrome ceiling, probably by one of Thornhill's assistants, matches the quality of the master's work, with musical instruments and agricultural tools representing the seasons of the year separated by *trompe-l'oeil* domes and shells.

Vernon's square red-brick house, begun *c.*1700 and probably designed by a local mason, is a typical example of Restoration domestic architecture, with dormers in the hipped roof and a central cupola. Pavilions in the French or Dutch style project from all four corners. The design of the striking pedimented entrance facade, with a central bay set between Corinthian columns and decorated with flowing carving, may have been influenced by the treatment of a grand house such as Thoresby Hall in Nottinghamshire, which had been remodelled in the 1680s for the Duke of Kingston. An unusual detached long gallery has two ornate Jacobean overmantels made up of carved woodwork brought from elsewhere. Domed gazebos at the corners of the entrance court are Victorian.

Hanbury's original contents were mostly sold in 1790 after the dissipation of the family fortunes during the disastrous marriage between Emma Vernon and Henry Cecil, later Lord Exeter. Some family pieces, such as the two Dutch marquestry chests of drawers in the Blue Bedroom, have returned in recent years and all the portraits, including works by Reynolds, Kneller and John Vanderbank, are now back in the house, hanging in the hall and dining room. Generally, most of the interiors, including a sitting room in the idiom of the 1920s, have been re-created, but a flavour of the early eighteenth century comes through in a panelled bedroom and dressing room, the latter still with its original corner chimneypiece. And in the smoking room at the back of the house, once Thomas Vernon's office, a painting of Hanbury commissioned by Bowater Vernon, Thomas's heir, from John Wootton, shows the house in the setting of its early

eighteenth-century landscape, with long avenues of trees stretching into the distance.

Nearby hangs a bird's-eye view of the estate in 1732 by Joseph Dougharty showing both the avenues and Vernon's compartmental formal garden, both part of a grand design by George London. Later changes destroyed all but remnants of London's layout but, using this bird's-eye view and surviving plans, the avenues have now been replanted and the garden, with its sunken parterre, grove, wilderness, bowling green and fruit garden, re-created. A handsome orangery was a mid-eighteenth-century addition to the design.

OPPOSITE Serene Hanbury Hall, built of brick with stone dressings and finished off with a little cupola, is a typical Restoration country house.
BELOW LEFT Hanbury's decorated staircase, executed in c.1710, was painted by the great James Thornhill, then at the height of his career, and would have been seen as an important status symbol.
BELOW RIGHT The fireplace in the dining room is surrounded by a trellis of elaborate rococo woodwork that was probably carved by a talented local craftsman, using designs from pattern books.

Hardwick Hall

Derbyshire
6½ miles (10.4 kilometres)
west of Mansfield, 9 ½ miles
(15.2 kilometres) south-east
of Chesterfield

This cathedral of a house stands tall and proud on the top of a windswept hill, its distinctive, many-towered outline lifting the spirits of those hurtling past on the M1. As the huge stone initials set along the roofline proclaim, this is the house of Elizabeth Shrewsbury, better known as Bess of Hardwick, the formidable and ambitious squire's daughter who rose from relatively humble beginnings to become one of the richest and best-connected people in Elizabethan England.

By the time Hardwick was begun, Bess was already approaching 70 and had four marriages behind her, each of which had advanced her social position and increased her wealth. Her last husband was George Talbot, 6th Earl of Shrewsbury, the head of the oldest, grandest and richest family in England. By 1583, when she bought the family estate from her brother James, she and Shrewsbury were estranged and Bess initially embarked on remodelling the manor house where she had been born, the romantic ruins of which (in the guardianship of English Heritage) still crown the crest of the ridge just to the south-west of the New Hall. Although built piecemeal, on a cramped and awkward site, this first venture was in many ways a trial run for what was to come, incorporating features, such as the enormous windows lighting the Great Chambers on the top floor, which Bess would use again. This house was still unfinished when, in 1590, Bess's situation was transformed by the earl's death. It is possible the foundations for the New Hall had already been laid a few weeks before, but now Bess had the funds to fully finance her new project. Whereas the Old Hall had been produced piecemeal, the New Hall rose on virgin land and was designed as one by Robert Smythson, the most original of Elizabethan architects. It is a prodigy house, in a class of its own, but it was never large enough for all Bess's household.

Even after the new building was finished, in 1597, servants and guests were still accommodated in the Old Hall.

Both houses are built of limestone quarried from just down the hill, but whereas the gabled and irregular outlines of the Old Hall reflect the remodelling of an existing building, the profile of the New Hall is clean and symmetrical. Windows that become progressively larger up the house enhance the strong vertical thrust of the six towers, giving Hardwick the appearance of a glittering glass lantern. Inside, a broad, tapestry-hung stone staircase, to the same innovatory design as one in the Old Hall, weaves its way majestically to the state apartments lit by huge windows on the third floor. These rooms are still very much as Bess left them. Her High Great Chamber for the reception and entertainment of important guests was designed round the tapestries that still hang here, purchased new in 1587. The goddess Diana with her court on the three-dimensional plaster frieze above was intended as a tribute to Elizabeth I, whom Bess always hoped would visit Hardwick (she never did).

A tapestry-hung door leads into the atmospheric long gallery, where some of the 80 pictures covering the walls were here in Bess's time. Portraying royalty, family, friends and patrons – evidence of her good connections – they include three of Bess's husbands and a glittering representation of the queen herself, her famous red hair piled high and her dress decorated with sea creatures and birds and studded with pearls. Here, too, is a memorable painting of the philosopher Thomas Hobbes, tutor to Bess's grandson, the 2nd Earl of Devonshire. Hobbes is shown just a few years before he died at Hardwick in 1679, toothless in extreme old age.

Elizabethan tapestries and paintings are complemented by an important collection of embroideries dating from 1570–1640, many of which were worked on by Bess herself and which include pictorial wall hangings made out of a patchwork of velvets and silks and exquisite cushion covers worked in cross stitch. There is also some exceptional original furniture, such as the eglantine table in the High Great Chamber, inlaid with a mosaic of musical instruments, playing cards and board games, even the setting of a four-part motet, that was probably made to celebrate Bess's marriage to the Earl of Shrewsbury in 1568, and, in the adjoining room an inlaid walnut table that is carried on carvings of sea dogs and tortoises.

Hardwick's unique character owes much to the 6th Duke of Devonshire, who inherited in 1811 and deliberately enhanced the antiquarian atmosphere of the house, promoting the legend that Mary Queen of Scots stayed here and filling it with additional furniture, paintings and tapestries from his other properties, particularly from Chatsworth some 15 miles (24 kilometres) to the west.

Formal gardens to the south were laid out in the late nineteenth century. A little Elizabethan banqueting house was used as a smoking room by the 6th Duke's private orchestra, who were forbidden to smoke in the Hall itself. Buildings grouped round a stableyard beyond the garden include a smithy that existed in Bess's time, and a great barn (now the restaurant) and ox-house (now the shop) that date back to the early seventeenth century. Grain threshed in the barn would have been taken to be ground at the mill at Stainsby, in the northern part of the estate, where the present building is stll in working order.

The 800-hectare (1,990-acre) estate embraces two different landscapes. At the back of the hall, a formal stretch of grass focused on a central basin looks out across the flat, partly cultivated land on the limestone plateau east of the house. To the west is the oak-wooded, hillier terrain of the former deer-park, with a series of fishponds and a partly restored duck decoy.

OPPOSITE Many of the embroideries at Hardwick, such as this red velvet panel, are decorated with Bess's ES monogram, standing for Elizabeth of Shrewsbury. BELOW Hardwick Hall, one of the greatest of all Elizabethan houses, stands high on a windswept ridge.

Hatchlands Park

Surrey
East of East Clandon, north of the
A246 Guildford–Leatherhead road

In the late 1750s Edward Boscawen, second son of the 1st Viscount Falmouth and Admiral of the Blue, used prize money from victories over the French in the Seven Years War to finance a new house. The architect of his square red-brick Georgian mansion, probably Stiff Leadbetter, ingeniously designed it with seven different floor levels. Looking at the house from the south-west, three storeys on the west front change mysteriously into two on the south. Sadly, the admiral did not live to enjoy his new mansion, dying only a year or so after he and his wife moved in.

Hatchlands contains the earliest recorded decoration in an English country house by Robert Adam, who was engaged in 1758, just after he had returned from his Grand Tour. Appropriately, his plaster ceilings in the saloon and library have nautical themes, the motifs used ranging from mermaids, dolphins and seahorses to drums, cannon and anchors. At the end of the century Joseph Bonomi made alterations to the staircase and the garden entrance, and a hundred years later Sir Reginald Blomfield added the music room in seventeenth-century style for Stuart Rendel, who was at one time a managing partner in London of Sir William Armstrong's engineering firm and became Lord Rendel of Hatchlands.

Apart from a few pieces from the Rendel collection, such as the eighteenth-century gilt pier tables in the saloon, Adam's interiors are now complemented by pictures, furniture and keyboard instruments lent by the collector and musician Mr Alec Cobbe, who is the National Trust's tenant at Hatchlands. Red silk panels in the saloon set off works by Carlo Dolci, Rubens, Frederick de Moucheron and a rare sixteenth-century altarpiece by the Florentine Alessandro Allori, and a number of portraits in the house include canvases by Gainsborough, Wright of Derby, Angelica Kauffmann and Hoppner. Among the collection of keyboard instruments by European makers from the period *c.*1750–1840 are an Erard pianoforte reputedly made for Marie Antoinette, one of the few French harpsichords to escape destruction in the years after the Revolution, and a very rare quadruple-strung piano by Conrad Graf, one of only three known such instruments by this maker. The collection is maintained for performance and visitors may be lucky enough to hear the distant sound of music by Mozart, Couperin or Schubert.

BELOW LEFT The grandiose music room at Hatchlands, where recitals are given, was an addition of c.1903 in the style of the late seventeenth century by the architect Reginald Blomfield.
BELOW Hatchlands Park, with a little pediment marking the entrance front, was built in the 1750s for Admiral Boscawen, who financed his new house out of prize money won in action against the French.

Hill Top

Cumbria
At Near Sawrey, behind the
Tower Bank Arms

The young Beatrix Potter met virtually nobody and went almost nowhere. The one bright spot in a stifling existence with her domineering parents in London was the annual family holiday, in her early years to houses in Scotland, but from 1882, when she was 16, to the Lake District. These brief episodes, and the freedom they brought, fuelled a longing for the country which emerged in meticulously observed watercolours of wild creatures and plants and in the beginnings of the animal fantasies that have delighted children and adults for over a century.

Beatrix's purchase of this small, largely seventeenth-century farmhouse in 1905 was a momentous step. Presented to her parents as nothing more than a good investment (which it was), to their lonely 39-year-old daughter the rough stone building with a view over Sawrey to the fells beyond represented the possibility of escape from an increasingly dreary and unchanging regime. Although she was only able to snatch weeks here in the eight years that followed, this period was to see her best work, with the production of thirteen of the stories in which rabbits, mice, squirrels, hedgehogs and other creatures become humans in miniature, all of them illustrated with Beatrix's charming and individual paintings.

Anyone who has read these nursery classics will recognise Hill Top and its well-furnished, homely rooms, filled with accumulated clutter. The long sloping garden flanking the steep path to the house, with rows of vegetables on one side and a medley of traditional flowers on the other, is still as it appears in *The Tale of Tom Kitten* and *Pigling Bland*. The old-fashioned kitchen range with a black kettle bubbling away strikes a reassuring note in several animal holes and burrows, the nineteenth-century dresser is featured in *The Tale of Samuel Whiskers*, and the grandfather clock with a cheerful sun on its face was the model for the one in *The Tailor of Gloucester*. Peter Rabbit's red-spotted handkerchief and the doll's house food – dishes of oranges and pears and a large ham – stolen by Hunca Munca and Tom Thumb are in one of the upstairs rooms. Some grander pieces of furniture, striking an unexpected note, were acquired after Beatrix's mother died, and one of the bedrooms is hung with her brother Bertram's landscape paintings.

For the last 30 years of her life, during which she was contentedly married to William Heelis, a local solicitor, Beatrix lived as a prosperous farmer in the nearby Castle Cottage (not open), reserving Hill Top, which was kept unchanged, for those times when she wished to be alone with her memories. During this period, she became increasingly concerned about the conservation of the fells and began to buy land to save it from being broken up or developed. In 1895 her friend Canon Rawnsley founded the National Trust and her substantial landholdings, with their farmhouses and cottages, came to the Trust on the death of her husband in 1945.

BELOW The young Beatrix Potter with Spot the spaniel, one of the many family pets which she drew and painted from an early age and which fed her later animal creations.

ABOVE Disraeli turned the arcade on Hughenden's entrance front into a conservatory and filled it with 'marble vases, busts, ferns and flowers'.
OPPOSITE, RIGHT When the Disraelis came to Hughenden in 1848, they set about giving the house a fashionable Gothic flavour and inserted ribbed and vaulted plaster ceilings in several of the rooms.

Hughenden

Buckinghamshire
1½ miles (2.4 kilometres) north of High Wycombe, on the west side of the Great Missenden road

The six years of Tory government from 1874 saw some of the greatest successes enjoyed by any ministry of Queen Victoria's reign, including progressive social reforms and an imperialist foreign policy that gained the queen the title of Empress of India. These achievements owed much to the vision, skill and persuasive passion of the Prime Minister, Benjamin Disraeli, who was already 70 when the new parliament began. His greatest international triumph, which earned him the admiration of Bismarck, was at the Congress of Berlin in 1878, where Disraeli's diplomatic skills were largely responsible for a settlement that checked Russian expansionism, one of the key issues of the day. A writer as well as a politician, his radical domestic policies had been foreshadowed some 30 years earlier in his political novels, *Coningsby* and *Sybil*, which were concerned with the condition of the rural and urban poor.

Disraeli had acquired Hughenden in 1848, the year after his election as MP for Buckingham and the year before he became leader of the Conservative Party. At a time when political power was largely in the hands of the landed aristocracy, he had increasingly felt the need for an estate to bolster his political ambitions, but he had only been able to make the purchase with the help of Lord Bentinck and his brothers, who loaned two-thirds of the sum involved. The grandson of an Italian Jew who had come to England looking for work, Disraeli had little in the way of financial resources himself.

Disraeli and his wife Mary Anne, twelve years his senior, lived at Hughenden until their deaths, in 1881 and 1872 respectively. The plain, three-storey Georgian house they acquired was gothicised with the help of Edward Buckton Lamb, who has been described as one of the most perverse and original architects of his day. Stucco was removed to reveal the blue and red brickwork behind, stepped battlements and pinnacles were added and the interior was enhanced with plaster vaulting and grained woodwork. Because of alterations by Disraeli's nephew Coningsby, who inherited the house, and the sale of some of the contents, Hughenden is no longer as the Disraelis had it, but the richly coloured High Victorian interiors reproduce some of their decorative schemes, such as the deep red walls of the hall and staircase, and portraits that were here in Disraeli's day, of friends and those Disraeli admired, as well as of close family, and original furnishings can be seen in almost every room.

Hughenden stands high above a steep Chiltern valley, looking out over parkland and ancient woods. An obelisk on a near hillside, erected by Mary Anne in 1852 in memory of Disraeli's father, would have reminded him of the two people who influenced him most and his writings show how he loved this place, valuing the solitude and escape it offered. Disraeli never let political ambition destroy his humanity and he was the only premier other than Melbourne to be honoured with a visit from the queen.

In recent years, Hughenden's vital secret role in the Second World War has come to light. Requisitioned by the Air Ministry in 1941 and renamed Hillside, the house was used to produce maps for night-time bombing missions, among them the Dam Busters raid and the operation to sink the battleship *Tirpitz*. A hundred people were stationed in the house, and the maps they produced were dispatched at night in trucks that were kept in the stable yard. A basement room is now devoted to this riveting period in Hughenden's history and Disraeli's ice-house in the grounds, where the maps were photographed, has been fitted out to evoke its wartime role. A vast air-raid shelter carved out of the hill below for the use of those working here has been colonised by bats.

Ickworth

Frederick Augustus Hervey, 4th Earl of Bristol, must rank as one of the Church's more remarkable bishops. Appointed to the see of Derry, the richest in Ireland, in 1768 when only 38, his sympathy with both Roman Catholics and Presbyterians made him enormously popular, despite a sometimes light-hearted approach to his duties which once led him to organise a curates' race along the sands at Downhill, rewarding the winners with vacant benefices. A large income coupled with an inherited fortune allowed the 4th Earl to embark on extensive foreign tours, now commemorated in Hotels Bristol all over the Continent, during which he amassed the works of art he intended to display in his new house on the family's Suffolk estate.

Ickworth is as grandiose and flamboyant as its creator. A larger version of the 4th Earl's earlier house at Ballyscullion, it was inspired, like the little Mussenden Temple at Downhill, by the circular Belle Isle on an island in Windermere. A huge domed rotunda decorated with classical columns and terracotta friezes is linked by curving corridors to rectangular wings, the whole building stretching some 183 metres (600 feet) from end to end. But Frederick was never to see his house completed. Work on Ickworth began in 1795 to the designs of the Italian architect Mario Asprucci the Younger, but came to a halt on the 4th Earl's death from gout in an outhouse in Italy in 1803 (from where his body was shipped back to England, labelled as an antique statue). Tragically, the bishop had had his magnificent collection appropriated by Napoleonic troops in Rome in 1798.

The 4th Earl's ambitious plans were realised by his son, created 1st Marquess of Bristol in 1826. The superb paintings, porcelain and furniture now displayed here largely represent the slow accumulation of several generations of Herveys, who have owned the estate since the mid-fifteenth century. Many followed brilliant political careers, as did Frederick's gifted eldest brother George, the 2nd Earl, who acquired gilt furniture and paintings while he was on diplomatic postings to Turin and Madrid. It was the 1st Earl, Frederick's grandfather, another prominent politician, who bought the early eighteenth-century Huguenot pieces among the silver displayed in the Museum Room, the relatively restrained hand of Paul de Lamerie contrasting with more ornate rococo Italian work. One case here is devoted to a shoal of silver fish, some designed as ornamental pendants, others as scent containers, their realistic, scaly forms including a whale and a swordfish as well as more mundane species. The landing outside is used to show some of the fan collection acquired by Geraldine Anson, who married the 3rd Marquess.

The 1st Marquess housed the bulk of the collection in the grand state rooms in the rotunda rather than in the wings, as his father had intended. The largest room in the house is the hemispherical library across the south front, notable for its rare late seventeenth- and early eighteenth-century political periodicals and ornamented with busts of Pitt, Canning, Fox and Liverpool and Benjamin West's portrayal of the death of General Wolfe, which the artist painted specially for the Earl-Bishop. Hogarth's *Holland House Group* in the Smoking Room, showing Frederick's father, Lord Hervey, in the centre of a group of friends that includes the 3rd Duke of Marlborough, is one of a number of outstanding portraits in the house. A painting of a grave little boy with two greyhounds and a huge mastiff at his feet is Velázquez's study of the Infante Balthasar Carlos, son of Philip IV of Spain, and there is a full-length canvas by Gainsborough of the colourful Augustus John Hervey, Vice Admiral of the Blue, who briefly succeeded as 3rd Earl between his two brothers. It seems this philanderer deserved his wife, Elizabeth Chudleigh, whose bigamous marriage with the Duke of Kingston in 1769 gave rise to one of the most famous scandals of the eighteenth century. Quite different in character is the charming self-portrait by Madame Vigée Lebrun, commissioned by the Earl-Bishop in Naples in 1791, the artist's severe black dress setting off a vivacious face crowned with a mop of curly hair that is loosely caught up in a white handkerchief. The most extraordinary exhibit is Flaxman's marble group, *The Fury of Athamas*, based on a scene from Ovid's *Metamorphoses*, which dominates the staircase hall. Commissioned by the 4th Earl, Athamas is here shown holding his young son over his shoulder by an ankle, about to dash him to death. A second child clings to their mother, terrified.

From the 1st Marquess's orangery, the only part of the west wing to be completed, floor-length windows lead out onto a terrace looking south over the heavily wooded garden, where

ABOVE Ickworth, with its palatial central rotunda, was the creation of the flamboyant and eccentric 4th Earl of Bristol, who had already built a vast house in Ireland to a similar design.

tall cypresses, yews, evergreen oak and box create the illusion of an Italian landscape. Artfully contrived vistas give enticing glimpses of the rotunda. From the long raised terrace walk beyond the trees, created in *c.*1870 to shield the garden, there is a sweeping panorama over clumps of mature beeches and oaks in the park, many of them probably planted by 'Capability' Brown for the 2nd Earl. In the foreground, partly hidden in a dip, is Ickworth church, while an obelisk just visible above a wooded ridge on the far horizon was erected by the people of Derry in affectionate memory of their bishop.

Ightham Mote

Kent
6 miles (9.6 kilometres) east of
Sevenoaks, off the A25, and
2½ miles (4 kilometres) south
of Ightham, off the A227

A steep path from the car park leads down to this magical house set in a deep, wooded valley in the Kentish Weald, its walls rising sheer from a surrounding moat. Half-timbered upper storeys project from the facade here and there, a little hump-backed stone bridge crosses the water to an old wooden door, and the roofline is a medley of steeply pitched gables, massive brick chimneys and moss-stained tiles. Ducks paddle about beneath the walls.

Built round three courtyards and dating originally from the 1320s, Ightham Mote has retained its medieval appearance, despite many later alterations, because additions were piecemeal, were always made using local oak and Kentish ragstone and were sympathetic to the ancient building. The great hall filling one side of the cobbled main courtyard was the core of the early house and still has its early fourteenth-century timber roof. Tudor improvements, when the house was owned by the courtier Richard Clement, account for the armorial glass inserted as a tribute to Henry VIII in the great window of the hall. The Tudor rose and the pomegranate of Catherine of Aragon, the king's first wife, which appear both here and on richly carved oak bargeboards facing onto the courtyard, must have been in place well before Henry cast Catherine aside and married Anne Boleyn in 1533, a ceremony at which Richard Clement officiated.

Sir Richard Clement was also responsible for decorating the long, half-timbered room on the first floor that is now a chapel, but was probably originally designed as a grand guest chamber. Its arched barrel roof is exuberantly painted, again in honour of Henry and Catherine, with vividly coloured badges and emblems in red, orange, green and white representing the royal houses of England, Spain and France. The colours have faded now, but it is easy to imagine how glowing they must once have been. The room appears to have become a chapel in the 1630s and seems to have been fitted out gradually, resulting in a beautiful array of fine woodwork – linenfold panelling, a richly carved pulpit, choir stalls and pews – of various dates. There is sixteenth-century stained glass in the windows and a remarkable late fifteenth-century oak door at the west end.

Across a landing from the chapel is the drawing room and a startling change in atmosphere and style. The room is dominated by a monumental Jacobean fireplace decorated with carved Saracen heads and painted in black and gold, and is lit by an eighteenth-century Venetian window. The walls are covered in hand-painted Chinese wallpaper of *c.*1800 and the room as a whole has a distinctly exotic flavour, although, as in the rest of the house, the furniture, with the exception of a few pieces, has been added since 1951, when the original contents were sold.

The drawing room fills one end of the early fourteenth-century west range. On the other side of a central gatehouse tower are the simply furnished bedroom and dressing room that were used by Charles Henry Robinson, the American bachelor who bought Ightham Mote in 1953, having spotted a sale advertisement in a back number of *Country Life*, and gave it to the National Trust in 1985. The library, with its alcove bookshelves, is also as he had it. His desk sits in one of the alcoves and the pictures include drawings of his house in Maine.

An extensive lawn stretches up the combe north of the house, its regular outlines marking the site of a medieval stewpond that was once fed by the stream that now tumbles over a cascade and crosses the grass to fill the moat and a lake below the house. A raised walk fringing the lawn leads to another lake hidden in the trees beyond. Near the house a long border is crowded with traditional English flowers and there is a paved Fountain Garden. This consciously old-fashioned garden, based on a medieval layout, reflects the late nineteenth-century's romantic view of the Middle Ages and also the influence of William Morris's Arts and Crafts movement. There are romantic views of the house from walks through the woodland and always there is the constant sound of running water, like soothing background music.

OPPOSITE A half-timbered range overlooking the cobbled courtyard at the heart of Ightham Mote has bargeboards carved with the emblems of Henry VIII and his first wife, Catherine of Aragon. RIGHT Romantic Ightham Mote, hidden away in a deep wooded valley in the Kentish Weald and surrounded by a moat, is built of an attractive mix of local ragstone, oak and brick.

Kedleston Hall

Derbyshire
3 miles (4.8 kilometres) north
of Derby, easily reached and
signposted from the A38
Derby bypass

No one could describe this grand Neo-classical palace as homely. But then, it was always intended as a show place. On the impressive entrance front, looking north over a sweep of open pasture, a massive pedimented portico adorned with classical sculpture rises the full height of the three-storey central block. To either side are substantial rectangular pavilions, linked to the main building by curved corridors. A tower peeping above the west pavilion flags a medieval church, all that remains of the village swept away when the landscape park was created.

Sir Nathaniel Curzon, later 1st Lord Scarsdale, began the house in 1759, only a year after he had inherited the estate.

A cultivated man who was interested in the arts, he saw it as a setting for his paintings and sculpture, a collection that was on view to visitors from the day the house was built. The formal reception rooms and guest suite filling the central block were never intended to be used except for the entertainment of important visitors. The family lived in one pavilion; the kitchen and domestic offices were in the other.

Although work began under the direction of Matthew Brettingham and James Paine, by 1760 these two architects had been superseded by the young Robert Adam, recently returned from Rome, who transformed his predecessors' rather conventional designs. Adam's monumental Marble Hall, with ten alabaster columns like tree-trunks on both sides and classical statues in niches along the walls, is top-lit to suggest the open courtyard of a Roman villa. The adjoining rotunda known as the Saloon, its coffered dome rising to a height of 19 metres (62 feet), was based on the Pantheon in Rome, one of the most admired buildings of classical antiquity. To either side lie formal reception rooms, Adam's hand evident in virtually every detail of their decoration. Delicate plaster ceilings were executed by the Yorkshireman Joseph Rose, paintings were grouped and hung according to Adam's schemes – plaster frames built into the walls in some rooms ensure his arrangements have survived – and the furniture, some of it by Adam, some designed by the London cabinetmaker John Linnell, some with inputs from both men, picks up on decorative themes. In the State Withdrawing Room, carved and gilded dolphins, merfolk and sea nymphs on the four great sofas echo nautical touches in the ceiling. Made by Linnell, they are based on an Adam design, but one that Linnell radically altered.

The paintings hanging double-banked in all the principal rooms, including a number of epic canvases such as Benedetto Luti's *Cain and Abel* or Salomon Koninck's *Daniel before Nebuchadnezzar*, illustrate Lord Curzon's taste for seventeenth-century Italian and Dutch art. Family portraits dating back to the sixteenth century adorn the guest apartments, among them a charming study by Nathaniel Hone showing the 1st Lord Scarsdale walking in the grounds

LEFT Robert Adam designed a dramatic portico resembling a Greek temple for Kedleston's north front, with a windowless facade ornamented with lead figures in niches and carved stone medallions as a backdrop to the columns.

with his wife. Thomas Barber's portrayal of the elderly Mrs Garnett, the housekeeper who took Boswell and Dr Johnson round Kedleston in 1777, is also memorable.

Bluejohn vases and ornaments are part of a notable collection of this prized Derbyshire stone, and Kedleston was further enriched in the early twentieth century by Marquess Curzon of Kedleston, who acquired Indian and oriental artefacts during travels in Asia and while he was Viceroy of India from 1899 to 1905. In his will, the marquess left half the collection to the Victoria and Albert museum. The other half, on show in the house, is dominated by the peacock dress that was worn by Lady Curzon, its pattern of glistening peacock feathers created by embroidering cloth of gold with metal thread and jewels.

The long drive from the great arched gateway of Adam's north lodge runs through his idealised landscape park, with its carefully placed clumps of trees and a chain of serpentine lakes crossed by a three-arched stone bridge. Adam also designed the fishing pavilion on the upper lake, a Venetian window facing north over the water enabling ladies to cast a line into the pool below while being shielded from the sun.

To the south of the house, a broad open lawn bounded by a ha-ha marks the eighteenth-century informal garden and there are uninterrupted views across the park beyond as it rises gently to a belt of trees. A hexagonal summerhouse and orangery were both designed by George Richardson in the late eighteenth century and a pair of gates leads into a winding 3-mile (4.8-kilometre) circuit of the park, with views back towards the house from the section following the wooded skyline.

ABOVE Robert Adam's vast saloon at Kedleston, modelled on the Pantheon in Rome and hung with paintings of Roman ruins, was occasionally used for balls, but its main purpose was to impress visitors.

Killerton

Devon
On the west side of the B3181,
formerly the A38,
Exeter–Cullompton road

Below the steep wooded slopes of Killerton Clump, the highest point for miles around, is the sprawling, two-storey house of the Acland family. Later additions mask the plain Georgian block that was built in 1778–9 for Sir Thomas Dyke Acland, 7th Baronet, by the architect John Johnson to replace an Elizabethan house on more or less the same site. This house was only intended to be a temporary residence while a grandiose mansion by the much more fashionable James Wyatt was built on the hill, but Wyatt's plans never got further than the drawing board, and Johnson's modest building ended up being considerably expanded in the early nineteenth century and again in Edwardian times. At the foot of the drive are his magnificent stone stables, with an elegant cupola rising over the pedimented archway leading into the courtyard. Another Sir Thomas, the 10th Baronet, was responsible for the Victorian Norman Revival chapel by C.R. Cockerell to the north of the stables. This was built to supersede the tiny Elizabethan building on the other side of the hill that is almost all that remains of a former Acland seat at Columbjohn.

Killerton's interiors, much altered over the years and as unpretentious as the exterior, reflect domestic life and country living between the First and Second World Wars. A music room

in the centre of the house, lit by a window bay added in the 1820s, was the main focus of family activities. Music by Samuel Sebastian Wesley on the chamber organ that dominates the room is dedicated to the wife of the 10th Baronet, who took lessons from Wesley when he was organist of Exeter Cathedral.

ABOVE The elegant corridor leading to Killerton's original front door, on the south side of the house, has eighteenth-century fanlights designed by John Johnson and is little changed.
LEFT The modest Georgian house which forms the core of Killerton (right) was greatly extended in the 1820s by Sir Thomas Acland, who built new rooms for his children with direct access to the garden.

Dinner in the dining room on the west front, looking onto the garden, was always eaten in evening dress, with bare arms for the ladies however cold the weather and a place near the fire for the most privileged. The room is decorated with Johnson's eighteenth-century plaster frieze and with two terracotta roundels by the Danish sculptor Bertel Thorvaldsen, and it is hung with family portraits celebrating the 6th Baronet's advantageous marriage, to the heiress Cecily Wroth, in 1721. Wooden columns frame a connecting door to the library, where the books now include some of those that belonged to the Rev. Sabine Baring-Gould (1834–1924), the larger-than-life parson of the Devon village of Lewtrenchard, best known for his hymn 'Onward Christian Soldiers'. In a corner of the room is a set of false book-backs with fanciful titles.

A massive Edwardian staircase leads to the second floor and the rooms used to display the costume collection of Paulise de Bush, who rescued many eighteenth- and nineteenth-century items from a house in Berkshire during the Second World War. The changing displays feature carefully composed tableaux to show the life and society of the day.

Sir Thomas Dyke Acland, who built the Georgian house, also engaged the young John Veitch – he was not yet 21 – to lay out the grounds. Veitch, who went on to become one of the greatest nurserymen and landscape designers of his day and had a life-long association with Killerton, planted an arboretum on the slopes of Killerton Clump with paths climbing ever upwards through the trees and a beech walk following the contours of the hill.

The 10th Baronet, who presided over Killerton from his coming of age in 1808 and who did so much to create this exceptional place, is remembered by the granite cross that stands high up on the western edge of the garden and which was erected by 40 of his friends in 1873.

Killerton sits at the centre of an extensive estate in the fertile valleys of the Clyst and Culm. A mix of farmland and sizeable areas of woodland, it also includes the villages of Broadclyst and Budlake. There are many traditional buildings, among them Marker's Cottage in Broadclyst, a small cob and thatch house dating back to the fifteenth century which has a contemporary cob summerhouse and some mid-sixteenth-century paintings on a wooden screen. A few minutes' walk away, on the River Clyst, is the working Clyston Mill, probably

built in the early nineteenth century but occupying an ancient site, and half a mile (0.8 kilometre) north up the B3181 is Budlake village, where a small thatched cottage still has its 1950s Post Office Room.

ABOVE The laundry at Killerton, with racks which could be pulled out from the wall in the drying room, was in use until 1940 and kept three of the female members of staff fully occupied.

Kingston Lacy

Dorset
On the B3082 Wimborne–
Blandford road, 1½ miles
(2.4 kilometres) west of Wimborne

Home of the Bankes family from 1663, when Sir Ralph Bankes built a house here to replace the earlier seat at Corfe Castle, ruined in the Civil War, Kingston Lacy is a monument to the eccentric and original William John Bankes (1786–1855), friend of Byron. With the aid of Sir Charles Barry, architect of the Houses of Parliament, William transformed the house into an Italianate palazzo and filled it with paintings and other works of art he had acquired during his extensive travels in the Mediterranean. But he had little opportunity to enjoy what he had created. In 1841 he was accused of behaving indecently with a soldier in a London park and he fled to Italy, where he spent the rest of his life. Nevertheless, although unlikely ever to see his house again, this extraordinary man continued to concern himself with its furnishing and decoration.

Kingston Lacy still retains the shape of the double-pile Restoration mansion built by Sir Roger Pratt for Ralph Bankes, but has been much altered. The hipped roof, pierced by prominent dormers, is crowned with a balustrade and cupola by Barry and his tall chimneys at each corner give the house the look of an upturned footstool. On the south front, Barry's broad Italianate terrace sweeps right across the facade, with central steps flanked by urns and guarded by lions descending to a lawn dotted with Venetian well-heads. His impressive marble staircase leading up to the principal rooms on the first floor is also of Italian inspiration. Bronze figures set in niches in the airy loggia on the half-landing include a depiction of brave Lady Mary Bankes, who twice defended Corfe Castle for Charles I in the Civil War. She is shown holding the key of the castle, the actual keys to which are displayed over the fireplace in the library.

No traces of Roger Pratt's house survive inside, but some rooms still remain from R.F. Brettingham's remodelling in the 1780s for Henry Bankes. The painted ceiling by Cornelius Dixon in the saloon arches over the room like elaborate wrapping paper, delicate curves and spirals of foliage echoing the rich floral borders on the opulent Savonnerie carpet. The paintings hanging two and three deep include Rubens's portraits of Maria Pallavicino and Maria Grimaldi that were acquired by William: one encased in her gleaming wedding-dress like an exotic beetle, the other pictured with her dwarf. The library, with a fine collection of leather-bound books dating from the mid-seventeenth century, is also largely as designed by Brettingham. Now returned to the layout and decorative scheme shown in a photograph of 1904, this room is dominated by a ceiling painting by Guido Reni that William Bankes acquired from a palazzo in Bologna in 1840. Executed in 1599, the painting illustrates the description of the first day in Genesis, when the darkness was separated from the light, and is a rare example of Reni's early work. Taken down from the ceiling when the National Trust took over Kingston Lacy in 1981, this fragile painting, one of the most significant in the house, was stripped of nineteenth-century retouching and painstakingly restored in 2007.

More recently, in 2010, a vast mythical painting by Tintoretto was restored and put on display for the first time in the dining room. Painted in 1570–9, it was probably acquired by Bankes from a Venetian palazzo and, like the Guido Reni, has been in store since 1981. Sebastiano del Piombo's unfinished *The Judgement of Solomon*, which hangs nearby, was painted about 50 years earlier and was probably also intended for a Venetian setting.

While the dining-room panelling dates from the late nineteenth century, the adjoining Spanish Room is as William created it, with works he procured during his travels in Spain at the time of the Peninsular War set against gilded leather hangings and seen beneath a sumptuous coffered ceiling, thought to be one of those Scamozzi added to the Palazzo Contarini on the Grand Canal in Venice. Papal power and splendour shine through Velázquez's portrait of Cardinal Massimi, clothed here in peacock blue.

A naturalistic late eighteenth-century landscape park, dotted with mature trees and grazed by North Devon cattle, surrounds the house. The Edwardian garden restored by the Trust includes a brightly coloured parterre to the west of the house and a Victorian fernery to the east. A cedar walk lined with trees planted by visiting notables, including the Duke of

Wellington, leads to the lime avenue and an arboretum beyond. A pink granite obelisk, one of four in the garden, was brought here by William Bankes from a temple on the Nile.

Kingston Lacy is also the centre of an extensive agricultural estate in the valley of the River Stour. Including some fourteen farms and parts of the villages of Shapwick and Pamphill, this is a historic rural landscape, dotted with earthworks and rich in vernacular buildings. White Mill, a substantial brick and tile corn-mill on the Stour, was largely rebuilt in 1776 but is probably on the site of one of the eight mills recorded on the river in Domesday Book. It still has its original and now very rare elm and applewood machinery.

OPPOSITE The opulent Spanish room was created by William Bankes to show off his Spanish paintings, the finest of which is a portrait by Velázquez.
RIGHT The east front of Kingston Lacy looks out over a formal Dutch garden, with balls of golden yew, which was laid out in 1899.

Knightshayes

Devon
2 miles north of Tiverton
on the A396

The drunken mob that destroyed his Leicestershire factory on 28 June 1816 prompted the young John Heathcoat to move his revolutionary new lace-making machines to the safety of Devon, where he set up his works in one of the Tiverton mills left empty by the decline of the wool industry. The profits from what was to become the largest lace factory in the world enabled his grandson, John Heathcoat-Amory, the 1st Baronet, to purchase the Knightshayes estate and to build the idiosyncratic Gothic house that overlooks the little town in the valley below. Dating from 1869 to 1874, it is a singular place. Built of dark-red Hensley stone, the house rises forbiddingly from the terraces to the right of the drive in a frontage of pointed gables, large mullioned windows and prominent gargoyles.

A rare example of the domestic architecture of William Burges, the High Victorian medievalist who is much better known for his churches, such as the masterpiece at Studley Royal, this rather dour exterior was planned to conceal interiors of exceptional richness. Although Burges's designs were mostly rejected by his client, who thought them too extreme, the schemes produced by his more conventional replacement, John Diblee Crace, were by no means subdued and, too bold and colourful for Sir John's taste, were largely covered up in later years. Where possible, the National Trust has sought to restore the nineteenth-century work. Maxims by Robert Burns in bold gold lettering run round the frieze in the dining room, where rich red and green wallpaper designed by Crace complements the dark half-panelling. Above is a beamed and painted ceiling supported on corbels carved with creatures from the Devon countryside: a badger, a fox and an otter with a fish. The medievalism of the hall, with its Gothic arches, gallery, timber vault and whimsical carvings, is even more striking. This was the only room to be completed largely as Burges planned, and he also designed the painted bookcase with panels by Burne-Jones and Rossetti that stands here and is on loan from the Ashmolean Museum in Oxford. Recently,

LEFT The Gothic south front of Knightshayes, with its gables and gargoyles and an oriel window tucked into an angle of the facade, looks over formal terraced gardens on this side of the house.

too, a bedroom has been decorated on the basis of his original drawings and shows clearly the richness of his planned interiors. A wide painted frieze filled with birds perched on stylised branches echoes a motif used by Burges at his London house and a golden bed and painted cabinets, all on loan from the Victoria and Albert Museum, were also made to his designs.

The drawing room and morning room, both of which have boldly painted, compartmental ceilings, are hung with the nucleus of the art collection acquired in the years after the Second World War, when Knightshayes became a convalescent home for American airmen, by the 3rd Baronet (1894–1972) and his wife, the former golfing champion Joyce Wethered, whom Sir John had married in 1937. Vivid red poppies like a scarlet splash on the wall are one of two flower pictures attributed to Constable, a misty river scene in Picardy by Richard Parkes Bonington is complemented by a copy of a Turner seascape, and a Madonna and Child by Matteo di Giovanni is one of a number of early religious works. The original fireplace having been lost, the restored nineteenth-century decoration in the drawing room is now set off by a massive carved marble chimneypiece which was designed by Burges for Worcester College, Oxford, where it remained until 1966, and which the college has given to the Trust.

Although based on a nineteenth-century design by Edward Kemp, the garden owes much to the 3rd Baronet and his wife, who greatly enlarged it, creating the extensive woodland garden, and made it one of the finest in the county. A formal layout near the house includes a water-lily pool in a battlemented yew enclosure and a topiary hunt on the hedges framing the lawn to the south, one of the pursuing hounds shown gathering itself to leap a leafy obstacle. West of the house, a little valley has a show of daffodils in spring, and there is a large walled kitchen garden, with unique stepped walls, which was designed by Burges.

RIGHT, TOP This richly decorated bedroom at Knightshayes, with birds perching on stylised branches in the painted frieze and a patterned ceiling, typifies the lavish interiors which Burges planned for the house.
RIGHT, BOTTOM No original fittings or decoration survive in this bathroom at Knightshayes, which has been re-equipped with appropriate period pieces, many of them from Lanhydrock in Cornwall.

Knole

Kent
At the south end of Sevenoaks,
just east of the A225

A sudden opening between the buildings lining the main A225 through Sevenoaks signals the unpretentious gateway to Knole. The drive from this modest entrance emerges unexpectedly into the glorious park surrounding the house, scored with deep valleys, planted with ancient oaks, beeches and chestnuts, and grazed by herds of fallow and sika deer. As the road breasts a rise, there is a view of what looks like a compact hilltop town, with rabbit-cropped turf running almost up to the walls and a jumble of chimneys, gables, battlements and red-tiled roofs rising behind.

Sprawled round several courtyards like an Oxford college, Knole could house the retinue of a medieval prince. The main ranges are of rough Kentish ragstone, but hidden away in some of the minor courts are half-timbered facades, like those that can be seen in a hundred villages round about. Inside, in contrast to the rather plain and rugged exterior, are furnishings and decoration of great richness and rarity.

The core of Knole was built by Thomas Bourchier, Archbishop of Canterbury, between 1456 and his death in

1486, when he bequeathed it to the see of Canterbury. Three more archbishops enjoyed and improved the splendid residence Bourchier had created before Archbishop Cranmer was forced to give it to Henry VIII in 1538. By this time, Knole had been enlarged by the addition of an outer courtyard with a turreted gatehouse, but it seems the covetous king spent little or no time here. Knole was later held briefly by Elizabeth I's favourite, the Earl of Leicester, but by 1605 the freehold of the house and estate had been acquired by the late queen's cousin Thomas Sackville, the 1st Earl of Dorset, who had also been

Elizabeth I's Lord Treasurer (a post to which he was reappointed by James I), and the earl's descendants, later Dukes of Dorset and then Lords Sackville, have lived here ever since. The 1st Earl transformed Knole, turning the medieval

OPPOSITE Knole's Spangle Bedroom takes its name from the sequins on the bed hangings, now blackened but once silver, and is lined with fine Jacobean panelling and seventeenth-century Brussels tapestries.
ABOVE Knole's long west front looking over the park, with its massive brick chimneystacks and turreted gatehouse, probably dates from the late 1400s, although the curved gables were later embellishments.

and Tudor palace into a Renaissance mansion. He employed James I's master plasterer, Richard Dungan, and, probably, the king's master carpenter, William Portington, to create the Jacobean ceiling and intricate carved screen in the great hall, and he established a series of state apartments on the first floor, each with its own long gallery, connecting them to the hall with a grand staircase decorated in grisaille.

All this remains, and in the late seventeenth century, after depredations during the Civil War, when Knole and its lands were seized and the contents largely sold, the house was filled with an outstanding collection of seventeenth-century furniture and textiles by the 6th Earl. As Lord Chamberlain to William III, the earl was entitled to take away discarded furnishings from the royal palaces and he also enriched Knole with the furniture acquired by his grandfather, the Earl of Middlesex, who was Master of the Great Wardrobe to James I. As a result, Knole's galleries and bedchambers are filled with state beds, tapestries, chairs and stools that would once have adorned the palaces of Whitehall, Hampton Court and Kensington. Blue damask chairs in the Brown Gallery are stamped WP for Whitehall Palace, brass locks in the Cartoon Gallery carry William III's monogram, and a state bed hung with watery green Genoa velvet that was made for James II may have been the one in which the king spent his last night

in Whitehall Palace, on 17 December 1688, before fleeing to exile in France. Some of the rarest and finest pieces are displayed in the King's Room. A silver looking-glass, table and candlestands shine brilliantly in simulated candlelight, drawing the eye away from the magnificent great bed with its cloth of silver and gold and matching chairs and stools.

In the late eighteenth century, Knole was enriched again by the cultivated and handsome 3rd Duke, who added a notable picture collection of his own to the many paintings already in the house, among them portraits by Mytens, Dobson and Van Dyck from the early seventeenth century and John Wootton's panoramic landscape in the great hall, showing the 1st Duke and his retinue arriving at Dover Castle in 1728, its period frame adorned with two prominent Sackville leopards. The 3rd Duke acquired a number of Old Masters and patronised English painters of his day, in particular his close friend Joshua Reynolds, whose many canvases at Knole, most of them hung two deep in the Crimson Drawing Room, include a self-portrait, which Reynolds gave to the duke, and likenesses of Samuel Johnson and the playwright and poet Oliver Goldsmith and of the Duke's Chinese page. In an age when great houses all over the country were being remodelled in the newly fashionable classical style, the 3rd Duke also stands out for his appreciation of the ancient mansion he had inherited, which he did not alter and, less exceptionally, for his long relationship with the Italian dancer Giovanna Baccelli, who is immortalised in a plaster statue at the foot of the grand staircase, where her nude form, introduced at one time as that of 'a close friend of the family', reclines provocatively on a couple of tasselled plaster cushions.

This remarkable house is still much as it was in the 3rd Duke's day and has something to fascinate in every corner. Even the drainpipes have ornate leadwork heads, some in the form of a tiny castle, each one subtly individual. And each gable on the entrance front is crowned with a carved Sackville leopard. A major programme of building and conservation work that started in 2012 has closed parts of the house, but visitors can see newly opened rooms and work in progress.

LEFT Knole's Brown Gallery is hung with a set of sixteenth- and early seventeenth-century portraits showing famous people of the age and lined with chairs and stools acquired from royal palaces by the 6th Earl.

Lacock Abbey, Fox Talbot Museum and Village

Wiltshire
3 miles (4.8 kilometres) south of Chippenham, just east of the A350

This romantic house, with ranges of golden stone set round a grassy court, lies in a leafy pastoral setting beside the River Avon. Twisted Tudor chimneys break the roofline and a prominent octagonal tower juts out at one corner. This unusual and evocative place has a history going back almost 800 years, with many echoes of the nunnery for Augustinian canonesses founded in 1232 by the redoubtable Ela, Countess of Salisbury, in memory of her husband William Longespee. At its suppression by Henry VIII's commissioners in 1539, the nunnery was acquired by the duplicitous and self-seeking William Sharington, a rather unattractive man who seems to have behaved with more than the usual dishonesty in his public life, but who showed both sensitivity and imagination in converting his purchase into a house. Although he demolished the abbey church, the outlines of which are now marked by long grass in the south lawn, Sharington kept many of the nunnery's original rooms and also incorporated innovative Renaissance features that were rare in England at this date. Beautiful fifteenth-century cloisters, with carved bosses punctuating the stone vaulting, still frame the court at the heart of the house. The daughters of well-to-do families who formed the community sunned themselves on the stone seats set into the walls or stretched out their hands to the blaze in the great fireplace preserved in the warming room, one of a set of fine, mostly stone-vaulted thirteenth-century chambers, including the sacristy and chapter house, opening onto the east cloister walk. The ghost of the nunnery is also evident in the thirteenth-century vaulted undercroft in the west range, part of which became the servants' hall; in a huge blocked medieval fireplace in the kitchen; in wall-paintings of St Christopher and the crucifixion of St Andrew in the chaplains' room; and in the Brown Gallery, which Sharington created out of part of the refectory and where original corbels still support the roof, although this is now hidden by the ceiling.

The wide Stone Gallery which Sharington fashioned from part of the nuns' dormitory to give views over his formal garden on the east side of the house is still much as he left it, lit by largely Tudor windows and with a delicately carved classical chimneypiece. More Renaissance features adorn Sir William's three-storey octagonal tower, where a narrow angled passage leads to a high-ceilinged chamber on the first floor. A place where Sharington could keep important papers and display precious objects, this tiny cupboard of a room, possibly the only one of its kind surviving in England, was both a strong-room and an early equivalent of the *studiolo* of an Italian Renaissance prince, where books and treasured works of art would be kept. It is almost filled by an elaborate octagonal stone table supported on the shoulders of four satyrs and carved with the scorpions of the Sharington crest, their vicious tails and matchstick legs also recognisable in pendants studding the vaulted ceiling. This exceptional stone carving may be the work of John Chapman, who worked for Henry VIII, or by a foreign craftsman from the Tudor court.

The newest architectural fashions were again introduced to Lacock in the middle of the eighteenth century, when John Ivory Talbot, a descendant of Sharington's niece, made extensive changes to the house and grounds. Sanderson Miller's Gothick hall, commissioned in 1753 and completed in 1755, is entered by a prominent double flight of steps on the west front. Below the painted heraldic ceiling, decorative niches with pinnacled canopies are filled with terracotta figures made in 1755–6 by the Austrian sculptor Victor Alexander Sederbach, whose strange company, two nuns, a bishop, a knight and a grisly skeleton among them, is dominated by Ela in heroic pose over the fireplace, a bird perching on her outstretched left arm. The adjoining dining room was also remodelled by John Ivory Talbot, in 1751–2, but here, in contrast to the drama next door, the decoration is coolly classical.

In the lovely South Gallery, hung with family portraits, including a painting of Sir William dressed in black with a long, red beard, a brown, indistinct photograph placed by one of the oriel windows shows the bare outlines of the lattice panes. This blurred print was produced from a tiny negative, the world's first, made in 1835 by the pioneer photographer William Henry Fox Talbot, who inherited the estate as a baby in 1800. Although he did not come to live at Lacock until 1827, he conducted many of his early experiments at the abbey. The earliest photograph was taken by Joseph Niépce in 1826, but Fox Talbot was responsible for inventing the negative–positive

process which paved the way for the development of modern photography.

The ground floor of the converted barn at the abbey gates is devoted to this exceptional man's life and work, displaying the skeletal forms of leaves and flowers captured in early experiments as well as portraits of his family and life at Lacock. Fox Talbot's achievements in other areas are also recorded, from his translation of the cuneiform inscriptions discovered in 1847 at the palaces of the Assyrian kings in what is now Iraq to his work on microscopy, demonstrated by magnified insect wings and plant sections. Also a prominent mathematician and astronomer and a Fellow of the Royal Society, Fox Talbot's scientific interests were accompanied by an appreciation of the artistic possibilities of photography, as clearly illustrated by his plates in *The Pencil of Nature* (1844–6), the first book to include photographs. The museum also exhibits examples of the work of other pioneers in this field, such as Daguerre, Niépce and Wedgwood, and early photographic equipment.

Beyond the Fox Talbot museum is the village of Lacock, now a picturesque assemblage of well-preserved buildings from the fourteenth to the late eighteenth century and primarily a tourist attraction, much used for filming period dramas, but for hundreds of years a busy and prosperous place. There has been a permanent settlement here since Saxon times and probably even earlier, but the present layout, with four main streets forming a square, dates from the thirteenth century, when a planned village was established for workers on the abbey estates. Its inhabitants grew rich on the medieval wool industry and the weekly market initiated by Ela. Lacock was ideally placed for both, being within a day's journey of prime grazing lands on the Cotswolds and Marlborough Downs and a staging-post on the road linking centres of the wool trade in the West Country. There was also access to the sea via the River Avon, which meanders past to the east. At its height in the late Middle Ages, Lacock's continued prosperity after the decline of the wool trade owed much to its position on a through route between Marlborough and Bristol, which brought wealth to the village and travellers to fill its many inns until the mid-eighteenth century. From then onwards Lacock stood still. Lack of development in the nineteenth century, when many nearby settlements expanded rapidly, was largely due to the Talbot family, who ensured no railway lines came too near the village. Lacock fossilised, resulting in one of the most pleasing and individual places in England.

Reflecting the village's origins, the irregular terraces that line the streets are all built on narrow medieval house plots running back from the frontages. There are timber-framed buildings with mullioned windows and jettied upper storeys, seventeenth-century stone cottages and elegant Georgian brick mansions, such as the two examples dated 1719 and 1779 in East Street, but many of the apparently later buildings are older than they look and were originally timber-framed.

Of the numerous inns, the timber-framed Angel in Church Street retains its medieval layout and the passage through which horses would be led to the yard behind, while the George in West Street has an original dog-powered spit. A magnificent fourteenth-century tithe barn would once have stored rent paid to the abbey in the form of corn, hides and fleeces. Standing slightly apart is the battlemented and pinnacled church of St Cyriac. Largely rebuilt when the village was at its most prosperous in the fifteenth century, it contains the grandiose Renaissance tomb of Sir William Sharington. A narrow lane leads from the church to the eighteenth-century packhorse bridge over the Bide Brook and to the Avon beyond, where a medieval bridge crosses the river.

Fox Talbot's granddaughter Matilda gave the abbey and the village to the National Trust in 1944, and members of the Talbot family continued to live in the abbey until 2011.

ABOVE Cloister walks of the fourteenth and early fifteenth century, when Lacock was an Augustinian nunnery, frame a grassy court at the heart of the abbey
OPPOSITE The octagonal tower which William Sharington added to Lacock Abbey contains a strong-room where he kept his precious books and other valuables.

Lanhydrock

Cornwall
2¹/₂ miles (4 kilometres) south-east of Bodmin, overlooking the valley of the River Fowey

Lanhydrock is lost in a long Victorian afternoon. No one is at work in the cool, tiled dairy, or in the huge stone-flagged kitchen, and buckets and brushes are lined up in the housemaids' closet ready for the next day. No sound comes from the extensive servants' quarters, where a pair of black boots stands neatly by a bed and the footman's livery lies ready to wear, while in the nursery wing all is still. Pipes lie waiting in the masculine confines of the smoking room and the dining-room table is laid for ten, the menu already handwritten in French. The period feeling is so strong that it would be no surprise to meet a scurrying maid with a tray or to hear the Robartes family and their guests, or their nine children, coming in from the garden.

Lanhydrock's interiors vividly evoke gracious living in the 1890s. The house itself, with three battlemented ranges of silver-grey granite set round a courtyard and mullioned windows, is much older, but was largely rebuilt at the end of the nineteenth century after a disastrous fire in 1881. Although, to avoid the risk of another fire, no gas or electricity was installed, the designs by Richard Coad, a local architect who had trained in London, incorporated the latest comforts and conveniences, such as the massive radiators featured in almost every room. The hill behind the house was cut away to accommodate a full range of service rooms and a steam generator in the cellar powered the jets for scouring greasy pots in the scullery and a range of equipment in the airy, high-ceilinged kitchen, where butterscotch walls reflect the late nineteenth-century colour scheme. Ice was brought by train from Plymouth for the ice chests in the pantry and spring water from the hill above the house was channelled along runnels in the slate and marble slabs in the dairy where jellies and custards were put to stand.

At the same time, as he was instructed, Coad restored the Jacobean exterior of the rather old-fashioned house built here by Sir Richard Robartes and his son between 1630 and 1642, his new work merging beautifully with the one wing that was not extensively damaged in the flames. An enchanting detached gatehouse still stands at the head of a beech and sycamore avenue leading away across the park, as it has done since the seventeenth century, and obelisks crowning this little architectural conceit are echoed by more on the main building and on the low wall enclosing formal gardens around the house.

Only the north wing, which survived the fire intact, gives a flavour of the original interiors. A sunny 35.5-metre (116-foot) gallery running the length of the second floor and lit by windows on both sides suggests what might have been lost. The barrel ceiling arching overhead is covered with magical plasterwork dating from just before the outbreak of the Civil War. Although the 24 panels illustrating incidents from the Old Testament take centre stage, the delightful creatures surrounding them are far more memorable, furry porcupines, bears, armadillos and peacocks rubbing shoulders with

LEFT In the dairy, spring water from the hill above the house was channelled along runnels in the marble and slate slabs to keep butter, cheeses and puddings cool.

ABOVE A disastrous fire in 1881 destroyed most of the main house at Lanhydrock, but the delicious gatehouse, built in 1651 as a hunting lodge from which to watch the pursuit of deer, was untouched.

mythical beasts, such as dragons and centaurs. The gallery is hung with portraits, including works by Thomas Hudson, who was a West Country painter, and George Romney, and this room houses an exceptional collection of early books dating from 1590 to 1700, among them a four-volume atlas of 1694 with delicate watercolour maps showing the Cornish landholdings of the 2nd Earl of Radnor.

Like Coad's interiors, Lanhydrock's garden reflects Victorian taste. In front of the house, clipped yew marks the corners of six geometric shapes planted with roses in George Gilbert Scott's formal layout of 1857 and more yew studs his intricate parterre beside the north wing, bedded out twice a

year. Beyond the obelisks and castellations of the surrounding parapet, a large informal garden dating from the 1860s covers the steep slopes rising above the house. Winding paths through shrubs and trees, including exceptional displays of large Himalayan magnolias, rhododendrons and camellias, lead ever upwards, past the well used by the monks of St Petroc's Priory at Bodmin, who held Lanhydrock before the Dissolution, and the strong spring feeding the stream that runs down the slope. Vistas over the house and the wooded valley of the Fowey culminate in magnificent views from the broad terrace walk at the top of the garden and there is a network of paths across the wood- and parkland of the estate.

Lyme Park, House and Garden

Cheshire
On the south side of the A6;
6½ miles (10.4 kilometres)
south-east of Stockport, entrance
on the western outskirts of Disley

Used to the blinding sun and hard shadows of his homeland, the Venetian architect Giacomo Leoni must have found it hard to contend with the grey skies and misty distances of the bleak Peak moors at Lyme when Peter Legh engaged him to remodel his largely Elizabethan mansion in 1725. As at Clandon Park, Leoni responded by bringing a touch of Italy to the English countryside.

The courtyard of the Tudor house was ringed by shady arcades and given a double flight of steps rising to the pedimented entrance, as if it were the *cortile* of a grand *palazzo*. The Mediterranean effect was later enhanced by the addition of a marble pavement and an Italian Renaissance well-head.

BELOW The Venetian architect Giacomo Leoni, who was commissioned to remodel Lyme Park in the 1720s, was responsible for the Italianate south front.

The long south front is entirely Leoni. Built of rose-tinted stone, it is dominated by a classical portico extending the full height of the house. Giant lead figures of Venus, Neptune and Pan set along the pediment stare at their reflection in the lake below and six bays separated by pilasters stretch away on either side. Something of the grand Elizabethan house survives on the north, where a towering Tudor gateway leads into Leoni's courtyard.

Despite much later remodelling, two Elizabethan interiors survive: a light and airy panelled long gallery hung with seventeenth- and early eighteenth-century portraits and a richly panelled Tudor drawing room. In the eighteenth century, although he was primarily involved with the exterior of the house, Leoni also created some internal spaces, of which his oak-panelled saloon, lit by windows looking over the park through the columns of his portico and adorned with a gilded rococo ceiling, has all the elegance of the period. Pale three-dimensional limewood carvings decorating the panelling were introduced from elsewhere in the house by Lewis Wyatt, in an entirely sympathetic idiom, in the early nineteenth century. One of these realistic compositions, which are traditionally attributed to Grinling Gibbons, cunningly intertwines an artist's palette and brushes, a partly folded chart and navigation instruments. In another, a beautifully embroidered lace handkerchief falls in naturalistic folds.

A full-length portrait of the Black Prince in Leoni's grand classical entrance hall is a vivid reminder that the land of Lyme was won for the Legh family in 1346 on the battlefields of France. Lyme was to remain the home of the Leghs for 600 years and many other aspects of the family history are reflected in the contents. A copy of Velázquez's *Las Meninas* portrays the celebrated mastiffs that were bred here until the twentieth century and were traditionally presented as royal gifts to the courts of Europe. The ancient Greek sculptures in the library, one of the interiors fashioned by Wyatt, were excavated in the early nineteenth century by the intrepid Thomas Legh, whose portrait in oriental costume enlivens the staircase. His grandest find, a stele of Melisto and Epigenes of *c.*350BC, has pride of place over the fireplace, but the little tombstone of the same date in the window bay, commemorating a mother and her newborn babe, is more memorable. A tragedy of a different kind is recalled in the Stag Parlour, where faded red covers on the Chippendale chairs were reputedly made from the cloak

ABOVE The attractive long gallery at Lyme Park, with its fine Jacobean oak panelling and seventeenth- and early eighteenth-century family portraits, dates from the building of the Elizabethan house but has been altered since.

Charles I wore on the scaffold. In the late twentieth century the house was enriched by the magnificent collection of seventeenth- and eighteenth-century bracket and longcase clocks acquired by Sir Francis Legh, who was born at Lyme in 1919, the earliest of them an instrument by Ahasuerus Fromanteel of 1658, which was one of the first pendulum mechanisms ever produced. Five clocks by the outstanding London maker Thomas Tompion from the collection of Mr M.H. Vivian are now also on display. Most recently, the rare illuminated Missal that was printed for William Caxton in 1487, and probably acquired by Sir Piers Legh V on publication or soon afterwards, has been bought back for the house.

There has been a garden on this unpromising site, carved out of moorland, since the seventeenth century. But the present layout and planting are essentially Victorian and owe much to William John Legh, 1st Lord Newton, who inherited in 1857 and took advice from the garden writer and theorist Edward Kemp. A sweep of grass running down to a naturalistic lake below the terrace on the south front and the informal semi-wild area along the deep ravine carved by the stream feeding the lake contrast with a series of formal gardens with massed bedding, one of which is overlooked by an orangery designed by Lewis Wyatt.

From the south terrace there are views across the lake to Lyme's medieval deer-park. Set dramatically on a windswept ridge broods Lyme Cage, its stark outlines relieved by little domed turrets at each corner. Probably built to designs by Leoni as a hunting tower and banqueting house, it was modified in the early nineteenth century by Lewis Wyatt.

Montacute House

Somerset
In Montacute village, 4 miles (6.4 kilometres) west of Yeovil, on the south side of the A3088, 3 miles (4.8 kilometres) east of the A303

Montacute invites the kind of elaborate compliment paid by one sixteenth-century visitor, who thought the fronting stone terrace superior to St Mark's Square in Venice. Probably finished by 1601, it is a tall and confident H-shaped Elizabethan house of local honey-brown Ham stone, with a huge display of glittering glass. Designed by a local stonemason, the gifted William Arnold, it was built for Sir Edward Phelips, an upwardly mobile lawyer who would become Master of the Rolls and Chancellor to the Household of Prince Henry, Charles I's ill-fated elder brother.

Long facades facing east and west rise three storeys to a roofline fretted with delicate chimneys, parapets and pinnacles and adorned with curved Flemish gables. Classical details on the entrance front, such as the nine curiously lumpy statues in Roman dress, betray the influence of the Renaissance, slowly filtering north from its beginnings in Italy. The other side of the house is even more engaging. Here stonework from nearby Clifton Maybank, a splendid sixteenth-century mansion that was partly dismantled in 1786, ornaments the two-storey front grafted on between the existing wings in the late eighteenth century. The roofline parapet is crowded with heraldic beasts on pedestals, the shadows cast by these decorative features and by the advancing and retreating wall surfaces giving the house a sculptural quality. Montacute's fantasy outline is continued in the spiky balustrade and the two delightful Elizabethan pavilions topped with obelisks that border the entrance court.

Although hardly any of the original contents survived the decline in the Phelipses' fortunes, which led to Montacute being put up for sale in 1929, fine furniture and tapestries from the Sir Malcolm Stewart bequest give the rooms an authentic atmosphere. In the medieval-style great hall the early morning sun casts richly coloured pools through the

LEFT The local honey-coloured limestone of which Montacute is built is now attractively weathered and lichened.
ABOVE In the 1780s, the Elizabethan west front of Montacute House was embellished with an ornamental facade from another Tudor house, which now forms an arresting and dramatic frontispiece.
OPPOSITE Early seventeenth-century plasterwork in the great hall shows a village drama, in which a man is punished after his wife caught him drinking when he should have been minding the baby.

heraldic glass in the east-facing windows. Phelips family portraits hang above the original panelling and an elaborate stone screen with columns framing rusticated arches runs across one end. Rams' heads with extravagant curling horns are carved on the capitals of the columns. A rare early seventeenth-century plaster panel on the north wall gives a tableau of rural life: a hen-pecked husband caught by his wife drawing beer from a barrel rather than attending to the baby is punished by being paraded round the village astride a pole.

A rich collection of hangings includes a fine fifteenth-century French *millefleurs* tapestry showing a knight on horseback against a beautifully detailed carpet of flowers, and the importance of domestic needlework in past centuries is shown in a changing display of samplers from the collection formed by Dr Douglas Goodhart, which ranges in date from 1609 to the twentieth century. The room where Lord Curzon slept when he leased Montacute in the early twentieth century has an ingenious bath concealed in a Jacobean-style cupboard and the former great chamber, with its majestic carved chimneypiece, the finest in the house, has the only original furniture, a set of six early eighteenth-century walnut cane-back armchairs.

A magnificent long gallery, the largest surviving Elizabethan example in Britain, runs over 50 metres (170 feet) down the length of the third floor. Used for entertaining important guests and for exercise in inclement weather, the gallery is hung with Tudor and Jacobean paintings from the National Portrait Gallery that echo the portraits of family and notables that would once have hung here. A set of stiff kings and queens like a pack of playing cards contrasts with more realistic works, such as the delightful picture showing Robert Carey, 1st Earl of Monmouth, with his family, the five adults posed as if in a photograph, or the portraits of the handsome, curly-headed Robert Sidney, 1st Earl of Leicester (1563–1626),

and of little Henry, Prince of Wales (1594–1612), the child's creamy pallor emphasised by his rich crimson dress. There are panoramic views from the two great oriel windows, framed by orange trees in pots, at either end of the gallery.

Although now incorporating both nineteenth- and twentieth-century features and planting schemes, the extensive garden still follows the outlines of the original layout. The oriel window at the north end of the long gallery looks down on a formal rectangle of trees and grass which lies on the site of the Elizabethan garden. Raised walks framing the sunken lawn with its nineteenth-century balustraded pond probably date from when the house was built and a border of shrub roses under the retaining wall includes species in cultivation in the sixteenth century. The cedar lawn, with an arcaded garden house to which Lord Curzon may have added the Elizabethan facade, lies on the site of an old orchard.

An avenue of mature cedars, beeches and limes, fronted by clipped Irish yew, frames the west drive created in 1851–2, its lines continued in the wide grassy ride edged with limes which stretches away across the park to the east.

Mottisfont

Hampshire
4½ miles (7.2 kilometres) north-west of Romsey, ¾ mile (1.2 kilometres) west of the A3057

Those lucky enough to acquire monastic houses at the time of the Dissolution in the 1530s were then faced with the problem of transforming them into domestic residences. Most chose to adapt the monks' living quarters, but a few ambitious men sought to incorporate the church itself into their conversions. One such was William Lord Sandys, Lord Chamberlain to Henry VIII, who was granted the priory of Mottisfont in exchange for the villages of Chelsea and Paddington and whose descendants were to move here from The Vyne after the Civil War. The north front of his Tudor house, built of silvery stone, runs the full length of what was the nave of the church, ending in the truncated crossing tower. The outline of the arch leading to the north transept shows clearly on the wall of the tower. Original mullions survive on the ground floor, but sash windows were inserted above as part of extensive Georgian alterations. These also account for the eighteenth-century stone balls crowning the medieval buttreses, transforming them into ornamental pilasters.

The cultured world of the 1740s is far more pronounced on the south side, where an elegant red-brick Georgian facade with a central pediment is framed by two shallow bayed wings stepped out from the main body of the house. Three storeys here, in contrast to two on the north, reflect the sloping site.

Few traces of the Tudor interior escaped the Georgian remodelling, but the ghost of the priory emerges in the atmospheric early thirteenth-century cellarium, where columns of Caen stone, now partly buried, support a vaulted roof. The most individual feature of the house, the Whistler Room over the cellarium, is a much later addition. This enchanting drawing room takes its name from Rex Whistler's elaborate *trompe-l'oeil* murals, imitating Gothick plasterwork, which he painted in 1938–9, after the completion of his mammoth work at Plas Newydd. More theatrical backdrop than room decoration, Whistler's work includes the illusion of a smoking urn and of a paint pot abandoned high on a cornice. At Mottisfont Whistler had also been commissioned to design the furniture, but he never returned from the Second World War to complete his assignment.

Whistler's sketches for the drawing-room murals, and some idyllic landscapes that were offered as an alternative decorative scheme, are now part of an exceptional assemblage of late nineteenth- and twentieth-century art shown in the house. Apart from the Whistler drawings, these are all from the collection of the artist Derek Hill (1916–2000), whose friend Mrs Gilbert Russell gave Mottisfont to the National Trust. Hung in the library, morning room, entrance hall and west corridor, the pictures, many of them drawings, pastels or gouaches, are by artists who inspired Hill in his own work or who reflect his interest in his contemporaries. There are representative works by Bonnard, Vuillard, Seurat, Corot and Degas, but most of the names shown here are British, with several paintings by Hill's former students at the British School in Rome, where he was art director in the 1950s. On the whole, these are intimate pieces, ranging from a drawing of a surgical operation by Barbara Hepworth, a gouache by Graham Sutherland and a gentle portrait of his sister Gwen by Augustus John to studies of trees, leaves and pears. A number of landscapes include many works by Hill himself, among them scenes from the west of Ireland, where the artist had a house in Co. Donegal, and Italian landscapes that were captured when he was living near Florence on the estate of the art historian Bernard Berenson. Further twentieth-century works and contemporary art are shown in changing exhibitions in the light and airy gallery on the top floor of the house.

Lying low on sweeping lawns by the River Test, the abbey is the centrepiece of beautiful wooded gardens. Many of the mature walnuts, sycamores, Spanish chestnuts, beeches and cedars for which the property is now famous were part of the eighteenth-century grounds, but some are even older. A little Gothick summerhouse also dates from the eighteenth century and incorporates medieval floor tiles and a corbel from the priory

Mr and Mrs Gilbert Russell, who came to Mottisfont in 1934, introduced features designed by Geoffrey Jellicoe and, later, Norah Lindsay, among them the paved octagon surrounded by clipped yew and the box- and lavender-edged parterre. There is also a magnolia garden and a beech circle, and two walled gardens contain Mottisfont's renowned collection of roses. On the far side of the grounds, crystal-clear water still gushes from the spring that attracted the Austin canons to this sheltered spot nearly 800 years ago.

RIGHT A former entrance hall at Mottisfont Abbey was decorated in 1938–9 by Rex Whistler, whose *trompe l'oeil* fantasy, set off by the rich green velvet curtains, includes trophy panels painted in grisaille.

Mount Stewart

Co. Down
15 miles (24 kilometres) east of Belfast on the A20 Newtownards–Portaferry road, 5 miles (8 kilometres) south-east of Newtownards

This long, low house looking south over Strangford Lough is associated with two exceptional men, the architect James 'Athenian' Stuart and the politician Viscount Castlereagh, but it is alive with the spirit of Edith, Lady Londonderry, the vivacious and brilliant wife of the 7th Marquess, who redecorated and furnished most of the house between the First and Second World Wars.

The main block, built of dark grey local stone and with a huge classical portico looking onto the balustraded entrance court, was designed in the mid-1830s, to replace the original eighteenth-century house, by the Irish architect William Vitruvius Morrison for the 3rd Marquess of Londonderry. Morrison's grandiose octagonal hall, lit from above by a huge dome and with a black-and-white chequered floor and classical statues framed by Ionic pillars, fills the centre of the house. A bust immortalises the linen merchant Alexander Stewart, the 3rd Marquess's grandfather, who acquired the estate in 1744, while the rust-coloured early eighteenth-century Chinese dinner service displayed here was inherited by Stewart's wife, whose brother was Governor of Bombay. Morrison's vast drawing room divided by screens of green Ionic columns is similarly imposing and gave Lady Londonderry just the setting she needed for her lavish entertaining.

George Dance's west wing, created for the 1st Marquess in the early nineteenth century and built of the same grey stone as the later work, has a lighter and more intimate touch. The delightful music room, the least changed of his interiors, has an inlaid floor by John Ferguson, with a scalloped octagon of oak and mahogany surrounded by radiating boards of mellow bog fir enclosing a central motif like a Catherine wheel. Delicate plasterwork on the ceiling reflects the design. Double doors lead into Dance's elegant staircase hall, which is dominated by George Stubbs's intriguing painting of the racehorse Hambletonian. Stubbs shows the horse after his win at Newmarket in 1799, a race in which the artist felt the animal had been driven too hard. Hambletonian is depicted in an impossible pose, standing on his two left legs, his groom's right arm stretched like elastic over his neck.

The principal bedrooms called after European cities (Rome, Moscow, even Sebastopol), the mementoes in the Castlereagh Room and Empire chairs used by delegates to the Congress of Vienna in 1815, including those occupied by Wellington and Talleyrand, recall the proud and austere 2nd Marquess, Foreign Secretary for ten years, who died so tragically by his own hand in 1822, misunderstood by the nation to which he had devoted his life. The main architect of the Act of 1801 that united Great Britain and Ireland until the creation of Eire in 1921, Castlereagh went on to play a major role in the war against Napoleon and in the Congress of Vienna that concluded it, regarded as the world's first summit. It is a measure of Castlereagh's achievement that the European boundaries established at this time were to endure until the start of the First World War.

The 6th and 7th Marquesses also followed prominent political careers, and both Edward VII and the future George VI were entertained at Mount Stewart. As Secretary of State for Air from 1931 to 1935, the 7th Marquess promoted the Hurricane and Spitfire fighter planes, which were to prove so crucial in the Battle of Britain in 1940, and introduced legislation to establish air corridors. And in the late 1930s he made several private visits to Germany to meet Hitler and other Nazi leaders in an effort to promote Anglo-German understanding.

Leading politicians, among them Sir Arthur Balfour, Harold Macmillan and Ramsay MacDonald, featured at the celebrated house parties that Lady Edith gave in the interwar years. Her flamboyant 1920s decor, the backdrop for these glittering occasions, survives in most of the principal rooms. Salmon-pink walls in Morrison's drawing room set off a green grand piano and comfortable chairs and sofas are spread invitingly on the pink Aubusson carpets. Subdued low-level lighting comes from lamps of every description, some made out of classical urns, others once altar candlesticks. Chinese tea caddies converted into lamp stands, chinoiserie screens and other oriental pieces were brought back from a trip to China in 1912.

Two chairs in this room and the friendly stone animals sitting on a terrace on the south front, four plump dodos, a grinning dinosaur, a hedgehog and a frog among them, recall the Ark Club, formed from those who attended Lady Londonderry's gatherings for political and military figures at the family's London house during the First World War.

Members of the club, all of whom were given the name of some exotic creature, included Sir Arthur Balfour (the albatross), Winston Churchill (the warlock), and Lord Hailsham (the wild boar). Appropriately, Lady Londonderry was Circe the Sorceress. This legendary beauty, whose charm is if anything enhanced by the drab khaki uniform she is wearing in the portrait showing her as head of the Women's Legion, was also largely responsible for Mount Stewart's enchanting 31.5-hectare (78-acre) garden, which flourishes with subtropical luxuriance in the temperate climate of the Ards peninsula. Many of the tender trees and shrubs cultivated here are rarely seen elsewhere in the British Isles and there is a notable collection of evergreens and other species from the Southern Hemisphere. Around the house a formal garden is laid out as a series of varied outdoor rooms. An Italian garden, with steps descending to fountain pools, was designed by Lady Londonderry and is enhanced by imaginative statuary, including mischievous monkeys and winged dragons perched on columns. The more intimate sunken garden to the west of the house is based on a design by Gertrude Jekyll, with rose-hung pergolas and scalloped beds, and the secluded, shady Mairi Garden laid out in the shape of a Tudor rose recalls Lady Mairi Bury, the 7th Marquess's daughter, who gave Mount Stewart and many of its contents, together with an endowment, to the National Trust in 1976.

Away from the house the planting is informal, with magnificent trees, shrubs and herbaceous plants lining the walks round the lake created by the 3rd Marquess, part of a nineteenth-century layout which Lady Londonderry embellished. Conical roofs glimpsed above the trees on the summit of the wooded hill beyond the lake mark the Londonderrys' burial ground, Tir Nan Og, which contains the graves of the 7th Marquess and his wife.

The octagonal Temple of the Winds, on a prominent knoll in the woods to the south of the house, is a replica, like its counterpart at Shugborough, of the Tower of the Winds in ancient Athens and the only building in Ireland by the pioneering Neo-classical architect James 'Athenian' Stuart. Erected by the 1st Marquess between 1782 and 1785, it was designed as an eye-catcher and banqueting house. The sumptuously decorated upper room has another star-like marquetry floor by John Ferguson, the design again echoed in plaster on the ceiling, and a dew-drop chandelier hangs from the central medallion. On the floor below, long sash windows can be lowered into the basement to give an uninterrupted view over the island-studded waters of Strangford Lough to the prominent silhouette of Scrabo Tower on the north shore, built in memory of the 3rd Marquess.

ABOVE The centre of Mount Stewart is filled by a vast octagonal hall designed by William Vitruvius Morrison, with classical nudes by Lawrence Macdonald at either end of the room.

Nostell Priory and Parkland

West Yorkshire
On the A638 out of Wakefield towards Doncaster

Sir Rowland Winn, 4th Baronet, commissioned two houses at Nostell in the mid-eighteenth century. One of them, a classical building only a few feet high, stands at the foot of the south staircase of the priory. Like the similarly fine dolls' house at Uppark, it is fully furnished in period style, and was built to delight an adult as much as to enchant a child. Marble chimneypieces are copied from plates in James Gibbs's *Book of Architecture* of 1728, carved mouldings and cornices in the principal rooms are picked out in gilt, and the furnishings are accurate in every detail. Little figures representing the family are looked after by servants in the Winn livery of grey and yellow, and there is even a glass mouse under the kitchen table. If family tradition is correct, this minor masterpiece was the work of two young men closely associated with Rowland Winn's new mansion: James Paine, who executed and modified the plans of the gentleman-architect Colonel James Moyser; and the cabinetmaker Thomas Chippendale, both then still in their teens.

The estate had been acquired by the Winns, a family of London merchants, in 1650, ten years before a baronetcy was granted by Charles II, and has been held by the family ever since. The present house, built to the north of an earlier building formed out of the old priory, was created over 50 years, beginning in 1735, with a strong contrast between James Paine's rococo decoration for Sir Rowland and the more severe classical designs of his successor, Robert Adam, later to oust Paine again at Kedleston, for Sir Rowland's son. Fine interiors include paintings by Antonio Zucchi that are among his earliest work in England, plasterwork by Joseph Rose the Younger and furniture by Chippendale.

Because only one of Adam's planned extensions to Paine's pedimented classical house was ever completed, the exterior of the priory is pleasingly asymmetrical. Adam was also responsible for lifting the main entrance facade by adding the substantial terrace reached by two flights of gracefully curving steps. Inside, however, it is Paine's rooms that are the more flamboyant. Adam's beautiful hall is a serenely graceful room, with Rose's delicate plasterwork picked out against a subtly darker background. The library, decorated with nine stylised classical paintings by Zucchi and with the Winn family's important collection of books housed in the pedimented bookcases, is dominated by a superb desk by Chippendale. The outstanding book collection overflows into the billiard room next door, where an intriguing longcase clock is an early piece by the young John Harrison, who made the mechanism for the clock almost entirely out of wood. The son of the estate carpenter at Nostell, Harrison went on to make his name by inventing the first timepiece that was accurate enough to enable seamen to determine their longitude, for which he received a reward of £20,000.

Adam's restrained treatments only serve to heighten the opulence of Paine's rooms. Zucchi's playful cherubs in the elaborate panels over the doors in the dining room and the plaster frieze of vines and satyrs' masks suggest an appreciation of the good things in life. Paine was also responsible for the splendid ceiling in what is now the state bedchamber, with its

ABOVE The austere east front of Nostell Priory, with the projecting portico of Robert Adam's family wing at the north end.
OPPOSITE The plasterer Joseph Rose the Younger and the decorative painter Antonio Zucchi executed Adam's delicate ceiling designs.

trio of music-making cherubs, but the exquisite Chinese paper, with brightly coloured birds of all sizes and varieties perching on branches laden with flowers and foliage, was chosen by Chippendale to complement his rich green and gold lacquer furniture, among his most unusual work.

Fine paintings hang throughout the house, among them a copy of Holbein's group portrait of Thomas More and his family that was painted by Rowland Lockey in 1592, a characteristic landscape by Pieter Breughel the Younger, with a procession of diminutive figures accompanying Christ on his way to Calvary (recently saved by public appeal and support from the Art Fund and National Heritage Memorial Fund), and a self-portrait of 1791 by Angelica Kauffmann, in which she portrays, in classical symbolism, her decision to abandon a promising operatic career in favour of painting.

The house is set off by a pastoral landscape that still has traces of Stephen Switzer's formal design of 1730 for the 4th Baronet, but which was developed in a more naturalistic style over the next hundred years. The main view from the house looks across a sweep of grass to a lake and the little hump-backed bridge built in 1761 to carry the main Wakefield to Doncaster road. A Gothick menagerie that was probably designed by Paine but has additions by Adam stands in the pleasure grounds to the west of the lake, and Adam designed three lodges for the 5th Baronet, one of which is in the form of a pyramid.

Nymans

West Sussex
On the B2114 at Handcross,
4½ miles (7.2 kilometres) south
of Crawley, just off the M23/A23
London–Brighton road

The enchanting compartmental garden set high in the Sussex Weald that was devised and nurtured by three generations of the Messel family is laid out round an apparently ancient house. Now largely a picturesque ruin, with climbers smothering the buttressed walls, mullioned windows that are now glassless and empty and roofless gable ends, this romantic backdrop is all that remains of the southern side of a pastiche Tudor manor that was built here in 1928 by Leonard Messel, whose father Ludwig created the original garden.

Ludwig and his wife, who had come to Nymans in 1890, had commissioned the architect Sir Ernest George to enlarge an existing early nineteenth-century villa, which was given an Italianate tower, a huge conservatory and other improvements, such as a billiard room. Leonard and his wife Maud, who took over Nymans in 1916, longed to live in a West Country manor and they engaged Norman Evill and subsequently Sir Walter Tapper to transform the existing building into a convincing reproduction of a medieval and Tudor house. Then, in February 1947, in the middle of an exceptionally hard winter, the house caught fire and, the standpipes being frozen, the flames could not be brought under control until water was pumped up from a pond at the bottom of the park. The whole southern side of the building, with the great hall and other principal rooms, was gutted and almost all the contents, including a valuable collection of botanical books, lost. Although damaged, the north and west parts of the house survived, and the family rooms were re-created in a more intimate setting with furniture salvaged from the fire and other pieces that were brought down to Sussex after the Messels' London house was sold. Miraculously, much of the planting on the south front also withstood the flames, including the great *Magnolia grandiflora* that now smothers the end of the ruined great hall.

After Leonard's death in 1953 and that of his wife in 1960, Nymans became the home of their daughter Anne and her second husband, the 6th Earl of Rosse, who did much to nurture and enrich the garden. The house is shown as the countess had it, with many echoes of her brother, the theatre designer Oliver Messel, and of her son by her first marriage, the photographer Lord Snowdon, who advised on the arrangement of the rooms. A door in the ruined wing opens into a long, wide, low-ceilinged corridor, more hall than passage, which links the main rooms in the range beyond. Arched openings reveal a comfortable sitting room, with a Broadwood grand piano covered in family photographs at one end, and the little book room, where the television that belonged to Oliver Messel has been given curtains and a proscenium arch, as if it were a theatre. There are irregular Tudor stone flags in the hall, heavy arched wooden doors, great fireplaces and other period touches, some of them, such as a narrow archway, survivals from a genuinely ancient house on this site, the scant remains of which were embraced by the villa; others, such as a timber partition, which came from a barn, brought here from other medieval buildings. The atmosphere of antiquity is enhanced by the Messels' collection of tapestries and seventeenth-century furniture and by a Flemish panel painting of Christ blessing the children, with figures in robes of luminous scarlet. These pieces are mixed with many twentieth-century touches, among them Norman Evill's drawing of the house, a sketch of the actress Merle Oberon by Oliver Messel and a dramatic self-portrait by Lord Snowdon. This last is among another show of family photographs in the comfortable library, complete with drinks trolley, at the end of the passage. The countess, who died in 1992, used to write here at the desk under the window that looks out onto the little stone-walled court on the west side of the house, with a delicious octagonal dovecote in one corner.

RIGHT The romantic Tudor-style ruins at Nymans, with the traceried windows of the great hall on the right, are smothered in climbers, some of which survived the fire which gutted the house in 1947.

Osterley Park

Middlesex
Just north of Osterley station,
on the western outskirts of
London (Piccadilly tube line)

This grand Neo-classical villa was created in the mid-eighteenth century out of a mansion built by Sir Thomas Gresham, Chancellor of the Exchequer to Elizabeth I. The ghost of the sixteenth-century courtyard house still lingers on in Osterley's square plan, with three ranges of warm red brick looking onto a central courtyard. But the delightful corner turrets crowned with cupolas are later additions, there is nothing Elizabethan about the sash windows and balustraded roofline, and on the fourth side of the courtyard, where once there would have been another range, a wide flight of steps leads up to a magnificent double portico stretching between the wings. The courtyard itself is raised, to give direct access to the principal rooms on the first floor.

Although there were alterations to Gresham's mansion in the late seventeenth and early eighteenth centuries, the house was transformed from 1761 by Robert Adam, who spent 20 years working on Osterley. Statues of Greek deities standing in niches and 'antique' vases on pedestals in Adam's cool grey and white entrance hall introduce the classical theme of the house. In the airy library, paintings depicting the world of ancient Greece and Rome by Antonio Zucchi are set into plaster frames built into the walls above the pilastered and pedimented bookcases. Marquetry furniture attributed to John Linnell includes a pedestal desk inlaid with trophies representing the arts, and there is a delicate Adam ceiling. Close by is an eating room arranged in the eighteenth-century way, with the chairs against the walls and no large central table. The kitchen in the basement below, where five servants were employed in the mid-eighteenth century, was originally set in the opposite corner of the house, so diners were not disturbed by noise and cooking smells.

Adam also designed the three rooms that form the state apartment on the south front. The most original decorative scheme is in the Etruscan dressing room, where ochre-coloured dancing figures and urns set beneath arches look as if a series of Greek vases has been flattened on the walls. In contrast, and despite its Adam ceiling, the antechamber has a French flavour. All claret and gold, it is hung with Gobelins tapestries.

Red-brick Tudor stables just north of the house, with original staircase turrets in the angles of the building, survive largely intact, apart from some alterations to doors and windows and the addition of a clock tower in the eighteenth century. Behind are the eighteenth-century pleasure grounds, where a Doric temple and Adam's semicircular garden house are set off by lawns, serpentine gravel paths and a re-creation of a Regency flower garden. The park stretches away, with majestic cedars planted in the eighteenth century shading a lake and cattle grazing beneath the trees in the Great Meadow to the west. Despite the proximity of Heathrow and the M4, Osterley still feels like a country estate.

Adam was employed by Francis Child, whose grandfather had purchased the estate in 1711 after rising from obscurity to found one of the first banks in England (now subsumed in the Royal Bank of Scotland). After Francis's early death at the age of 28, his brother Robert completed Osterley, but he also died prematurely, perhaps partly as a result of anxiety about his only child Sarah Anne, who eloped with the 10th Earl of Westmorland at the age of 18. When mildly rebuked by her

LEFT When commissioned to remodel Osterley, Robert Adam's masterstroke was to design a grand double portico to close the internal courtyard and provide an imposing entrance.

mother, who pointed out she had better matches in mind, the high-spirited girl replied, 'A bird in the hand is worth two in the bush.' The father forgave his only child, but altered his will to leave Osterley and most of his fortune to Sarah Anne's second son, or eldest daughter, thus cutting out the Westmorland heir.

In the event, Osterley passed, through Sarah Anne's daughter, to the Earls of Jersey, and it was the 9th Earl who gave the house to the National Trust in 1949. Sadly, a collection of exceptional paintings, including works by Rubens, Van Dyck and Claude, which were displayed in the gallery were almost all destroyed in a fire while en route to the earl's new home in Jersey. The present hang in the gallery, based on loans and gifts, has been devised to conjure up the eighteenth-century arrangement and is strong on later seventeenth- and eighteenth-century Venetian painting. Some enormous eighteenth-century Chinese jars and vases spaced down the room are part of an important collection of ceramics in the home, while the Child and Jersey family silver, gold plate and other valuables, dating back to the 1740s, are shown in cabinets in the strong room in the basement, where traces of the original Tudor brickwork can still be seen in the wine and beer cellars.

ABOVE The decoration in Adam's Etruscan dressing room at Osterley was created by Pietro Maria Borgnis, who painted the motifs on paper and then pasted them on canvas for fixing to the walls and ceiling.

Oxburgh Hall

Norfolk
At Oxburgh, 7 miles
(11.2 kilometres) south-west of
Swaffham, on the south side of
the Stoke Ferry road

This romantic moated house is set on what was once an island in the East Anglian fen. The land around is now criss-crossed with drainage dykes and cultivated, but when Edward IV gave Sir Edmund Bedingfeld licence to build his fortified manor house at Oxburgh in 1482, the site was on a promontory in the marsh. Apart from a brief period in 1951–2, when Oxburgh was sold and then bought back and given to the National Trust, Bedingfelds have lived here ever since, the gradual impoverishment of the estate that resulted from their adherence to the Catholic faith also ensuring that the house survived unaltered through the sixteenth and seventeenth centuries.

Even in this remote corner of England, Sir Edmund was more concerned with display and comfort than defence. The best-preserved part of his fifteenth-century courtyard house is a piece of early Tudor showmanship: a seven-storey gatehouse with battlemented turrets and stone-mullioned windows rising sheer from the moat. Flemish-style stepped gables and twisted terracotta chimneys on the brick ranges to either side, which contribute so much to the romantic character of the place, seem to be all of a piece; in fact they were added by J.C. Buckler as part of extensive restoration in the mid-nineteenth century for Sir Henry Paston-Bedingfeld, the 6th Baronet. Buckler was also responsible for the beautiful oriel window that fills two storeys of his convincingly medieval battlemented tower at the end of the east range.

The interior of the house includes both Tudor survivals and atmospheric Victorian rooms. The brick-walled King's Room in the gatehouse tower, warmed by a great fireplace, was where Henry VII slept when he came to Oxburgh in 1487. A priest's hole in the floor of a former garderobe off this room is an evocative reminder of the family's religious sympathies. Oxburgh's most prized possession, needlework by Mary Queen of Scots, is displayed in a darkened room nearby. Her rich embroidery, set onto green velvet, is mostly devoted to delightful depictions of a wide assortment of beasts, birds and fishes ranging from the unicorn to the garden snail. Wrought by the queen while she was in the custody of the Earl of Shrewsbury after her flight to England, these enchanting pieces are very rare illustrations of her skill.

The nineteenth-century interiors, with designs by J.C. Buckler and J.D. Crace, are among the best examples of Catholic High Victorian taste in Britain. Crace's heraldic ceiling in the drawing room incorporates delicately painted foliage and flowers in blue, pink and green. More heraldic devices – crimson fleurs-de-lis – are woven into the carpet of the low-ceilinged library, picking up the red in the flock wallpaper. A neo-Tudor fireplace dominating this room has a carved overmantel made up of medieval fragments from continental churches, including some delicate fan vaulting. The small dining room is another rich Victorian interior, still looking exactly as it did in a watercolour of the early 1850s, the dark lustre of the panelling and of the elaborate sideboard with its crest of writhing birds relieved by vivid blue, orange and red tiles round the fireplace.

In the chapel, which was built in 1836 for the 6th Baronet, Victorian and medieval craftsmanship are again combined. The heraldic glass in the south window, dominated by a great red Bedingfeld eagle, was commissioned from Thomas Willement, but the splendid altarpiece is crowned by a sixteenth-century painted and carved triptych purchased by the Bedingfelds in Bruges in about 1860.

Apart from the nineteenth-century Wilderness Walk to the west of the chapel and mown grass around the moat, most of the garden lies to the east of the house, where Buckler's tower looks out over a florid French-style parterre flowering in swirls of blue and yellow. A yew hedge beyond the parterre fronts a colourful herbaceous border. Behind is the fanciful, turreted wall of the Victorian kitchen garden, now planted as a formal orchard with climbers on the walls.

LEFT A priest's hole in the medieval gatehouse was used by the Bedingfelds to shelter fellow Catholics during the religious persecution of the sixteenth century.

Packwood House

Warwickshire
2 miles (3.2 kilometres) east of
Hockley Heath on the A34, 11 miles
(17.7 kilometres) south-east of
central Birmingham

This tall, many-gabled house looking over a grassy forecourt was built in the late sixteenth century for John Fetherston, a prosperous yeoman farmer. The original timber-framing has now largely been rebuilt in brick and rendered over, but the house still has its massive Elizabethan chimneystacks and there is an array of mullioned casement windows and a delightful red-brick stable block at right-angles to the house that was added by another John Fetherston in *c*.1670. Never a prominent or county family, the Fetherstons, it seems, lived quietly here, although they were caught up in the Civil War, apparently offering shelter and succour as seemed expedient. Cromwell's general, Henry Ireton, slept here the night before the Battle of Edgehill in 1642 and there is a family tradition that Charles II was given food and drink at Packwood after his defeat at Worcester in 1651.

When it was sold by the last of the Fetherstons in the later nineteenth century, the house had been greatly altered, with sash windows replacing the original casements and other 'improvements'. In 1905, when it was sold again, it was also much in need of repair. The buyer was the wealthy industrialist Alfred Ash, a genial man who owned a string of racehorses and is said to have viewed life 'from the sunny side – and from the interior of a gorgeous Rolls-Royce'. His son, Graham Baron Ash, a connoisseur and collector, used his father's fortune to restore the house in the 1920s and 1930s, sweeping away Georgian and Victorian alterations and painstakingly acquiring features that would give Packwood a period feel, rescuing leaded casements, floors, beams and chimneypieces from other old buildings. To complete his romantic vision of how a Tudor house should be, he also added the splendid long gallery and fashioned the great hall, complete with oriel window, out of an existing barn, leaving the room open to the original rustic timber roof. He filled Packwood with period furnishings, including fine Jacobean panelling and an exceptional collection of tapestries, such as the seventeenth-century Brussels hanging depicting a cool terraced garden with splashing fountains and urns filled with orange trees. A long oak refectory table in the great hall and a Charles II oak cupboard inlaid with mother of pearl in the dining room are two of the many pieces that Baron Ash bought from the Ferrers family, whose moated manor house, Baddesley Clinton, is just 2 miles (3.2 kilometres) away and who, in the 1930s, were much in need of funds.

The house Graham Baron Ash created is as contrived and self-concious as a work of art. The garden, too, is a showpiece. On the south side of the house, across a large sunken lawn, brick steps lead up to a terrace walk and the exceptional topiary garden where a throng of mature clipped yews, most rising well above the heads of visitors, is said to represent the Sermon on the Mount. At the far end of the garden, a mound is crowned by a single yew tree; twelve more, similarly massive, are crowded below. These, representing the Master and his disciples, were part of the seventeenth-century garden, but many of the multitude dotting the smoothly mown grass below, each tree characterised by its own lumps and slants, were planted in the mid-nineteenth century.

A sunken garden in front of the house, also dating from the seventeenth century, has brick gazebos at each corner, one ingeniously designed so that its fireplace can be used to warm fruit trees growing on an adjacent wall. There are yew-hedged enclosures, walls and steps of mellow brick, wrought-iron gates, some with glimpses into the park, and a vivid herbaceous border.

BELOW Although originally Elizabethan, and still boasting massive period chimneystacks, Packwood House is largely a creation of the 1920s and '30s and represents an idealised vision of a Tudor manor house.

Penrhyn Castle

Gwynedd
1 mile (1.6 kilometres) east of
Bangor, at Llandegai off the A5

From the long upward climb off the Bangor road there is a sudden view of Penrhyn's great four-storey keep rising above the trees, with battlemented turrets at each corner. The rest of the creeper-clad building stretches away across a bluff in an impressive array of towers, battlements and crenellations. Round-headed windows ornamented with a carved zigzag motif seem to have been lifted from a Norman church. The interior is even more dramatic, with long stone-flagged corridors, high ceilings and heavy doors and panelling. Carved stone is everywhere: surrounding arches and doors and forming bosses, corbels, friezes and capitals.

A strange population looks down from the forest of slender pillars creating blind arcades on the walls of the staircase. Each head is different. Here is a bearded wild man, there an elf with pointed ears, somewhere else a gargoyle with interlocking teeth. Look carefully and what appears to be writhing foliage becomes a contorted face. At the foot of the

staircase, the curve of the door into the drawing room is echoed by a semicircle of carved hands around the arch. Another opening leads into the galleried great hall, where Romanesque arches soar heavenwards like the transept of a cathedral. In the evening the polished limestone flags of the floor are warmed by pools of multicoloured light from the recessed stained-glass windows.

Penrhyn is a late Georgian masterpiece, the outstanding product of a shortlived neo-Norman revival. Designed by Thomas Hopper, a fashionable architect who had been employed by the Prince Regent to build a Gothic conservatory at Carlton House, it was commissioned in 1820 by G.H. Dawkins Pennant to replace the neo-Gothic house by Samuel Wyatt he had inherited from his uncle Richard. Whereas Richard Pennant had the benefit of a fortune made from Jamaican estates (as a result of which he strongly opposed the abolition of the slave trade), his nephew built lavishly on the profits of the Penrhyn slate quarries in Snowdonia, which were exporting over 12,000 tons a year by 1792. A slate billiard table with cluster-column legs in the library and the grotesque slate bed weighing over a ton echo the basis of his prosperity.

G.H. Dawkins Pennant seems to have allowed his architect ample funds for building the castle and also for decorating and furnishing the rooms. As a result, Penrhyn is uniquely all of a piece. In the oppressive Ebony Room, original green and red curtains and upholstery and faded red damask wall-hangings give some relief from the black ebony furniture and the black surrounds to the fireplace and doorways. Huge plantain leaves on the firescreen recall the Jamaican estates. Here, too, is Dieric Bouts's delightful painting of St Luke sketching the Virgin and Child, the arches behind the apostle framing a sylvan landscape with a walled city. In the much lighter drawing room next door, mirrors at each end reflect two immense metalwork candelabra.

The house was greatly enriched in the mid-nineteenth century by the Spanish, Italian and Dutch paintings collected by Edward Gordon Douglas, 1st Baron Penrhyn of Llandegai, including a Canaletto of the Thames at Westminster, Rembrandt's portrait of a plain, middle-aged merchant's wife and Palma Vecchio's *Holy Family*. Lord Penrhyn's son, the 2nd Baron, commissioned the elaborate brass King's Bed for the future Edward VII when he was a guest here in 1894.

This royal visit, over three days in July, saw the house staff at full stretch, required to produce gastronomic dinners of eight or nine courses and to attend to 35 house guests. At this date, Lord Penrhyn employed some 40 servants, including the men in the stables, which was by no means a lavish establishment for the period. The servants' quarters, shown as they were after rebuilding in 1868, illustrate what went into keeping the household going.

A warren of rooms giving onto an inner courtyard is centred on the kitchen, which would have been presided over by a French chef in the late nineteenth century and which still has its roasting range, pastry oven and original ash-topped table. Penrhyn slate forms cool work surfaces in the pastry room and dry larder, and tops the butter table in the dairy larder where milk, cream, butter and eggs were delivered from the home farm every morning. Fitted cupboards are stacked with fine china; candlesticks and oil lamps are ready for cleaning and trimming in the lamp room; and there are top hats for sprucing up in the brushing room. In the outer court, close to the back gate, is the Ice Tower, where a deep pit in the basement was packed with ice in the winter, some of it cut from a lake high in Snowdonia, for use in the warmer months.

Beyond the back gate is the sizeable stable block, designed for 36 horses, and with Penrhyn slate between the stalls and used for the mangers. Part is now given over to a collection of dolls from all over the world; a museum of industrial locomotives associated with the slate industry also accommodated here includes *Charles*, a saddle tank engine that once worked the railway serving the Penrhyn family's quarries, and *Fire Queen*, built in 1848 for the Padarn Railway.

The siting of Penrhyn is superb, with views south to Snowdonia and the slate quarry like a great bite out of the hills and north over Beaumaris Bay to Anglesey. A terraced walled garden sloping steeply into a valley below the castle shelters many tender shrubs and plants and includes a bog garden at the lowest level. Throughout the grounds, fine specimen trees are mixed with mature beeches and oaks and there is a ruined Gothic chapel placed as an eye-catcher on a prominent knoll. A row of headstones in the dogs' cemetery by the chapel commemorates Annette, Suzette, Wanda and other pets.

OPPOSITE Penrhyn Castle, with an impressive array of towers and battlements set against the backdrop of the Welsh mountains, is an early nineteenth-century vision of a Norman stronghold.

ABOVE Penrhyn's vast hall, with soaring stone arches, a paved floor and stained glass in the windows, seems more like the interior of a church than the centre of a house.

Petworth House

West Sussex
In the centre of Petworth

A luminous landscape by Turner at Petworth shows the park at sunset. Dark clumps of trees throw long shadows over the lake and in the foreground a stag stoops to drink, its antlers silhouetted against the sun-tinged water. Turner was inspired by 'Capability' Brown's masterpiece, one of the greatest man-made landscapes created in eighteenth-century Europe. This sublime wooded park, with its serpentine lake, enfolds a late seventeenth-century palace filled with an exceptional collection of works of art, including fine furniture, *objets* and sculpture as well as paintings. This great house, in a French baroque style, was the creation of the unlikeable Charles Seymour, 6th Duke of Somerset (the Proud Duke), who set about remodelling the manor house of the earls of Northumberland on his marriage to the daughter of the 11th and last earl, probably to designs by Daniel Marot. Petworth's impressive west front, over 90 metres (300 feet) long and with projecting bays at each end, has the Seymour family symbol – a pair of angel's wings – displayed over every window. Although, apart from the Grand Staircase, only two seventeenth-century interiors survive intact, these fully reflect Charles Seymour's self-importance. The major feature of the florid baroque chapel is the family pew filling the west end. Supported by classical columns, it is surmounted by carved and painted drapery on which angels bear the duke's arms and coronet to heaven. By contrast, the coldly formal marble hall with its black-and-white chequered floor must have quelled the spirits of the few thought worthy to set foot in the Proud Duke's house.

As well as remodelling the house, Charles Seymour also added to the art collection established by the earls of Northumberland, which included a series of portraits by Van Dyck and works by Titian and Elsheimer. And he commissioned Grinling Gibbons to produce the limewood

carvings of flowers, foliage, birds and classical vases which now cascade down the walls of the Carved Room, and Louis Laguerre to paint the Grand Staircase.

On the Proud Duke's death, the estate passed by marriage to the Wyndham family, and it was Charles Wyndham, 2nd Earl of Egremont, who employed Brown to landscape the park. A cultivated man who had profited from the Grand Tour and time in the diplomatic service, he was largely responsible for Petworth's collection of Italian, French and Dutch Old Masters. He also acquired the impressive array of ancient sculpture from Greece and Rome. Now of particular importance because it is one of only three such collections of

LEFT This candelabra is just one of the many works of art at Petworth.
ABOVE When the grand staircase had to be rebuilt after a fire in 1714, the 6th Duke of Somerset employed Louis Laguerre to paint the walls, a commission for which Laguerre received £200.

the period to have survived intact, it includes the sensitive sculptured head fashioned in the fourth century BC known as the Leconfield Aphrodite, and some good Roman portrait busts and copies of Greek originals. The 2nd Earl's son, the philanthropic and benevolent 3rd Earl, who presided over Petworth for 74 years, from 1763 to 1837, left his stamp on almost every room, enriching them with his purchases of contemporary art and sculpture, and altering and rearranging furnishings and picture hangs in the pursuit of the perfect scheme. Best known as the patron of Turner, for whom he arranged a studio at Petworth, the 3rd Earl also acquired works by Gainsborough, Reynolds, Fuseli and Zoffany. And he augmented his father's sculpture collection, for which he twice extended the existing gallery, with works by English contemporaries such as Sir Richard Westmacott and John Rossi and by the Irish sculptor J.E. Carew. One of the most striking pieces is the vividly fluid representation of St Michael and Satan by John Flaxman that was finished in 1826, the year in which the sculptor died. Except for the spear that St Michael is about to plunge into his grovelling adversary, this powerful work, which cost the 3rd Earl £3,500, was all carved from one piece of marble.

In spite of a family tradition that paintings should be left as the 3rd Earl had them, many changes were made to the way they were arranged by Sir Anthony Blunt, then Honorary Adviser on paintings, when Petworth came to the National Trust in 1947. In recent years, helped by generous loans of pictures from the present Lord and Lady Egremont, the Trust has re-created the spirit of the 3rd Earl's crowded and eclectic displays. In some cases it has been possible to reconstruct the hangs as recorded in watercolour gouaches painted by Turner when he was living here. Thus, on the south wall of the square dining room, a large canvas by Reynolds is now framed on three sides by columns of small paintings and crowned by a Reynolds self-portrait, just as it was some 200 years ago. Similarly, four landscapes by Turner have been returned to the Carved Room for which they were commissioned. At the same time, again with loans from Lord and Lady Egremont,

additional contents have been brought in, such as the copper *batterie de cuisine* in the impressive service quarters.

Although the great storms of 1987 and 1989 brought down hundreds of trees, the park is still much as Turner painted it, with deer grazing beneath clumps of beeches, chestnuts and oaks. Trees still frame Brown's serpentine lake below the west front and crown the ridges shading imperceptibly into Sussex downland. Far in the distance on the horizon is the outline of a turreted Gothick folly, possibly designed by Sir John Soane. Brown's pleasure grounds to the north-west of the house, with serpentine paths winding through rare trees and shrubs, echo the boundaries of a vanished Elizabethan layout. A little Doric temple was probably moved here when the pleasure grounds were created, but the Ionic rotunda, perhaps designed by Matthew Brettingham, was introduced by Brown. Here, too, are some of the carved seventeenth-century urns on pedestals which the 3rd Earl placed strategically in the gardens and park.

RIGHT The magnificent west front of Petworth looks out over the serpentine lake and wooded landscape park which Capability Brown created to set off this house in the mid-eighteenth century.

Plas Newydd

Anglesey
1 mile (1.6 kilometres) south-west
of Llanfairpwll and the A5 on the
A4080, 2½ miles (4 kilometres)
from the Menai Bridge, 5 miles
(8 kilometres) from Bangor

'I tried repeatedly in vain ... to get some use made of my drawing.' So Rex Whistler explained his decision to join the Welsh Guards in 1940. Four years later he was dead, killed by a mortar bomb in Normandy at the age of 39. Fortunately for all who visit Plas Newydd, the house is full of works by this talented artist, who spent some of his happiest and most creative hours here. His panoramic seascape, 18 metres (58 feet) wide, fills an entire wall of the dining room. Painted on a single piece of canvas that Whistler had had specially made, it looks across the choppy waters of a harbour to an Italianate town 'bristling with spires, domes and columns' set at the foot of wild and craggy mountains, a vision that echoes Plas Newydd's own setting on the shores of the Menai Strait, with the mountains of Snowdonia rising steeply from the water on the other side.

Reproductions of Whistler's massive work never capture the sweep and scale of the composition or the wealth of detail it includes, with plentiful allusions to buildings the artist had seen on his continental travels and to the family of his patron, the 6th Marquess of Anglesey, of whom he was very fond. Every corner contains some delightful cameo. At the far end of the *trompe-l'oeil* colonnade on the left-hand side people are going about their business in a steep street running up from the water. Two women gossip; an old lady climbs slowly upwards with the help of a stick; a boy steals an apple from a tub of fruit outside a shop. A girl leaning out of an upstairs window to talk to a young man below, as if she were Juliet and he Romeo, alludes to Whistler's unrequited love for the beautiful Lady Caroline, the marquess's eldest daughter, and the artist has portrayed himself as the gardener sweeping up leaves in the colonnade.

The exhibition of Whistler's work in the room next door shows the range of his talent. Here are his illustrations for *Gulliver's Travels*, examples of costume and stage designs, bookplates and caricatures, and rebus letters he sent to the 6th Marquess's young son. Here, too, are drawings he did as a child, the horror of those inspired by the First World War heralding his own experiences some 20 years later. A painting of Lord Anglesey's family grouped informally in the music room is one of many examples of Whistler's skill at portraiture, his sensitive studies of Lady Caroline, eight years his junior, betraying his feelings for his sitter.

Whistler's mural was part of Lord Anglesey's extensive changes to Plas Newydd in the 1930s. He and his wife converted the house into one of the most comfortable of their day, following the 6th Marquess's maxim that 'every bathroom should have a bedroom', and employed Sybil Colefax to create Lady Anglesey's feminine pink and white bedroom, furnished with a white carpet, muslin curtains and bed-hangings and with a pink ribbon setting off the white bedspread. The long saloon with a view over the Menai Strait to Snowdon is also much as the 6th Marquess and his wife arranged it, with two large and comfortable settees either side of the fire and four pastoral landscapes by Ommeganck dominating the pictures.

Architecturally, Plas Newydd is intriguing. The original sixteenth-century manor built by the powerful Griffith family was substantially remodelled in the eighteenth century, most importantly in the 1790s for the 1st Earl of Uxbridge by James Wyatt and Joseph Potter of Lichfield, who produced the uncompromising mixture of classical and Gothick. There is a classical staircase leading to a screen of Doric columns on the first floor and a classical frieze by Wyatt appears boldly white against blue in the ante-room and against red in the octagon, but in the hall there is fan vaulting, with elaborate bosses at the intersection of the ribs. This stately room rising through two storeys with a gallery at one end opens into the even more splendid Gothick music room, the largest room in the house and probably on the site of the great hall of the manor.

An early artificial limb and mud-spattered Hussar trousers recall the 1st Earl's son, who was created 1st Marquess of Anglesey for his heroism at the Battle of Waterloo in 1815, where he lost a leg. He is also remarkable for the fact that he had 18 children and 73 grandchildren. Other members of the

family gaze down from a fine array of portraits, including works by Hoppner, Romney and Lawrence and a Grand Tour painting of the 1st Earl, a rather plump young man in a salmon coat. Many of these pictures came from Beaudesert, the family's Staffordshire house that was dismantled in 1935 and which was also the source of some of the fine furniture.

Plas Newydd is first seen from above, when the path leading down from the car park suddenly reveals the Gothick west front covered in red creeper and magnolia. Sweeping lawns and mature woodland set off the house, the mix of native trees and exotics here including many fine sycamores,

beeches and oaks that predate the planting undertaken with Humphry Repton's advice. A Venetian well-head and Italianate urns in the formal terraced gardens suggest a warmer sun than that which reddens the peaks on the far side of the water in the evening.

OPPOSITE This spiral staircase at Plas Newydd leads from the Gothick hall to the comfortable bedroom fitted out in pink and white in the 1930s for the wife of the 6th Marquess.
ABOVE Plas Newydd is gloriously set above the Menai Strait, with views over the water to the mountains of Snowdonia, and has its own private harbour, built in the 1790s.

Polesden Lacey

Surrey
5 miles (8 kilometres) north-west of Dorking, 1½ miles (2.4 kilometres) south of Great Bookham, off the A246 Leatherhead–Guildford road

Polesden Lacey is alive with the spirit of Mrs Ronald Greville, whose vivacious portrait greets visitors to the house. Those she invited to the legendary weekend parties held here from 1906 until the outbreak of the Second World War included Indian maharajahs, literary figures such as Beverley Nichols, Osbert Sitwell and Harold Nicolson, and prominent politicians. Edward VII was a close friend of the elegant society hostess, as were George V and Queen Mary, the latter often telephoning in the morning to invite herself to tea that afternoon. In 1923, the future George VI and Queen Elizabeth spent part of their honeymoon at Polesden Lacey.

Set above a deep valley on the edge of the North Downs, with views across the combe to sheep-grazed fields and hilltop woods, the house is a comfortable two-storey building sprawling round a courtyard. The white frames of generous sash windows on both floors stand out attractively against honey-coloured stucco. The flavour of the Regency villa built in the 1820s by Joseph Bonsor to the designs of Thomas Cubitt still lingers on the south front with its classical colonnade, but the house was much enlarged and the interior transformed after 1906 by Mewès and Davis, the architects of the Ritz Hotel, as an essential step in the realisation of Mrs Greville's social ambitions. Here she displayed her outstanding collection of paintings, furniture and other works of art, the nucleus of which she had inherited from her wealthy father, William McEwan, founder of the Scottish brewery that still bears his name.

The range and richness of the collection, which includes Flemish tapestries, French and English furniture, English, continental and oriental pottery and porcelain, and European paintings from the fourteenth to the eighteenth centuries, gives Polesden Lacey its extraordinarily opulent atmosphere, vividly evoking the charmed life of the Edwardian upper classes. Some of the finest pieces were intended for very different settings. In the sumptuously decorated drawing room glittering mirrors reflect carved and gilt panelling that once adorned an Italian palace. A richly carved oak reredos in the hall, a masterpiece by Edward Pierce, was originally intended for Sir Christopher Wren's St Matthew's church just off Cheapside in London, which was demolished in 1881. From her father Mrs Greville inherited some Dutch seventeenth-century paintings, but she acquired most of the British portraits in the dining room, among them Raeburn's charming study of George and Maria Stewart as children, the little girl shown holding a rabbit in the folds of her dress, and was also largely responsible for the best of the collection shown in the corridor round the central courtyard. The pictures hanging here include several early Italian works, such as an exquisite early fourteenth-century triptych of the Madonna and Child, sixteenth-century portraits in the style of Corneille de Lyon and a number of atmospheric Dutch interiors and landscapes, among them Jacob van Ruisdael's skyscape of the Zuider Zee in which diminutive figures on the shore are dwarfed by wintry grey clouds piled overhead.

Invitation cards, scrap albums and other mementoes in the billiard room and smoking room conjure up the world in which Mrs Greville lived. The menu book records the *salade niçoise* and orange mousse on which Ramsay MacDonald dined on 17 October 1936 and the *aubergines provençales* given to the Queen of Spain the following day. The same names appear again and again in the visitors' book and the same faces recur in the photographs, statesmen and royalty, such as Grand Duke Michael of Russia and Kaiser Wilhelm II, rubbing shoulders with figures from the worlds of entertainment and literature, a memorable shot showing Mrs Greville in Hollywood with Wendy Barrie and Spencer Tracy. Upstairs, Mrs Greville's bedroom apartment runs along the south front. As yet it is unfurnished, but from here the view over the valley is even more spectacular and there is a marble bath in the bathroom.

ABOVE Carolus Duran's vivacious portrait of Mrs Ronald Greville, who hosted legendary weekend parties here, greets visitors from the half-landing above the hall.

Powis Castle

Powys
1 mile (1.6 kilometres) south of
Welshpool, signed from the A483

Some time around 1200 the Welsh princes of Powis began building their new stronghold on this splendid defensive site, a great outcrop of limestone plunging steeply to the south with panoramic views over the River Severn to the hills of Shropshire. Although long since converted to a country house, Powis still has the trappings of a castle. Seen from across the valley, a massive Norman-style keep with three projecting towers rises to a battlemented skyline. To the left, a long range flanking the entrance court was created out of the substantial curtain wall that defended the inner bailey. In front of the castle, grand baroque terraces blasted out of the rock fall to a vast expanse of lawn.

A wide flight of steps closely guarded by twin drum towers leads up from the entrance court to a Gothic archway. Here the house takes over. The front door opens into seventeenth-century grandeur and opulence and the magnificent interiors fitted out for William Herbert, 3rd Lord Powis, 1st Earl, Marquess and titular Duke. A staunch supporter of the Stuart cause, Lord Powis spent his last years in exile with James II. The most remarkable of his formal apartments, possibly designed by the gentleman-architect William Winde, is the state bedroom, which was decorated with a profusion of gilt in the 1660s and 1680s. A deep alcove is almost filled with the canopied state bed, which is adorned with rich red hangings and gilt cresting and separated from the rest of the room by a finely carved balustrade. The only one of its kind in Britain, this barrier is a direct link with the formal etiquette of Louis XIV's Versailles that was closely imitated by the British aristocracy.

BELOW Although long since converted into a country house, Powis Castle, standing high above a series of magnificent Italianate terraces, still looks like the medieval stronghold it once was.

ABOVE The Elizabethan long gallery at Powis has an original plasterwork ceiling and elm floor and is designed in the shape of a T, giving the room a subtle play of light.
OPPOSITE The Clive collection of Indian treasures displayed at Powis includes a tent of painted chintz which belonged to Tipu Sahib, Sultan of Mysore, who was defeated by the 2nd Lord Clive.

Velvet-covered furniture, a painted ceiling and rich tapestries contribute to the opulent effect. A huge and much more accomplished ceiling by Antonio Verrio, based on Veronese's *Apotheosis of Venice*, with an assembly of deities seated on clouds, dominates the 1st Marquess's grand staircase.

There is no hint of this pomposity in the only surviving Elizabethan interior, a beautiful T-shaped long gallery dating from Sir Edward Herbert's acquisition of the castle in 1587. Young trees and tendrils of foliage branch across the plasterwork ceiling above the rather indifferent family portraits set against early seventeenth-century *trompe-l'oeil* panelling and the polished silver sconces forming pools of light down the room. A table carries a more than life-size marble cat, crouched aggressively over the body of a snake, ears pricked as it looks back over its shoulder, teeth bared and muscles rippling beneath its fur. This remarkable ancient Roman sculpture, perhaps modelled on a wild animal, came to Powis through the marriage of the daughter of the house to the eldest son of Clive of India in 1784. Indian curiosities acquired by the Great Nabob and his son, who was Governor of Madras, are shown in the Clive Museum that now adjoins the curiously elongated ballroom (originally almost twice as long), commissioned from T.F. Pritchard in 1775, in the range flanking the courtyard. Among the glittering exhibits are jewelled slippers that once adorned the feet of Tipu Sahib, Sultan of Mysore, a gold tiger's head from his throne, a jewelled hookah encrusted with rubies, diamonds and emeralds, and sumptuously decorated padded armour. The tone is set for this exotic display by the richly coloured mid-seventeenth-century tapestry filling one wall of the ballroom, showing an embassy to Cairo or Istanbul. A potentate on a gold couch greets the ambassador against the backdrop of an eastern city peppered with onion domes, the trees peeping over the walls conjuring up a sense of hidden gardens.

The final alterations to the castle were made for the 4th Earl of Powis in 1902–4 by G.F. Bodley, who was responsible for the Jacobethan-style panelling, plaster ceilings and other features in the dining room and oak drawing room, and for inserting mullioned windows to replace some existing sashes.

Powis's four great Italianate terraces ornamented with lead statues and urns hang over the valley below, forming a giant staircase descending the rock. Who designed them and when

is unclear, but it is likely they date from the 1680s and were the inspiration of William Winde, who created the grand arcaded terrace at Cliveden, with some of the work being carried out by the French gardener Adrian Duval in the early years of the eighteenth century. Clipped yews cluster closely below the castle, some lapping the terrace wall as if about to flow downhill. Rare and tender lime-tolerant plants flourishing here contrast with those planted in the wilderness laid out in the eighteenth century on the ridge across the valley, where the soil is acid and where there are panoramic views of the castle from winding wooded walks.

A wooded medieval deer-park surrounds Powis, its naturalistic contours and planting partly reflecting alterations by 'Capability' Brown's disciple William Emes, who was engaged to landscape it in 1771 and diverted a public road away from the castle. Although most of the great beeches, sycamores and limes were planted between 1800 and 1850, some of the massive oaks may be as much as 800 years old.

Quarry Bank Mill and Styal Estate

Cheshire
1½ miles (2.4 kilometres) north of Wilmslow off the B5166, 2 miles (3.2 kilometres) from the M56, exit 5, 10 miles (16 kilometres) south of Manchester

In 1769 Richard Arkwright started a revolution in the textile industry when he invented a water-powered machine that could spin cotton. In the 1780s there was another watershed when the patents protecting his invention were challenged and overthrown, opening the way for a huge expansion in factory-produced yarn. One of the first to take advantage of the new opportunities was the young Samuel Greg, who in 1780 had inherited one of the largest textile businesses in Manchester. He found a suitable site for a water-powered mill in the isolated Bollin Valley some 10 miles (16 kilometres) south of the city and had built his first mill here by 1784. As the mill prospered, it was enlarged, and a little village complete with school, shop and two chapels was built in the early nineteenth century to house the growing labour force.

This early industrial complex now lies at the centre of over 120 hectares (300 acres) of well-wooded park following the River Bollin. The surroundings seem delightfully rural, with grass and trees setting off the red-brick four-storey mill with its cupola, tall chimney and impressive rows of windows. Samuel Greg lived in the elegant white Georgian house next to the mill, and on the other side of the works is a smaller but no less comfortable residence that was inhabited by the mill manager, who controlled the flow of water powering the factory. At Quarry Bank House, where the modest rooms make clear that this was a home rather than a showplace, Samuel Greg and his family were very much part of the factory community and the mill with its soaring chimney dominates views from the ornamental garden running down to the Bollin. The upper, kitchen garden has recently also been acquired by the National Trust and is being restored. Dramatically set above a sandstone cliff with spectacular views over the valley, this garden has some of the earliest surviving cast-iron glasshouses, probably dating from the early 1820s, which were used for growing vines and peaches. Later generations of Gregs moved to a grandiose Victorian house high up on the side of the valley.

Although their approach was tempered by self-interest, the Gregs had an enlightened attitude to the care of their workers and this comes through in the design and layout of the village at Styal. Behind each red-brick cottage are the remains of a privy, a great luxury at a time when such facilities were usually shared between several families. The long gardens, now mostly given over to flowers, were once allotments in which tenants could grow their own vegetables. Some thatched, half-timbered buildings, including the impressive Oak Farm which once provided the village with fresh dairy produce, are remnants of a medieval settlement.

Close to the mill is the Apprentice House, built in 1790 to accommodate the children who then made up about a third of the workforce. By the 1830s, this double-gabled three-storey building was home to up to a hundred pauper apprentices. Brought in from workhouses, most of them were on seven-year contracts to work twelve hours a day, six days a week. Neat rows of vegetables in the organic garden, including the red-veined leaves of cottagers' kale, illustrate the traditional produce the children grew in their spare time, although their diet largely consisted of bread, milk, porridge and potatoes. On Sundays, they went twice to church, walking across the fields to Wilmslow.

Although none of the original machinery survives, the mill has been restored as a working museum of the cotton industry. At its heart is a giant iron waterwheel, the most powerful in Britain, which drives spinning machines and looms, these and other exhibits showing how cotton was transformed, first by hand, later by machine, into spun yarn and calico cloth. The noise in the weaving shed and the lack of space round the flying machinery give some idea of what conditions must have been like during the mill's heyday, when tired children could be disfigured for life if they nodded off over their work.

OPPOSITE Quarry Bank Mill has been much expanded since it was first opened in 1784, but still lies in an unspoilt sylvan landscape.
BELOW Samuel Greg lived with his family in this elegant white Georgian house beside his cotton mill; later generations of the family, though, moved further away from the works.

Rufford Old Hall

Lancashire
7 miles (11.2 kilometres) north of Ormskirk, in the village of Rufford on the east side of the A59

Like his father, grandfather and great-grandfather before him, Sir Thomas Hesketh married an heiress. Certainly no expense was spared on the half-timbered manor house he built in c.1530, establishing the family seat for the next 230 years. Although only the great hall survives in its original form – the west wing being now no more than marks in the grass and the east wing having been extensively rebuilt – this impressive Tudor interior speaks eloquently of wealth and position. The hall was built for show. Some 14 metres (46 feet) long and 6.5 metres (22 feet) wide, it rises to a richly carved hammerbeam roof in which each massive timber is fretted with battlements. Angels, all but one now wingless, look down from the ends of the supporting beams and carved roof bosses display the arms of the great Lancashire families with which Hesketh was allied.

Instead of a partition separating the hall from the screens passage, as was usual in houses of this date, there is a massive, intricately carved wooden screen. Three soaring finials look as if they might have come from a pagoda. This deliberately theatrical set-piece, backed by blind quatrefoils lining the upper wall of the passage and placed within a wooden arch supported by beautifully decorated octagonal pillars, must have delighted the young William Shakespeare, who very probably spent a few months here as part of Sir Thomas's company of players in 1581. A canopy of honour curves over the far end of the room, where the lord and his guests would have sat at high table, their special status further emphasised by the great bay window that bulges out to one side. A long refectory table, richly carved oak chests, and pieces from the Hesketh collection of arms and armour add to the hall's atmosphere. The exterior is similarly fine, an impressive display of studding, quatrefoils and wood-mullioned windows greeting visitors as they come up the drive.

A Carolean wing juts out at right-angles to the medieval great hall, its symmetrical gabled facade built of warm red brick contrasting strongly with the black-and-white half-timbering. A castellated tower peering over the angle between the two ranges is a later addition, a feature of the nineteenth-century building in Tudor Gothic style that joins the great hall to the Charles II wing and which was partly formed out of a 1720s rebuilding, using sixteenth-century timbers, of the east range. This part of the house includes a spacious drawing room stretching the full length of the first floor, which rises to an open timber roof and has a spy-hole looking down into the great hall below. As elsewhere in the house, richly carved court cupboards, spindle-backed rush-seated chairs and oak settles add to the antiquarian atmosphere, although not all are genuinely old. A show of family portraits includes Sir Godfrey Kneller's imposing likeness of the Thomas Hesketh who rebuilt the east wing and a number of landscapes are dominated by a huge canvas by the Flemish artist Gommaert van der Gracht, whose still-life is set against a distant formal garden and walled town beyond.

Throughout the house are displayed toys, household utensils, textiles and many other items from the unique Philip Ashcroft collection, which illustrates village life in pre-industrial Lancashire. Larger pieces of agricultural equipment from the collection are on show in the stables.

BELOW The hammerbeam roof in Rufford's great hall is decorated with carved angels.

Saltram

Devon
2 miles (3.2 kilometres) west of
Plympton, 3 miles (4.8 kilometres)
east of Plymouth city centre,
between the A38 Plymouth–Exeter
road and the A379
Plymouth–Kingsbridge road

Anyone who has travelled by train from Plymouth to London will know the pleasure of seeing the Saltram estate shortly after leaving the city, when the line suddenly emerges on the banks of the Plym estuary and the wooded slope of the park rises on the other side of the water. With a view over Plymouth Sound to the trees of Mount Edgcumbe, this is a perfect position for a house and the building created here lives up to its setting. Although dating back to late Tudor times, Saltram is essentially a product of the eighteenth century, the rooms with their original contents summing up all that was best about this elegant and civilised age.

The remodelling of the house was the work of John and Lady Catherine Parker, who wrapped three classical facades round the Tudor core, fragments of which are still visible in an interior courtyard, and the three-storey seventeenth-century block which John's father had purchased in 1712. Their son, John Parker, 1st Lord Boringdon, who inherited in 1768, was responsible for amassing the outstanding collection of pictures and for inviting Robert Adam to redesign some of the principal rooms. Already at work on Kedleston Hall and Osterley Park, Adam was at the height of his career and his interiors at Saltram, in which he was responsible for almost everything, including the door handles, are exceptional examples of his style. In the great Neo-classical saloon, delicate plasterwork attributed to Joseph Rose stands out white against the eggshell blue and burnt yellow of the coved ceiling. Blue damask lines the walls, setting off the four great looking-glasses and a show of portraits, Old Masters and Old Master copies, hung as Adam intended. A magnificent Axminster carpet echoes the design of the ceiling and gilded chairs and sofas line the walls. Double doors at the north end of the room give a vista into the equally elegant dining room, originally designed as the library, where romanticised depictions of ruins and rocky landscapes set into the walls and lunette paintings in Adam's delicate plasterwork ceiling are the work of Antonio Zucchi.

Another aspect of the eighteenth century is reflected in the more intimate and relaxed morning room, where a quartet of cloud-based cherubs makes music in the rococo plaster ceiling. Paintings hang triple-banked in the fashion of the day, their gilded frames glowing against red velvet.

Other delights at Saltram are the eighteenth-century Chinese wallpaper, some of it depicting those curiously elongated figures so familiar from Japanese prints, which decorates some of the first-floor rooms, and a show of topographical watercolours by Frances Talbot, who married the 1st Earl in 1809. A light and airy late eighteenth-century kitchen looking onto a rough-walled internal courtyard has a splendid, 1,000-piece array of gleaming copper pans and moulds.

A pleasantly informal Victorian garden to the west of the house is a soothing mixture of lawns, wooded glades, shrubs and grass walks. A Gothic belvedere at the end of a long lime avenue was probably built by Harry Stockman, the estate's talented carpenter. Stockman also created the chapel nearby, adding battlements, buttresses and pointed windows to what was originally a barn. The extensive deer-park formed in the mid-eighteenth century was landscaped in the style of 'Capability' Brown, but the magnificent views depicted in William Tomkins's delightful landscapes in the garden room have been ruined by Plymouth's urban sprawl. Shelter belts planted by the National Trust help to hide this intrusive reminder of the twenty-first century, but passengers on the main Plymouth to London line can still enjoy a glimpse of the amphitheatre, a mid-eighteenth-century folly nestling in the woods above the Plym estuary.

LEFT As at Nostell Priory, the plasterer Joseph Rose and the decorative painter Antonio Zucchi were employed to execute the delicate ceilings that Adam designed for Saltram.
BELOW The pediment on Saltram's south front contains the Parker family's coat of arms.

LEFT Robert Adam was responsible for almost everything in the saloon at Saltram, from the carpet echoing the design of the ceiling to the hang of the paintings.

Scotney Castle

Kent

1½ miles (2.4 kilometres) south of Lamberhurst on the A21

The magical garden created by Edward Hussey III from 1837 in a deep valley of the Kentish Weald owes much of its charm to the romantic buildings incorporated in the design. At the top of a steep bluff overlooking the valley is a nineteenth-century vision of an Elizabethan house, all gables, tall chimneys and mullioned windows, while far below, encircled by a lake-like moat beside the River Bewl, are the ruins of a genuinely ancient castle. Flowering trees and shrubs on the slopes frame carefully contrived views over the valley and from one building to another.

In a move against the fashion of the time, which was swinging away from the naturalistic layouts that had been in vogue since the eighteenth century, Edward Hussey, who had inherited the estate from his father while still a child, created an outstandingly successful example of the Picturesque style, whose exponents promoted artfully created landscapes, ideally including a romantic building or two, which gave the illusion of the beauty of nature untamed. At Scotney, the castle was the perfect eye-catcher. In fact the remnants of a fortified house that Roger Ashburnham constructed here in c.1378–80 during the troubled decades of the Hundred Years War, when men of substance in this part of England lived in fear of French raids, the castle consists of a massive round tower rising from the

LEFT The new house at Scotney, built in Elizabethan style, has a huge stone-mullioned window lighting the stairs on the garden front.
BELOW Scotney is an outstanding example of a Picturesque landscape, with carefully contrived vistas between the old castle on the valley floor and the new house, built in neo-Tudor style in 1837–43, far above.

ABOVE The wallpaper designed by Thomas Willement in the library at Scotney was originally brightly coloured, but has faded over the years.

lake-like moat, with a projecting parapet at roof level, and a ruined gatehouse. A brick Elizabethan range adjoining the tower is all that survives of sixteenth-century additions, and jagged walls with gaping windows mark the remains of a substantial seventeenth-century wing.

Instead of living in the castle, where his father had contracted the typhoid that killed him from the drains, the young Edward, still in his 20s, built a new house in neo-Tudor style in 1837–43, for which he engaged the rising young architect Anthony Salvin, who was not much older than his client. But the shaping of its surroundings and the actual site of the house were determined with the advice of the artist and landscape gardener William Sawrey Gilpin, who was a disciple of Richard Payne Knight and Sir Uvedale Price, the leading exponents of the Picturesque style. The natural drama of the valley was enhanced by the creation of a deep quarry, from which the streaky golden sandstone for the house was obtained, and the seventeenth-century wing of the castle was partly demolished, to focus the eye on the older remains and make them seem more romantic.

The new building, the design of which took 33 meetings between architect and client to thrash out, was devised to be both picturesque and practical. The tall, many-gabled facades are enhanced by a battlemented tower like a Northumbrian pele that dominates the entrance front and by the chimneys rising above the roofline, and there are great mullioned and transomed windows lighting the stairs and filling the bays looking over the garden. There are arresting details, too, such as the lead rainwater hoppers designed by the heraldic artist Thomas Willement, who is better known for his stained glass.

The well-designed interior, with stunning views from most of the main rooms, has been little altered since it was built and still has many of Salvin's decorative schemes and several pieces of furniture that he designed for Scotney. Most recently, the new house has been the home of the architectural historian and writer Christopher Hussey, Edward Hussey III's grandson, who inherited the estate in 1952 and gave it to the National Trust. The garden has been open since his death in 1970, and the house passed to the Trust, with all its contents, on his wife Betty's death in 2006. It is being presented as a welcoming and lived-in home, as Christopher and Betty had it, and with nineteenth-century furnishings blended with twentieth-century additions. There are inviting sofas and a drinks trolley in the spacious library, where the faded Willement wallpaper and the Jacobean-style plasterwork ceiling are both original, as are the bookcases designed by Salvin. In the book-lined study next door, where Christopher Hussey wrote his many articles for *Country Life* and other works, the ornamental ceiling features local Kentish hops, and there is more plasterwork by Salvin in the more formal dining room, where the huge buffet sideboard Salvin made for Edward Hussey III matches the richly carved panelling.

A few rooms were substantially altered by Christopher and Betty. Their sunny bedroom, with a bay window looking over the garden, was fitted with a walk-in wardrobe and en-suite bathroom in the 1950s and a restful blue and green bedroom, redecorated by Betty, is furnished with bamboo pieces purchased in 1951. Betty's sense of colour comes through again in the remodelled kitchen, where shelves are filled with her vibrant red and white china. The many paintings include likenesses of Christopher and Betty Hussey by their friend John Ward and views of both the new house and the old castle by John Piper, whom they also knew well. Most enchanting is the little room giving access to the garden, where blue and white Delftware vases are set against old Flemish panelling in the style of the seventeenth century.

One of the best views of the garden is from a semicircular bastion below the new house, which gives a vista down over the quarry and the slope of the valley to the moated remains of the old castle. The only modern note in the garden, hidden away on a little isthmus in the lake, is the *Reclining Figure* by Henry Moore, a tribute to the memory of Christopher Hussey.

Seaton Delaval Hall

Northumberland
2 miles (3.2 kilometres) north of Whitley Bay, off A190 between Seaton Delaval and Seaton Sluice

This arresting baroque house, set less than a mile (1.6 kilometres) from the sea on a bleak and windswept coast, was designed by Sir John Vanbrugh for Admiral George Delaval and built between 1719 and c.1730. Arcaded wings framing a deep and gently sloping forecourt set off the tall and dramatic central block. Placed by Vanbrugh on a mound, like a castle keep, it is four and a half storeys high, symmetrical and detailed for theatrical effect. Huge Doric columns, supporting nothing, frame the entrance, there are massive chimneys and heavy keystones over the windows and the pedimented top storey, designed as a penthouse for the admiral's use, resembles a classical temple. Naval guns, harpoons, sea creatures and other devices carved into the stonework and the porthole windows are allusions to the admiral's career. Vanbrugh, an architect of genius and the greatest exponent of the English Baroque, was both looking back to prodigy houses such as Hardwick Hall and setting out to create 'something of the castle in the air', a play house that could also be lived in. Gutted by fire in 1822, this central block is now an architectural shell, with a dramatic Piranesian interior of huge spaces, vistas to upper levels and shafts of light. Beyond the lofty entrance hall, with fire-blackened and crumbling sculptures set into blind arcading at the level of the first floor and an original marble pavement, is the monumental saloon, 23 metres (75 feet) long and 9 metres (29 feet) wide. Running the length of the south front, this great room looks out through a grand Ionic portico to a great obelisk half a mile (0.8 kilometre) away across the former park. Slender cast-iron shafts dividing the saloon, replacements for eight stone columns destroyed in the fire, were inserted by the Newcastle architect John Dobson, who roofed the ruined building in 1860 and carried out essential restoration. Two oval stone staircases wind up through the house to either side of the hall and descend to the Stygian, stone-vaulted basement, a section of twisted iron handrail on the east stair showing how fierce the fire must have been.

Sadly, neither the admiral, who died after a fall from his horse in 1723, nor Vanbrugh, who died in 1726, lived to see the house finished, and the work was probably completed under the supervision of William Etty, Vanbrugh's clerk of works at Castle Howard in Yorkshire, which was still being built in the early 1720s. Now-vanished wings to east and west of the main house which appear in mid-eighteenth-century paintings and engravings are of uncertain date, if, indeed, they ever existed. Those flanking the forecourt were built at the same time as the central block, but not entirely to Vanbrugh's design. On the east, offering another monumental interior, spanned by vast arches of stone, are the stables, the names over the stalls – Hercules, Julius, Zephyrus, etc. – referring to beasts housed here in c.1800. The west wing, originally designed as kitchen and servants' quarters, became the family's home in more recent years.

BELOW Vanbrugh's monumental entrance hall is decorated with blind arcading and statues representing the arts, geography and astronomy.

When Edward Delaval, the last of his line, died in 1814, the house passed to a nephew, Sir Jacob Henry Astley, whose main seat was at Melton Constable in Norfolk. After the fire, it was Sir Jacob's son, created 16th Lord Hastings in 1841, who employed John Dobson, although plans for fully restoring the house were never realised, leaving the shell that is seen today. The hall grounds were used for garden parties and church fêtes, and prisoners of war were housed here in the Second World War, but the family rarely came to Seaton Delaval until, in the 1950s, the 22nd Lord Hastings decided to restore the hall and make the west wing his home, furnishing the rooms with pieces from Melton Constable as well as with furniture and paintings originally in the hall. He finally settled here in 1990. What was once the kitchen, with massive pilasters supporting a high vaulted roof, is now a sitting room, with sofas ranged invitingly round the fireplace, and other rooms are in the former laundry and servants' bedrooms. Mainly eighteenth-century family portraits, among them works by John Vanderbank, Thomas Hudson and Francis Cotes, include a likeness, after Reynolds, of the profligate and philandering Sir Francis Delaval (1727–71), the most notorious of his line, who fathered several illegitimate children and died heavily in debt. Walnut Queen Anne sofas and chairs upholstered in

ABOVE Seaton Delaval was designed for theatrical effect, with huge Doric columns framing the entrance, windows weighed down with heavy keystones and a penthouse like a classical temple.

needlework, and two marble-topped pier tables that were once in the hall of the main block, are part of a collection of fine furniture, mostly of the eighteenth century, while a painting of Windsor Castle in c.1670 by Hendrik Danckerts was given to the Delavals by Charles II as a reward for their loyalty in the Civil War, as was a marble bust of the king attributed to Caius Gabriel Cibber. More recent family history is reflected in a sculpted head of the late Lord Hastings and in two stone sculptures from Zimbabwe, where he had a farm.

As well as restoring the fabric of the house, Lord and Lady Hastings also extended the gardens to the west of the main block, engaging James Russell to design a topiary parterre and embellishing the layouts with a fountain, urns and ornamental sculpture. On the death of both Lord Hastings and his wife in 2007, the National Trust was approached by their son, the 23rd Lord and, as a result of a major fund-raising campaign and a £6.7 million endowment from the Trust's own resources, the largest ever allocated, the house and gardens, much of the estate and the core of the collection passed to the Trust on 16 December 2009.

Shugborough Estate

Staffordshire
6 miles (9.6 kilometres) east of
Stafford on the A513 at Milford

The two Anson brothers born in the 1690s took very different paths in life. George, who went to sea at the age of 12, rose to be 1st Lord of the Admiralty and gained both fame and fortune on an epic four-year circumnavigation of the globe in the 1740s, during which he captured a treasure-laden Spanish galleon. Much of the admiral's wealth went to help his cultivated elder brother Thomas improve the three-storey, late seventeenth-century house on the banks of the River Sow which he had inherited in 1720. Among other changes and enlargements in the late 1740s and '60s, Thomas added charming domed pavilions with semicircular bay windows by Thomas Wright of Durham to frame the central block. The massive two-storey portico dominating the entrance front was a later addition, part of Samuel Wyatt's alterations for the 1st Viscount Anson at the end of the century that obliterated much of the earlier work. Similarly, Wyatt was responsible for the central bow on the garden facade, and for the verandahs on either side fronting the links to the pavilions, which he extended.

Thomas Anson was a leading spirit of the Society of Dilettanti, which promoted the art of classical antiquity, and this interest in the ancient world comes through in the interiors that survive from his time. Six huge, Piranesi-like paintings of classical ruins by Nicholas Thomas Dall strike a sombre note in the dining room, distracting the eye from Vassalli's arresting rococo plasterwork gently curving overhead, with medallion heads representing Egyptian and Greek deities. In Thomas Wright's low-ceilinged library, with a shallow arch set on Ionic columns dividing the room, marble busts set along the bookcases include a number of antique sculptures, among them likenesses of Plato and Hercules, as well as delightful nineteenth-century portraits of various members of the family, one of whom is depicted holding a rabbit.

The apartments lived in by the Lichfield family, which have been private since the National Trust took over the house in 1966, are now gradually being opened following the death in 2005 of the 5th Earl, the society photographer Patrick Lichfield. Situated mostly on the upper floors, these more intimate and lived-in spaces contrast with the grandeur elsewhere and show Shugborough in a different light. They are also full of mementoes of the 5th Earl and his glittering 40-year career, during which he immortalised iconic figures of the sixties such as Mick Jagger and Joanna Lumley, caused a stir by photographing the singer Marsha Hunt in the nude, and also took memorable images of his royal relatives (he was the Queen's cousin), among them shots of the exiled Duke and

BELOW Shugborough is the home of the Anson family, Earls of Lichfield, whose fortunes were founded in the 1740s by Admiral George Anson, who captured a treasure-laden Spanish galleon.

ABOVE The Red Drawing Room at Shugborough, the most impressive room in the house, was created in 1794 and is hung with the remains of a once-renowned picture collection, most of which was sold in 1842.
OPPOSITE The Tudor brick tower at the heart of Sissinghurst garden.

Duchess of Windsor and the official photographs of the wedding of the Prince of Wales and Lady Diana Spencer in 1981.

In the kitchen, which was fitted out in the late 1970s, a cupboard door is covered with business cards, and jams made from fruit grown on the estate, which Lichfield particularly enjoyed, are lined up on the windowsill of the light and airy circular breakfast room. Some of his most personal belongings, such as his spectacles and the boots and helmet he wore to ride his motorbike, are in the green sitting room, and here too is the collar of his dog Drum, beside the chair in which the 5th Earl used to sit. The bathrooms still have early twentieth-century plumbing and the elegant boudoir has the only hand-painted ceiling in the house and original 1794 wallpaper inlaid with silver leaf. Treasures on display, some brought out of storage and being shown for the first time, others on loan, include a collection of enamelled and gilded jardinières and urns that are said to have come from the Summer Palace in Peking.

And then there are the photographs. Some of them, as in the green sitting room, are of close family, others are of celebrities, among them some images taken on the Shugborough estate which have not been seen before. Also on show is Lichfield's studio from Oxford Gardens in west London, which has been faithfully reconstructed with his cameras and other equipment.

Formal terraced gardens lead down to the Sow, where the family's arboretum on an island in the river, formerly private, is now accessible. Thomas Wright's Picturesque ruin on the banks of the Sow, a crumbling array of columns and walls topped by the statue of a druid, is outclassed by the classical monuments based on buildings in ancient Athens in the park that Thomas Anson commissioned from James 'Athenian' Stuart. A triumphal arch stalks across the grass on a rise above the drive like a creature from outer space. Two pedimented porches with fluted columns project from the octagonal Tower of the Winds in the valley below and a shady knoll is crowned with the Lantern of Demosthenes, a cluster of columns topped by three dolphins supporting a tripod and bowl. No later development dulls the impact of these re-creations, only a gentle roar and tremors in the ground betraying the presence of the Stafford to Stoke railway line buried in a tunnel beneath the triumphal arch.

Sissinghurst

Kent
2 miles (3.2 kilometres) north-east
of Cranbrook, 1 mile
(1.6 kilometres) east of
Sissinghurst village on the A262

The lovely garden set high on a Wealden ridge owes much of its charm to the Tudor buildings of mellow pink brick around which it was created and which form a romantic backdrop to the planting. These evocative remains are all that survive of the great Tudor and Elizabethan courtyard house of the Baker family, who came to Sissinghurst in c.1490. There is also the ghost of an older manor here, its site marked by an orchard framed by three arms of a medieval moat.

Visitors approach Sissinghurst through a gabled archway crowned by three slender chimneys that was built in c.1535 by the high-flying Sir John Baker, who rose to be Chancellor of the Exchequer and made the family rich. The long ranges to either side, originally used for stabling and servants' lodgings, may be Sir John's too. Beyond, across a grassy court, rises the brick prospect tower that forms the focal point of the garden. Four storeys tall, with slender octagonal turrets, this glorified gatehouse was built by Sir Richard Baker in 1560–70 as part of a wholesale reconstruction of his father's house and once led into a courtyard lined by tall, gabled ranges. Elizabeth I, who stayed here for three days in 1573, would have ridden through Sir John's archway to be greeted by Sir Richard under the tower. A fragment of the Elizabethan mansion is now a cottage in the garden and there is a little sixteenth-century building where the family's private chaplain may have lived.

From the mid-seventeenth century, when the Baker family lost much of their wealth in the Civil War, Sissinghurst went into a long decline and was largely pulled down in 1764. Despite 200 years of neglect and decay, the evocative remains inspired the novelist and biographer Vita Sackville-West to purchase the property in 1930 and with the help of her husband, Sir Harold Nicolson, the diplomat and literary critic, to create one of the most individual and influential gardens of the twentieth century. The old walls and hedges were used to create a series of intimate open-air rooms, each one planted differently, and long linking walks provide a unifying framework.

The buildings were transformed into a singular and eccentric house, its various parts scattered round the garden. The stables in the long north wing of the entrance range were formed into an atmospheric library, lined with thousands of books, many of which were Harold Nicolson's review copies. The fireplace, which now has a de Laszlo portrait of the young Vita (disliked by her) hanging above it, was made out of Elizabethan fragments found in the garden and the furniture includes copies of pieces from Knole, Vita's childhood home. The family had their dining room and kitchen in the priest's house and Harold Nicolson worked in South Cottage, but the tower was Vita's retreat. Reached by a spiral staircase is the cluttered room where she wrote, its walls still lined with the books on gardening, history and travel that reflect her special interests. In summer, she would garden all day and then write into the night. From the roof there is a bird's-eye view of the garden and wider prospects over woods, fields and oast houses to a distant ridge of the North Downs, with the spire of Frittenden church in the middle distance.

Snowshill Manor

Gloucestershire
3 miles (4.8 kilometres)
south-west of Broadway, 4 miles
(6.4 kilometres) west of the
junction of the A44 and the A424

The old lady who showed her grandson the family treasures hidden away in her Cantonese cabinet on Sunday afternoons could not have known that this would inspire one of the most extraordinary collections ever assembled by one person. Charles Paget Wade, born in 1883, was clearly an unusual little boy and he grew up to be an exceptional man. A talented artist and craftsman as well as a professional architect, once he had inherited the family sugar estates in the West Indies he devoted his life to restoring the Cotswold manor house he bought in 1919 and to amassing the wide-ranging exhibits now displayed here.

Snowshill is an L-shaped building of warm Cotswold stone, with a warren of rooms on different levels leading off one another. The Tudor hall house of *c*.1500 at its heart, still evident in the huge fireplace on the ground floor and in two ceilings upstairs, was substantially rebuilt in about 1600 and altered again in the early eighteenth century, when the oddly attractive south front was created. Here, Georgian sash windows on the left side of the pedimented main entrance

contrast with mullioned and transomed casements to the right, giving the house a rakish air.

Every corner from ground floor to attics is devoted to Charles Wade's acquisitions, which are packed into rooms with bizarre names such as Dragon, Meridian, Top Gallant and Seraphim. Mr Wade did not set out to accumulate things because they were rare or valuable, but saw his pieces primarily as records of vanished handicrafts. As a result, the Snowshill collection is unique, displaying an unclassifiable range of everyday objects, from tools used in spinning, weaving and lacemaking to baby minders (one for use on board ship), prams, early bicycles, exquisite bone carvings made by French prisoners of war, eighteenth-century medicine chests cunningly contrived to carry a mass of little bottles and gaily painted model farm wagons. One room is devoted to pieces connected with the sea, such as compasses, telescopes and ship models, another to musical instruments, arranged as a playerless orchestra, and yet another (his Seventh Heaven) to many of the toys Mr Wade had as a child. Perhaps the most remarkable spectacle is in the Green Room, where suits of Japanese Samurai armour topped with ferocious masks threaten visitors in a theatrically staged display. A sense of order everywhere shows that this is no random, magpie collection but a reflection of a serious purpose.

The steeply sloping terraced garden was largely designed by Wade's friend M.H. Baillie Scott, a fellow architect with whom he had worked when employed by Raymond Unwin in London before the First World War, but Wade altered and adapted the original structure. It is laid out as a series of interconnecting but separate garden rooms, with arches and steps leading from one to another. Flagged paths, carefully contrived vistas down and across the slope, many features and centres of interest, among them a medieval dovecote with birds roosting on the steeply pitched roof, and Wade's old-fashioned planting schemes reflect the influence of the Arts and Crafts movement, with its preference for cottage-garden styles. And always there is the backdrop of a far wooded hillside across the valley.

At the top of the garden, just below the manor house, is the little cottage where Charles Wade lived. He had no electricity, a fireplace with two bread ovens being the only means of heating and cooking, and the walls and even the ceiling of his

kitchen/living room are covered with a multitude of useful objects, from bowls and tankards to farm tools. Seeing these spartan conditions and the workshop where he spent so many happy hours making, among other things, the model Cornish fishing village that is now on display, it is easy to believe, as Queen Mary said after visiting Snowshill in 1937, that the most notable part of the collection was Mr Wade himself.

OPPOSITE Charles Wade's interest in workmanship and good design led him to fill Snowshill with all kinds of humble artefacts, such as these leather fire buckets.
ABOVE This eccentric display in Seraphim sets an array of Balinese and Javanese dancing masks against a collection of fine cabinets.

Speke Hall

Merseyside
On the north bank of the Mersey, 8 miles (12.8 kilometres) south-east of the centre of Liverpool, 1 mile (1.6 kilometres) south of the A561, on the west side of the airport

A carved overmantel in the great parlour depicts the three generations of the wealthy gentry family who were largely responsible for this magical half-timbered moated manor house. Henry Norris to the left, accompanied by his wife and five children, carried on the building started by his father on inheriting the estate in about 1490. In the centre sits Sir William, whose considerable additions in the mid-sixteenth century may be explained by the nineteen children grouped at his feet (the son killed in battle is accompanied by a skull and bones). To the right is Edward, who recorded his completion of the house with an inscription dated 1598 over the entrance, and is shown with his wife and two of their children.

These men built conservatively, each addition merging perfectly with what had gone before and with no hint of the Renaissance influences that were becoming evident further south. Four long, low ranges enclose a cobbled courtyard, the jettied gables topped with finials that project unevenly and apparently haphazardly from the facades and the rough sandstone slabs that cover the roof all contributing to a charmingly crooked effect. Leaded panes show up as dark patches in a riot of black-and-white timberwork, among the finest in England. An Elizabethan stone bridge crosses the

BELOW Speke Hall, with four picturesque ranges enclosing a cobbled courtyard, is one of the most important timber-framed buildings in the north of England.

now grassy moat to the studded wooden doors which give access to the interior. Walking through is a surprise: two huge yews known as Adam and Eve shadow the courtyard, their branches rising above the house.

Surviving Tudor interiors live up to the promise of the exterior. In the light and airy T-shaped great hall rising to the roof, a number of plaster heads look down from the crude Gothic chimneypiece stretching to the ceiling. The naïve decoration here contrasts with the sophisticated carving on the panelling at the other end of the room, where busts of Roman emperors represented in high relief are set between elegant fluted columns. In the great parlour next door, panels in the fine early Jacobean plaster ceiling are alive with pomegranates, roses, lilies, vines and hazelnuts; bunches of ripe grapes and other fruits dangle enticingly and rosebuds are about to burst into flower. A spy-hole in one of the bedrooms and hiding places throughout the house reflect the Catholicism and royalist sympathies that brought the Norrises to the edge of ruin in the seventeenth century, when parts of the estate were sold.

After years of neglect following the death of the last of the family in 1766, the house was rescued in the late eighteenth century by Richard Watt, whose descendants introduced the heavy oak furniture in period style which contributes to Speke's unique atmosphere. The more intimate panelled Victorian rooms in the north and west wings were created by the shipping magnate F.R. Leyland, who leased the house and carried on Watt's restoration after his early death. A noted patron of the arts, Leyland was responsible for hanging the early William Morris wallpapers that are now a feature of Speke, and he also entertained the painter James McNeill Whistler here.

The house lies buried in bracken woodland beside Liverpool airport, forming a green oasis in the heart of industrial Merseyside. A wide ride leads to the great embankment that shelters the property to the south. Those who struggle up the steep grassy slope are rewarded by a panoramic view of the River Mersey stretching away in a shining sheet of water to the smoking stacks of Ellesmere Port on the other side of the estuary.

ABOVE When the shipping magnate Frederick Leyland lived at Speke in the 1860s, he invited some 80 children from the estate to a Christmas meal in the great hall, built in the 1530s.

Standen

West Sussex
2 miles (3.2 miles) south of
East Grinstead

Standen is a most unusual house, built in 1892–4 and yet not at all Victorian, built all of a piece and yet seeming to have grown out of the group of old farm buildings to which it is attached. This peaceful place on the edge of the Weald was designed by Philip Webb for the successful London solicitor James Beale, who wanted a roomy house for his large family for weekends and holidays. Standen was one of Webb's last commissions and, like Red House, which was his first, is among the few unaltered examples of his work. A lifelong friend and associate of William Morris, for whom Red House was built, Webb shared Morris's views on the value of high-quality materials and craftsmanship. His aim was to design good, plain buildings, with comfortable interiors that could be lived in, an ambition that Standen fulfils in every respect.

As shown in Arthur Melville's delightful watercolour, painted when he visited the Beales for a weekend in 1896, Standen sits on a terrace, with views south over the long lake of the Weirwood reservoir to the wooded hills of Ashdown Forest. The attractive five-gabled garden front is partly built of creamy sandstone from the hill behind, but the upper storeys are weather-boarded and tile-hung in the Wealden fashion, producing a red and white effect. An arcaded conservatory is joined onto this front and there are tall brick chimneys rising almost to the height of the tower holding the water tanks.

The light, airy rooms are furnished with Morris's wallpapers and textiles, with richly coloured William de Morgan pottery, such as the red lustreware in a cabinet in the stairwell, and with a pleasing mixture of antiques and beautifully made pieces from Morris's company. The house was lit by electricity from the beginning, and many of the original fittings still exist. Webb's delicate wall lights in the drawing room hang like overblown snowdrops, casting soft pools of light on the blue and red hand-knotted carpet and on the comfortable chairs covered in faded green velvet that were supplied from Morris's workshops. A sunflower motif on the wallpaper is echoed in the embossed decoration on the plates supporting the light brackets and in the swirls of foliage and sunflowers on the copper cheeks of the fireplace. A view through to the conservatory from this room shows cane furniture set enticingly amidst a profusion of plants. All the rooms reflect Webb's meticulous concern for detail. The dining room at the end of the south front has an east-facing breakfast alcove, where the little round table flanked by oak dressers lined with china is flooded with sunshine in the early morning. Curiously, the first floor reveals that the Beales were expected still to rely heavily on washstands and hip baths: only one bathroom was provided for twelve bedrooms.

The steep, south-facing garden reflects changes over several decades by a number of different hands. A fussy, gardenesque layout by the London landscape gardener G.B. Simpson, who was employed before Webb and planned his design to focus on a differently sited house, was then modified by his successor, who favoured a simpler approach concentrating on grass and trees and was responsible for the terraces that descend the hill in giant leaps, their outlines followed by stepped yew hedges. The planting, on the other hand, was undertaken by James Beale's wife Margaret. The end result, although based on no coherent overall plan, is both individual and charming, with many changes of level linked by flights of steps. The little quarry from which the stone for the house was taken is now attractively leafy and overgrown.

OPPOSITE, LEFT Standen has always been lit by electricity and many of the original fittings are still in the house, among them the delicate lights in the hall by W.A.S. Benson, William Morris's protégé.

OPPOSITE, RIGHT Wallpapers and textiles designed by William Morris, among them the 'Pomegranate' paper and cushion covers in the billiard room, add much to Standen's charm.

RIGHT Webb's water tower, which he provided with a viewing platform, links the entrance front to the weather-boarded servants' wing on the left.

Stourhead

Wiltshire
At Stourton, off the B3092,
3 miles (4.8 kilometres)
north-west of Mere

This fine Neo-classical house standing high on a ridge of the Wiltshire Downs looks out over the park to distant wooded hills. One of the first Palladian houses in England, it was built in 1721–4 by Henry Hoare I, whose wealth came from the bank founded by his father, Sir Richard Hoare, in 1672. Henry had purchased the estate in 1717, three years after it had passed out of the hands of the Stourton family who had lived here for 700 years. He immediately demolished the existing house and employed Colen Campbell, a leader of the fashionable Neo-classical revival, to design this replacement. The square main block, with its temple-like portico rising the height of the building, is flanked by pavilions added in the 1790s to house a picture gallery and library. The rather severe lines of the facade are softened only by three lead statues set above the portico and by two flights of steps rising to the entrance, their end pillars supporting stone basins surmounted by the Hoare eagle.

Sadly, fire gutted this central block in 1902, destroying much of the original decoration. More or less faithful Edwardian reconstructions of Campbell's intentions by the local architect Doran Webb and the more prestigious Sir Aston Webb who replaced him are now sandwiched between the Regency rooms in the pavilions, both of which survived virtually unscathed. The contents, a rich collection of family heirlooms with finely crafted furniture by Thomas Chippendale the Younger, reflect the interests of several generations of Hoares and the addition of pieces from Wavendon, the family's house in Buckinghamshire, in the nineteenth century.

The nucleus of paintings, sculpture and *objets d'art* acquired by Henry Hoare II to embellish his father's new house was greatly extended by his grandson Sir Richard Colt Hoare, who inherited in 1785. This eminent antiquary, scholar and county historian was an omnivorous collector, amassing a magnificent library in one of his purpose-built extensions and displaying the pick of his grandfather's art collection, together with his own acquisitions of works by Italian and British contemporaries, in the other. Although some of the finest were sold in the late nineteenth century, the paintings still hang triple-banked against pea-green walls, some simple gilt

frames contrasting with florid rococo creations on the end wall. Cigoli's *Adoration of the Magi* dominates the room, an expression of great tenderness lighting the face of the grizzled king in an ermine-fringed cloak who kneels at the Virgin's feet.

Similarly, although many of his books have now been dispersed, Colt Hoare's evocative green and white library is one of the most beautiful surviving Regency rooms in England, with the arch of the high barrel-vaulted ceiling echoed in the curves of the alcoves lined with books. Thomas Chippendale's rich mahogany furniture (including massive staircase-like library steps), gilded calf bindings and the deep-green and ochre carpet all contribute to a feeling of luxurious opulence, while the muted tones are lifted by flashes of colour from the painted glass high up in the lunettes at each end of the room. Of the other treasures in the house, perhaps the most memorable is the seventeenth-century 'Pope's cabinet' designed like the facade of a Renaissance church, a framework of ebony and bronze setting off a multicoloured inlay of marble, porphyry, jasper and other ornamental stones.

At the back of the house, a door from the saloon leads to handsome stone steps designed by Aston Webb, which fan out gently to a sweep of tree-framed grass. Beyond, hidden in the trees, the ground suddenly falls away into a steep-sided valley

and the magical landscape garden created here in the second half of the eighteenth century. Sheltered and enclosed by windbreaks along the rim of the combe is a serene arcadia, with classical temples and other eye-catchers set against wooded slopes and mirrored in an artificial lake. A grotto devised on the edge of the water has sombre rock pools and a sculpture of a river god. All around are the trees, with native species such as beeches and oaks mixed with exotics, among them the Norwegian maple, tulip trees, cedars, the dawn redwood and the Japanese white pine, *Pinus parviflora*.

Although later members of the family, in particular Sir Richard Colt Hoare, enriched the garden by widening the range of species and also made some more fundamental changes, Stourhead is primarily the creation of Henry Hoare II. Perhaps turned in on himself by the tragic loss of both his wives, the garden was to be Henry's absorbing interest for 40 years from 1741. The only professional engaged in its creation was the architect Henry Flitcroft, who designed the classical eye-catchers: the Doric Temple of Flora, which was the first building to be added to the garden; the domed Pantheon, with a broad flight of steps leading up to a pedimented portico; and the tall, circular Temple of Apollo, enclosed in a continuous colonnade. A Gothic cottage, its prominent traceried windows

and thatched roof almost buried in vegetation, was added by Sir Richard Colt Hoare in 1806 and Sir Richard was also responsible for the impressive castellated gateway through which the house is approached. Some two miles (3.4 kilometres) away, standing high on the chalk scarp overlooking Somerset, is the triangular brick folly known as Alfred's Tower, which was also designed by Flitcroft.

Tiled cottages with mullioned windows in the estate village on the edge of the valley stretch down to the Palladian bridge over an arm of the lake. Built by Henry Hoare, they were originally hidden behind a screen of trees so that they would not intrude on his design, but now this row of buildings forms another attractive feature. Opposite the cottages is the medieval parish church, picturesquely crowned with fretwork parapets and filled with monuments to the Hoares and their predecessors, the Stourtons. Just beyond the churchyard, dominating the view over the lake, is the slender column of the medieval cross that Henry acquired from the City of Bristol in the 1760s, its tapering length suggesting the spire of a buried church. Statues of medieval kings standing round the base are carved stone replicas of the originals, which are on loan to the Victoria and Albert Museum.

LEFT The central block of Stourhead's east front, with a grand portico looking over the park, was designed to resemble the villas built by Andrea Palladio around Vicenza in Italy in the sixteenth century.

Sudbury Hall and the National Trust Museum of Childhood

Derbyshire
6 miles (9.6 kilometres) east of Uttoxeter at the crossing point of the A50 Derby–Stoke and the A515 Lichfield–Ashbourne roads

Sudbury is the most idiosyncratic of the many great houses created during Charles II's reign. It is built to a consciously outdated E-shaped plan incorporating a great hall and long gallery and yet is fashionably decorated, with rich plasterwork and woodcarving of the highest quality. The message of the exterior is similarly contradictory. The stone-mullioned and transomed windows were not yet old-fashioned when Sudbury was begun, but the diapered brickwork and carved stone ornaments over the ground-floor windows suggest a Jacobean house. By contrast, the hipped roof and gleaming central cupola, visible for miles around, show knowledge of more up-to-the-minute styles, such as the design of Roger Pratt's Kingston Lacy. George Vernon, who started his new house soon after he inherited the Sudbury estate in 1660, seems to have acted as his own architect and to have adapted his original ideas over some 40 years, the result, perhaps, of being able to consult more sophisticated books and engravings and of a visit to London.

Competent but uninspired early work by local men contrasts with the skills displayed by the London craftsmen Vernon employed as time went by, in particular the woodcarvers Edward Pierce and Grinling Gibbons and the plasterers Bradbury and Pettifer. The balustrade of Pierce's virtuoso staircase, one of the finest and most elaborate of its date, is a mass of writhing foliage carved out of limewood, with baskets of fruit fashioned from elmwood set on the newel posts. Pettifer's plasterwork overhead, in which garlands of fruit and flowers and acanthus scrolls form three-dimensional encrustations, is similarly rich. And yet, 20 years after this work was finished, Vernon added a taste of the exuberant baroque style that was then popular at court by employing Louis Laguerre to paint mythological scenes in the plasterwork panels.

Another painting by Laguerre fills a plaster wreath on the ceiling of the saloon. One of the richest of Sudbury's interiors, this room is lined with family portraits, each of which is set in a gilded ornamental panel carved by Pierce, with swags of fruit and flowers above, below, and in some cases framing the pictures. But even his work is outclassed by the Grinling Gibbons carving over the fireplace in the drawing room next door, in which fruit, flowers, dead game and fish are all depicted with lifelike realism.

After so much unrelieved grandeur, the decoration of the sunny long gallery running the length of the south front is unexpected. At first glance, Bradbury and Pettifer's intricate plasterwork appears to repeat established motifs. But all is not what it seems. The classical busts portrayed along the frieze are humorous caricatures, while a lion, a horse, a boar and other animals leap gaily out of the swirls of foliage on the ceiling and grasshoppers dance playfully round the sunflower rosette in the central window bay.

The small family rooms at the east end of the house are a contrast to all this magnificence. Lady Vernon's cosy sitting room, with its leaf-green walls and tranquil view over the lake below the south front, has a communicating door to her husband's study. It is easy to imagine them talking through it, and walking together across the passage to eat in the small dining room.

Although Sudbury has lost some of its original contents, there are family portraits in almost every room, including works by Lawrence, Hoppner and J.M. Wright, and several other outstanding furnishings remain, among them walnut dining chairs of c.1735 which have been bought back for the house. In the long gallery, a seventeenth-century Flemish ebony cabinet is enchantingly decorated with scenes of the Creation by Frans Francken the Younger. The first panel shows a purple- and red-robed god hovering above an endless expanse of ocean, brooding on what he is about to unleash.

The nineteenth-century service wing by George Devey now houses the Museum of Childhood, which contains displays illustrating children's lives from the eighteenth century onwards and the Betty Cadbury collection of toys and dolls.

OPPOSITE Sudbury, built in the 1660s, is an idiosyncratic house with an old-fashioned Jacobean exterior but work by outstanding London craftsmen mirroring the taste of the day inside.

Tatton Park

Cheshire
3½ miles (5.6 kilometres) north of
Knutsford, 4 miles (6.4 kilometres)
south of Altrincham, 3½ miles
(5.6 kilometres) from the M6 at
the Manchester interchange

The 4th Lord Egerton, who inherited the Tatton estate in 1920, was a restless and individual man who was intrigued by the scientific discoveries of his day. Widely travelled, he staked a claim in the Yukon during the Gold Rush of the 1890s and once lived with a tribe in the Gobi Desert, but he also experimented with short-wave radio and was a pioneer aviator. His 1900 Benz proudly displaying the number plate M1 was the first car to be registered in Cheshire.

The 4th Lord's enquiring mind seems to have been an inherited trait. In all the plans for the remodelling of the house, on which Samuel Wyatt and his nephew Lewis were employed between 1774 and about 1825, the library is given particular prominence. A comfortable room filling the centre of the garden front, it was designed to be used, not admired. Books lie companionably on the reading chairs and stands, leather-padded armchairs are drawn up by the fire and a library ladder invites inspection of the topmost shelves. There is something for everyone here, including first editions of Jane Austen's novels, volumes of music, and illustrated works on the arts and classical antiquities, most of them finely bound. The nucleus of the collection is the sixteenth-century library acquired by Thomas Egerton, founder of the family fortunes, who rose from unpromising beginnings to become Lord Chancellor of England.

Lewis Wyatt's formal drawing room hung with cherry-coloured silk is much grander, with a relentless coffered ceiling and with specially commissioned gilt-framed chairs and sofas carved in a sinuous rococo style by Gillows of Lancaster that would not seem out of place in a Venetian palazzo. Van Dyck's *Martyrdom of St Stephen* seems curiously appropriate in these unrelaxed surroundings, cherubs hovering overhead to receive the saint's soul. Two moody Venetian views by Canaletto are full of delightful detail, such as the little white dog with a jaunty tail that trots purposefully along the quay in the scene in front of the Doge's Palace.

Lewis Wyatt was also responsible for the inspired treatment of the staircase in the centre of the house and for a theatrical vista through a colonnade-like series of arches on the first floor. The Regency lifestyle for which Tatton was designed emerges strongly here, every bedroom except one sporting a dressing room. Each suite was originally distinguished by the colour of its textiles and the wood of the furniture, the pieces in the principal apartment being of mahogany inlaid with ebony.

The Wyatts' exterior is a pure Neo-classical design, with a giant pedimented portico dominating the south front, a low-pitched roof and almost no decoration except for the chaste

LEFT As the centrepiece of the south front, Lewis Wyatt designed a pedimented portico, with Corinthian capitals supported on plain columns of Runcorn stone.

swags in panels over the sash windows. Only the dining room designed by T.F. Pritchard, with its superb rococo plasterwork, remains from the eighteenth-century house.

The atmosphere of opulent grandeur extends into the spacious gardens with their sweeping lawns, herbaceous borders and a rich variety of trees. Grassy terraces on the south front, with shallow flights of steps descending to a fountain surrounded by an Italianate parterre, were designed by Joseph Paxton and there is an impressive range of glasshouses, including Wyatt's classical conservatory and Paxton's fernery, the roof of which has been raised to allow for the huge New Zealand tree ferns which now reach to the glass. More informal planting surrounding the artificial lake known as the Golden Brook almost conceals the Japanese garden laid out here in 1910, with stone lanterns dotting a mosaic of water and islands. Another surprise is the small beech maze hidden behind a bank of rhododendrons beside the long avenue known as the Broad Walk.

The Home Farm at Tatton Dale was once the heart of the extensive Egerton estates, with pigsties, stockyards, stables and workshops surrounding the office from which nearly 1,000 tenant properties were administered. Humphry Repton produced a Red Book for the extensive park, but most of the landscaping probably dates from William Emes's work in the mid-eighteenth century, with some early nineteenth-century modifications by John Webb. There are deer and flocks of Soay and Hebridean sheep beneath the trees, and the remains of the medieval manor house are used to introduce visitors to the realities of pre-modern life.

BELOW Like other great country houses, Tatton Park was largely self-sufficient, generating its own electricity until 1961. This intriguing calorifier was used for heating the water. .

Tyntesfield

Somerset
Off the B3128, 3 miles
(4.8 kilometres) east of Nailsea

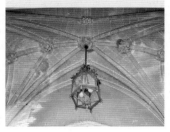

This romantic High Victorian mansion is set on steeply rising ground, with woods behind and a panoramic view south over parkland and the valley of the Yeo to the distant ridge of the Mendips. Still all of a piece with its original furnishings, decorative schemes and the accumulated possessions of the family that lived here for four generations, this memorable place is an unspoilt and largely unaltered example of a Gothic Revival country house. Windows are stone-mullioned and traceried, there are pepper-pot turrets, huge chimneystacks and fanciful Gothic dormers, and window bays and rooflines are finished off with carved friezes, pierced parapets, finials and gargoyles. Rising over the house is the steeply pitched roof of a sizeable chapel, with finialled buttresses between the Gothic windows and a west-end stair turret.

Together with 200 hectares (almost 500 acres) of gardens, park and estate, Tyntesfield was acquired by the National Trust in 2002 after a whirlwind campaign to save the property from being sold on the open market, which required the Trust to raise over £20 million in 50 days. This was only made possible by a huge public response, and a measure of the brinkmanship involved is that the contents had already been ticketed and sorted for sale by auction. Much-needed conservation and restoration has been going on ever since.

Tyntesfield is predominantly the creation of the entrepreneurial William Gibbs (1790–1875). Involved in the family firm, which had business interests in Spain and Latin America, from a young age, by 1842, when he was in his early 50s, William was in charge. In the same year, the firm's South American agent concluded the deal that was to make him a fortune, giving Gibbs and Sons a virtual monopoly in the shipment of Peruvian guano, then a fertiliser of prime importance. A growing family may have encouraged William and his wife Blanche, 28 years his junior, to look for a place out of London, and in 1843 William bought what was then a Georgian country house with some decorative Gothic touches. Twenty years later he commissioned the architect John Norton, who had learned his trade from a pupil and friend of Augustus Welby Pugin and so had direct links with the most influential figure of the Gothic Revival, to remodel Tyntesfield.

The house is built of golden Bath stone, with roofs covered partly in tiles, partly in heavy stone slabs quarried in Wiltshire. Carved stone decoration enlivening every facade includes some finely detailed, three-dimensional work by a certain Mr Beates, who realised the plants and creatures of the gardens and estate in stone. There are primroses, cobnuts and strawberries carved on corbels in the porch, and a capital carries a dormouse, bees and a lizard. As throughout the house, the craftsmanship is of the highest quality.

William's son Antony (1841–1907), an art collector and highly skilled amateur craftsman rather than a businessman, moved into Tyntesfield in 1890 after the death of his mother. He embarked on alterations, but his chosen architect, Henry Woodyer, also worked in the Gothic Revival style and Woodyer's changes, including the substantial verandah which he had added on for Blanche in 1883, were all in keeping with the earlier work. By the next generation, a shift in taste was reflected in changes made by George Gibbs, 1st Lord Wraxall (1873–1931), who was a prominent politician and socialiser and invited members of the government down for country-house weekends. Again, though, with the exception of the drawing room, the essential character of the place was retained.

The 2nd Lord Wraxall (1928–2001) succeeded to the title when he was only 3, and his mother Ursula, Lady Wraxall ran Tyntesfield for many years. At the end of his life, Lord Wraxall was living at Tyntesfield alone and many of the main rooms were shut up, but he maintained a keen interest in the gardens and estate and cared for the fabric of the place. Most importantly, although he sold some items, he did not follow the reaction against High Victorian art that led to other houses being stripped of their contents, and he added pictures and other objects to the collection.

The interior is of a piece, combining original decorative schemes with much surviving Victorian furniture, some of it, such as a richly ornamented rolltop desk, by the Warwickshire cabinet-makers Collier and Plucknett, who supplied the family with furniture in the later nineteenth century. Wood and stone have been used profligately: there are open timber roofs, decorative panelling and parquet floors; monumental

OPPOSITE The vaulted roof of Tyntesfield's cloister-like entrance hall.

ABOVE The exuberant Gothic south front, with the traceried windows of the library on the right and the substantial verandah to the left.

FOLLOWING PAGE The state-of-the-art table acquired for the billiard room in the late nineteenth century was centrally heated and connected to the electrically operated scoreboard on the far wall.

fireplaces, stone arches and doorways and pillars of polished marble. The main rooms are arranged around the toplit staircase hall, with clerestory windows beneath an open roof of English oak. Paintings hung thickly on the walls include a portrait of William, with white hair and side-whiskers, by his close friend Sir William Boxall, and a seascape by Sir Augustus Wall Callcott, all steely sky and blue-grey sea. The chenille stair carpet, in ribbons when the Trust acquired Tyntesfield, has been rewoven in wool, to the original design, for which 27 colours were required.

William's spirit is strong in the spacious library which fills one of the wings on the entrance front. A comfortable, welcoming room rising to an open oak roof, it has the original carpet, in deep reds and blues, by the fashionable decorators J.G. Crace and Son and this company also provided the deep-buttoned armchairs and sofa. William's seven children staged theatricals here, and the bookcases round the walls, carefully numbered in Latin numerals, are stuffed with the gilded bindings of his library. William's religious sympathies lay with the Oxford Movement, which was launched in the 1830s to return ceremony and ritual, and thus elements of beauty and mystery, to the Church of England. The main texts of the movement are here, and so too are key works on the Gothic Revival, with which it went hand in hand, including the writings of Pugin and Ruskin. Above the bookcases at the west end of the room is a striking display of Imari porcelain – blue and white, green and red.

The dining room, entered through a flamboyant carved stone doorway and lined with wallpaper imitating Spanish leather, is Antony's. But the drawing room, with a Renaissance-style fireplace and an original Crace carpet that has been dyed to match the crimson damask on the walls, was altered and refurnished by Antony's son George, 1st Lord Wraxall, and his first wife Via. Much more relaxed in spirit is the capacious billiard room, with an array of antlered heads on the walls, skins thrown casually over ageing sofas, and a centrally heated table with an electric scoreboard.

Upstairs, a run of bedrooms along the south and east fronts includes the room used by Via, who died at the tragically early age of 39. The rose carpet was installed for her, her dressing-table set is on display, and the room is furnished with Italian and Dutch marquetry pieces that she brought with her to the house. Because of the slope of the hill, the family could walk from these first-floor rooms straight into the chapel which William commissioned from Arthur Blomfield and which was only just finished when William died in 1875. Provided with a chancel and ornate screen and richly fitted out with gleaming mosaics, stained glass and an inlaid floor, it proclaims William's commitment to High Church principles. A silver communion set designed by William Butterfield in 1876 was commissioned by Blanche in memory of her husband.

The layout of the garden is still very much as it was when William died. Close to the house, billowing hollies lap the marble urns set along the lower terrace, and bright displays of bedding plants reflect the taste of the 2nd Lord Wraxall. A lone palm and luxuriant magnolias and camellias outside the billiard room mark the site of John Norton's huge conservatory, with an onion dome and gilded cupola, which was demolished after the dome collapsed in a storm in March 1916. A formal walk lined by mushroom domes of holly stretches away from the west front, past the former rose garden, and another long walk, marked by clipped Irish yews, echoes the line of the terraces, with views over the sadly waterless lake. Architectural stone Gothic seats punctuate the ends of the walks.

Everywhere in the landscaped grounds are huge specimen trees and a ha-ha allows uninterrupted views across the park and the valley beyond. Hidden from the house are the walled kitchen gardens, with greenhouses that are still very much in use, and a splendid classical orangery, of brick and stone. Cut flowers and fresh vegetables are still supplied to the house from these gardens as they always have been.

Uppark House and Garden

West Sussex
5 miles (8 kilometres) south-east
of Petersfield on the B2146,
1½ miles (2.4 kilometres) south
of South Harting

The serene two-storey house built in about 1690 for Ford, Lord Grey, Earl of Tankerville, owes its existence to his grandfather's invention of an effective method of pumping water to great heights, without which the commanding site on a crest of the South Downs would have been impractical. The amoral and duplicitous Lord Grey, who emerged remarkably unscathed from his involvement in the Duke of Monmouth's rebellion against James II in 1685, perhaps because he turned king's evidence, is one of many colourful characters connected with the estate. His new house, whose architect is uncertain, was in the latest Dutch style. Standing four-square like a giant doll's house, it is built of red brick with weathered, lichen-tinted stone dressings and dormer windows in a hipped roof. A pediment crowns the south front and detached mid-eighteenth-century stable and kitchen blocks balance the composition on either side.

The rich interior is mostly the work of Sir Matthew Fetherstonhaugh, who bought Uppark in 1747. This cultivated man, heir to the vast fortune of a distant relative, redecorated most of the principal rooms and enriched the house with a magnificent collection of carpets, furniture and works of art, much of it, such as portraits by Batoni and four harbour and coastal scenes by Joseph Vernet, purchased on a Grand Tour with his wife Sarah in 1749–51. The couple were responsible for the hauntingly beautiful white and gold saloon, with its delicate plaster ceiling and ivory silk brocade curtains framing the long south-facing windows, and with paintings set into fixed plasterwork frames in the Adam style. Fireplaces inlaid with Sienese marble warm both ends of the room, one of them carved with the Sienese wolf suckling Romulus and Remus. Sarah also introduced the finely crafted doll's house of c.1740, with three floors of rooms behind a pedimented facade. Every detail is accurate. Diminutive landscape paintings hang on the walls, hallmarked silver and glass gleam on the dining-room table and there are fire irons of silver and brass. Meticulously dressed dolls people the mansion, those representing the family identifiable by their wax faces, the lower orders depicted in wood.

Matthew's only son Harry inherited his parents' good taste and enriched their collection. But in other respects he was a prodigal young man, with a love of hunting and the turf which is echoed in his sporting pictures and silver-gilt cups. His close friend the Prince Regent was a guest at the lavish house parties staged at Uppark, with superb meals produced by Moget, Harry's French chef. It was on one of these occasions that the 15-year-old Emma Hart, the future Lady Hamilton, is said to have danced naked on the dining-room table. Sir Harry's liaison with Emma, whom he had discovered in London, was only brief and the letters she wrote to him after she had been sent away, six months pregnant, went unanswered. Decades later, Sir Harry caused another stir when, in his 70th year, he married young Mary Ann Bullock, his head dairymaid. Largely because of Mary Ann and her sister Frances, who joined the household, Uppark was to survive the nineteenth century little changed.

In the basement is an extensive range of service rooms. There is an authentically laid out butler's pantry, and the sunny room where H.G. Wells's mother presided as housekeeper from 1880–93 has easy chairs drawn up by the fire and tea laid on a tray. Long whitewashed tunnels, down which the young Wells chased the maids, lead to the eighteenth-century pavilions flanking the house. One was a stable block, the other a laundry and greenhouse where, in c.1815, Sir Harry installed a new kitchen. During most of the nineteenth century the present kitchen, with a long scrubbed table and gleaming pots and pans, was probably a still room, used for making cakes and drinks and for giving final touches to the dishes for upstairs after their long journey through the tunnel.

Much of Uppark's charm derives from its setting, with a great stretch of downland turf planted with mature trees sweeping away from the house and leading the eye across a rolling landscape to the sea. Humphry Repton, who added the pillared portico to the north front, was probably also responsible for Mary Ann's elegant dairy, its white tiles decorated with a blue and green frieze of clematis, and for the little Gothic summerhouse.

One of the more traumatic events in the National Trust's history was the fire at Uppark in 1989, from which most of the furniture and paintings were rescued but which destroyed much of their eighteenth-century setting. Restoration took

five-and-a-half years, and required the re-learning of traditional skills. Plasterwork was re-created, intricate mouldings and architraves re-carved, new curtains woven and wallpaper printed. From the outset, the Trust aimed to maintain the air of faded elegance that makes the house so attractive. New was carefully matched to old, even to the extent of imitating picture-protected patches of wallpaper and time-darkened white paint, but almost every room has also been left with scorched floorboards and chimneypieces and other reminders of the fire, or with unfinished, newly created detail, such as an ungilded ornamental cherub. Wherever possible, fire-mangled and shattered fittings were put back together: lanterns and chandeliers that had been reduced to twisted metal shapes and fragments of glass were painstakingly

reconstructed and a scagliola table-top was pieced together, bit by bit. The house itself seems unchanged. As before, the most enduring memory is of mellow pink brick and lichened stone against a life-enhancing view. And martins have returned to nest under the eaves.

ABOVE The south front of Uppark, with an elegant central doorway and the Fetherstonhaugh arms in the pediment above, looks over the former deer park and the downland landscape of Sussex towards the sea.
OPPOSITE The late eighteenth-century Saloon at Uppark, filling the centre of the south front, is one of the most serenely beautiful interiors of its date in the country.

Upton House

Warwickshire
1 mile (1.6 kilometres) south of Edge Hill, 7 miles (11.2 kilometres) north-west of Banbury, on the west side of the Stratford-upon-Avon road (A422)

Walter Samuel, 2nd Viscount Bearsted, was lucky enough to inherit a fortune from his father, who had profited greatly from the expansion of trade with the Far East in the late nineteenth century and, together with his brother, had developed the Shell organisation, building it up into an international corporation. One of the twentieth century's most generous philanthropists, the 2nd Viscount used his inheritance to benefit a long list of charities, hospitals and schools. At the same time, it also enabled him to pursue his great passion for painting and the decorative arts, and to acquire one of the finest art collections of his time.

Lord Bearsted bought Upton in 1927, shortly after the death of his father, as somewhere to display his collection. At the heart of the house, making up the central seven bays of the long, sash-windowed entrance front, is the mansion built in 1695 for Sir Rushout Cullen, but this was altered substantially in the eighteenth century, when the entrance bay acquired its baroque broken pediment, and in 1927–9 the architect Percy Morley Horder reworked the place for Lord Bearsted, giving the building a strong horizontal emphasis. Morley Horder's interiors were among the most luxurious of the period, but were deliberately bland and restrained in order to create a suitable setting for the collection. Only the first-floor suite created for Lady Bearsted, which includes a Chinese bedroom looking out over the garden and a striking Art Deco bathroom decorated in silver, red and black, has a strong character of its own.

Lord Bearsted's collection included tapestries, furniture, silver, miniatures and many other fine things, but the rooms at Upton are now largely devoted to displaying his paintings, including some inherited from his father, and his eighteenth-century soft-paste French and English porcelain. In both areas he had an eye for the unusual and outstanding. Among a number of works by fifteenth- and sixteenth-century masters is El Greco's *El Espolio* (Flagellation of Christ), the spears of the soldiers grouped behind Our Lord suggesting a crown of thorns. In another strongly atmospheric work, Brueghel's *Dormition of the Virgin*, Our Lady is shown receiving a lighted taper from St Peter in a dimly lit room. The use of grey and black alone gives the picture a ghostly quality. Serene Dutch interiors and landscapes with diminutive figures set against immense skies include Saenredam's cool study of St Catherine's Church, Utrecht, in which beetle-like clerics and two men inscribing a stone set into the floor are dwarfed by the soaring arches of the nave.

Sporting pictures feature in the dining room. Here, too, hang Stubbs's scenes from rural life, his *Haymakers*, *Reapers* and *Labourers*, the weariness evident in the horses about to take away a laden cart as real as the chill conjured up in Hogarth's portrayal of an early winter morning in front of St Paul's, Covent Garden, one of the paintings for his engraved series, *The Four Times of Day*.

The porcelain collection is similarly wide-ranging. Here, again, perhaps reflecting Lord Bearsted's essential humanitarianism, figures feature prominently, among the most memorable being two Chelsea pieces in the long gallery depicting a wet nurse suckling a swaddled baby and a shepherd teaching his shepherdess how to play the flute, holding the instrument for her as she blows. Embroidery on the eighteenth-century-style walnut chairs in this room, depicting people involved in weaving, grape-treading and other occupations, is the work of the 3rd Lord Bearsted, who started doing it as therapy after he was badly injured in the Second World War. Art of a different kind features in the display of scenic posters produced by Shell in the 1930s which are devoted to some of England's most beautiful buildings and landscapes, several National Trust properties among them.

While the house is bland and architecturally undistinguished, the gardens are full of character. Across

OPPOSITE As part of his remodelling of Upton House in the 1920s, the architect Percy Morley Horder created the long gallery out of several smaller rooms.
ABOVE To imitate silver leaf, which would have tarnished, Morley Horder covered the walls and ceiling of the Art Deco bathroom with aluminium leaf.

a broad double terrace and cedar-framed lawn on the south front, there is a sudden steep descent to a chain of ponds in the valley below. An Italianate balustraded stairway added in the 1930s leads into the depths of the combe, its lichen-stained steps overhung with wisteria. The mellow brick wall of the old kitchen garden on the slopes of the valley still carries espaliered fruit trees as it did in the seventeenth century and present renovation of the ornamental terraces above will give a 1930s flavour to the planting, with drifts of colour in the style of Gertrude Jekyll. A wilder bog garden fills a natural amphitheatre to the west of the house, sheep graze on the other side of the valley and over a mile (1.6 kilometres) away, just visible from the terrace, a lake reflects the columns of a little eighteenth-century Tuscan temple.

The Vyne

Hampshire
4 miles (6.4 kilometres) north of
Basingstoke, between Bramley and
Sherborne St John

This long red-brick house with purple diaperwork lacing the facades is set low in a hollow, looking north over an idyllic lake. There is a pedimented portico on the garden front and the original mullions have been replaced with mid-seventeenth-century sash windows, but the E-plan is that of a Tudor house. Dating from some time between 1500 and 1520, The Vyne was built for William, 1st Lord Sandys, whose long career in the service of Henry VIII culminated in his appointment to the office of Lord Chamberlain in 1526.

Sandys's battlemented chapel juts out conspicuously at the east end of the house. One of the most perfect private oratories in England, this lofty room rising the height of two storeys is still largely as it was built in 1518–27. Intricately carved canopied stalls facing across the chapel are fringed by intriguing early sixteenth-century Italian tiles: richly coloured in blue, yellow, orange and green, they were found in heaps in the grounds. Three magnificent stained-glass windows at the east end, seen at their best in morning sunlight, are equalled in importance only by those of similar date in King's College, Cambridge. One of them, showing Henry VIII with Catherine of Aragon, who is accompanied by a little dog, would have been hidden from view when the king came here with Anne Boleyn in 1535.

The Oak Gallery, stretching the length of the west wing on the first floor, one of the finest examples of its date in Britain, is another survival from the Tudor house. The delicate linenfold panelling which lines the walls from floor to ceiling carries a wealth of carved badges and devices, among them the Tudor rose and Catherine of Aragon's pomegranate. A more unusual emblem is the curious portcullis-like hemp bray that was used in the separation of flax fibres and which is included here because it was the crest of Sir Reginald Bray, uncle of Lord Sandys's wife. The white marble of a seventeenth-century classical fireplace in the middle of the east wall is picked up in a series of portrait busts set down the room, a mixed company in which portrayals of Shakespeare, Milton and Mary Queen of Scots rub shoulders with a typically arrogant Nero and a world-weary Seneca.

Lord Sandys's service to Henry VIII was rewarded at the Dissolution of the Monasteries with the gift of Mottisfont Abbey and it was here that the family retired when impoverishment in the Civil War forced the sale of The Vyne in 1653. The new owner was another successful and astute politician, Chaloner Chute, shortly to be Speaker in Richard Cromwell's parliament, who reduced the size of the house. He also added the classical portico on the north front, which is thought to be the earliest on a domestic building. His grandson Edward acquired the Queen Anne furniture and Soho tapestries now displayed in the house, such as the hangings in the room next to the gallery. Depicting oriental scenes, they are full of gay spotted butterflies and darting birds, and one shows a monkey sitting in a palm tree.

Chute's great-grandson John, friend of Horace Walpole, made notable alterations in about 1750, creating the theatrical classical staircase, with busts of Roman emperors on the newel posts, ornate fluted columns fringing a first-floor gallery and a moulded ceiling in pale blue and white. John Chute was also responsible for the tomb chamber off the chapel, built in honour of his distinguished ancestor. Here the Speaker lies immortalised in Carrara marble on the top of a box-like monument loosely disguised as a Greek temple. His lifelike effigy rests on an unyielding plaited straw mattress, his head supported on his right arm, one finger extended along the curve of his brow.

OPPOSITE, LEFT One of the Tudor stained-glass windows in the chapel at The Vyne shows Henry VIII, a deep blue cloak over his gilt-plated armour, kneeling in prayer beside his patron saint, Henry II of Bavaria.

OPPOSITE, RIGHT The chapel at the Vyne, built between 1518 and 1527, is a largely unaltered Tudor interior.

ABOVE The Tudor long gallery filling the first floor of The Vyne's west wing is the finest interior in the house.

Waddesdon Manor

Buckinghamshire
6 miles (9.6 kilometres) north-west of Aylesbury, on the A41, 11 miles (17.7 kilometres) south-east of Bicester

The great châteaux of the Loire made such an impression on the young Ferdinand and future Baron de Rothschild, grandson of the founder of the Austrian branch of this famous banking family, that he determined to model any house he might build on what he had seen in France. This magnificent palace designed by Gabriel Hippolyte Destailleur and built in 1874–9, when the baron was in his late 40s, fulfilled the youthful Ferdinand's dreams, its pinnacles, mansard roofs, dormer windows, massive chimneys and staircase towers reproducing the characteristic features of Maintenon, Blois and other French Renaissance châteaux. The hill on which Waddesdon is set was purchased from the Duke of Marlborough, a platform was carved out for the mansion and the slopes were planted with half-grown trees. Building materials were brought up by cable, while the timber was hauled laboriously up the hill by teams of horses.

This pastiche château has similarly extravagant, French-inspired interiors, with a procession of high-ceilinged reception rooms re-creating the elegant splendour of the pre-Revolutionary regime. Profiting from Baron Haussmann's remodelling of Paris for Napoleon III, Ferdinand was able to obtain panelling from the great eighteenth-century houses that were destroyed to form the city's new boulevards, and this elaborately carved woodwork can be seen in almost every room. Royal fleurs-de-lis feature prominently on the Savonnerie carpets, a representation of the Sun King himself appearing on one from a set that Louis XIV commissioned for the long gallery of the Louvre. Eight pieces of furniture were made for the French royal family by the great Jean-Henri Riesener, the leading cabinetmaker of his day, including a marquetry writing-table created for Marie Antoinette and a drop-front secretaire ordered for the queen by Louis XVI. Elegant little tables with delicate gazelle-like legs contrast with the baron's massive cylinder-top desk that once belonged to the dramatist Beaumarchais and a monumental black and gold secretaire surmounted by a clock and crowned by a huge gilt eagle. Tear-drop chandeliers are reflected in mirrors with ornate gilt frames and every surface is crammed with clocks, Sèvres and

Meissen porcelain and *objets d'art*, among them a gold snuffbox that once belonged to Louis XV's mistress, Madame de Pompadour, with her pet dogs, Ines and Mimi, shown cavorting on the lid. Paintings by Watteau, Lancret, Boucher and Greuze help to create a sense of pre-Revolutionary France.

These French pieces are harmoniously combined with a fine collection of eighteenth-century English portraits by Gainsborough, Reynolds and Romney, and with a number of seventeenth-century Dutch paintings, such as Jan van der Heyden's tranquil view of an Amsterdam canal, with stepped red-brick gables reflected in the still waters, a garden scene by de Hooch, and Rubens's dreamy *The Garden of Love*. One of the two galleries leading from the main entrance is dominated by two huge canvases of Venice by Francesco Guardi, one a view to Santa Maria della Salute and San Giorgio Maggiore, two gilded and canopied gondolas gliding across the water between them, the other looking towards the Doge's Palace from across the lagoon. Oenophiles are tantalised by a 'library' of Rothschild vintages on view in the wine cellars; there is a display of Sèvres porcelain and a recently acquired silver dinner service that was made in Paris for George III; and a tower room is hung with panels commissioned by the late James de Rothschild from the stage designer Leon Bakst, who incorporated portraits of the family and their friends in paintings illustrating the story of Sleeping Beauty. Also shown is the Bachelor's wing, complete with smoking and billiard rooms, where Ferdinand entertained his male guests.

An extensive programme of restoration undertaken by the Rothschild family at the turn of the century returned Waddesdon's Bath stone to its original striking yellow and the house is set off by an exceptional Victorian garden. Steps from the south front lead down to a parterre with an ornate Italian fountain. The wooded park beyond, with rich plantings of specimen trees and some contemporary sculpture, is part of the extensive grounds designed by the French landscape gardener Lainé, while artificial rockwork by Pulham and Sons bordering the approach north of the house shelters an aviary in eighteenth-century style, its presence heralded by chirruping from the exotic inhabitants, many of which were bred here. The aviary is the heart of the west garden as Baron Ferdinand conceived it, with flamboyant beds and hedges giving way to tranquil glades.

ABOVE Waddesdon Manor, built on a hill above the Vale of Aylesbury in 1874–9 for Ferdinand de Rothschild, was designed to look like a château of the Loire and is set off by a great formal parterre.

Wallington

Northumberland
12 miles (19.3 kilometres) west of
Morpeth on the B6343, 6 miles
(9.6 kilometres) north-west of
Belsay on the A696

Many country houses are hidden behind walls or screens of trees, but there is nothing secluded about Wallington. The pedimented south front of this square stone building crowns a long slope of rough grass, in full view of the public road through the park. Nor is there a lodge or an imposing gateway. The pinnacled triumphal arch built for the house was found to be too narrow for coaches and now languishes in a field.

Wallington is largely the creation of Sir Walter Calverley Blackett, 2nd Baronet, who commissioned the Northumbrian architect Daniel Garrett in *c*.1738 to remodel his grandfather's uncomfortable house. Garrett's cool, Palladian exteriors are no preparation for Pietro Lafranchini's magnificent rococo plasterwork in the saloon, where delicate, feminine compositions in blue and white, with winged sphinxes perched on curling foliage, garlands of flowers and cornucopias overflowing with fruit, suggest an elaborate wedding cake.

Oriental porcelain in the alcoves on either side of the fireplace is part of a large and varied collection, much of it the dowry of Maria Wilson, who married into the family in 1791 just a few years after Wallington had passed to Sir Walter's nephew, Sir John Trevelyan. A bizarre Meissen tea-set in the parlour features paintings of life-size insects nestling in the bottom of each cup. Even more extraordinary is Wallington's Cabinet of Curiosities, which Maria also introduced, its strange exhibits ranging from a piece of Edward IV's coffin to stuffed birds set against painted habitats and a spiky red porcupine fish like an animated pin cushion.

The hall rising through two storeys in the middle of the house reflects another era. Created in 1853–4 out of what was an internal courtyard, this individual room was the inspiration of the talented Pauline Trevelyan, whose vivid personality attracted a stream of artists and writers, including Ruskin,

Swinburne and Rossetti. Under her influence, Rossetti's friend William Bell Scott was commissioned to produce the eight epic scenes from Northumbrian history which decorate the walls, the subjects portrayed including the death of the Venerable Bede and Grace Darling in her open boat rescuing the men of the *Forfarshire*. In the canvas showing the landing of the Vikings, savage heads on the prows of the fleet emerge out of the gloom over the sea like an invasion of prehistoric monsters. Ruskin and Pauline herself, among others, painted the delicate wild flowers – purple foxgloves, brilliant-red poppies and yellow columbine – on the pillars between the pictures. The family's later connection with the Macaulays brought associations with scientists and politicians as well as artists and writers, and Lord Macaulay wrote his monumental history of England here.

Sir Walter Calverley Blackett's spirit lives on in the extensive estate, which embraces several parishes. This he transformed, laying out roads, enclosing fields, building cottages, planting woods and devising follies. His formal pleasure grounds were later converted into a naturalistic landscape park, possibly with the advice of the young 'Capability' Brown, who was born nearby and went to school on the estate and who, in about 1765, was employed to design the setting for the ornamental

lake at Rothley. But Sir Walter himself was responsible for damming the River Wansbeck and for James Paine's imposing three-arched bridge below the house.

Sir Walter also laid out the walled garden that lies in a sheltered dell half a mile (0.8 kilometre) east of the house. Once a vegetable garden, it is now an unexpected delight of lawns and mixed herbaceous beds following the lines of the valley, with a little stream running out of a pond in a stone niche that was created in 1938. To one side a raised terrace walk carries a little brick pavilion, surmounted with the owl of the Calverley crest, and Sir George Otto Trevelyan's 1908 conservatory. A hedged nuttery on the slopes below marks the site of the former vegetable patch, while across the valley is a broad, sloping mixed border. Although this must be one of the National Trust's coldest gardens, roses, honeysuckles, clematis and sun-loving plants thrive against the south-facing walls.

OPPOSITE The Northumbrian architect Daniel Garrett, who remodelled Wallington in the mid-eighteenth century, made the south front more imposing by adding a pediment and deepening the entablature.
BELOW Wallington's vast central hall was created out of what was a courtyard in 1853–4 and is painted with murals by William Bell Scott illustrating scenes from Northumbrian history.

West Wycombe Park and Village

Buckinghamshire
2 miles (3.2 kilometres) west
of High Wycombe, on the A40

Everything about West Wycombe bears the stamp of the man who created it, the mercurial eighteenth-century dilettante Sir Francis Dashwood. Armed with the fortune his father had made trading with Africa, India and the East, Sir Francis interleaved several visits to Italy with tours as far afield as Russia and Turkey. Months of foreign travel not only gave him opportunities to indulge in the practical jokes he was fond of but also an appreciation of art and a depth of learning that led him, in 1732, to be a founder member of the Dilettanti Society, which was to have an important influence on English taste. Now remembered chiefly for his connection with the notorious Hellfire Club, which met in caves burrowed into the hill rising steeply to the north of West Wycombe, the more serious side of his character comes across in his successful political career. Although disastrous as Chancellor of the Exchequer in 1762, he proved himself a more than able joint Paymaster General in the years that followed.

Between 1735 and Sir Francis's death in 1781, the square, red-brick Queen Anne building he inherited was transformed into a classical mansion and filled with paintings and furniture acquired on his Grand Tours. The architect John Donowell supervised the remodelling until 1764, but it is not clear who was responsible for designing the house. Sir Francis undoubtedly had strong ideas of his own, but he may also have had expert advice from Giovanni Servandoni, Roger Morris and Isaac Ware, and Nicholas Revett was involved in the later stages of the work. In his remodelling, Sir Francis was no more than a man of his time; but the architecture and decoration with which he enriched West Wycombe give the house its highly individual and theatrical character. An unusual double colonnade rising to roof height stretches almost the full width of the long south front, rivalling the huge porticoes decorated with frescoes, one of which was designed by Revett in imitation of a Greek temple, that dominate the east and west facades. The richly decorated interior, with gilded mirrors reflecting glittering vistas through the house, mixes illusion with fine craftsmanship. Sensual baroque painted ceilings by the Italian Giuseppe Mattias Borgnis, who was brought to England specially for this commission, adorn some of the principal rooms, his *Triumph of Bacchus and Ariadne* in the Blue Drawing Room a riot of overweight cherubs, heavily muscled bodies and flowing drapery. Paint was also used to imitate marble, fine plasterwork and joinery of burr walnut and satinwood and Sir Francis's Neo-classical hall and dining room, with illusionistic coffered ceilings by Giuseppe's son Giovanni, marbled walls and elaborate stone floors, were intended to evoke the houses of Roman antiquity. The hall was even fitted with hypocaust heating.

Some delicate rococo plasterwork is the real thing, and elaborate marble chimneypieces in many of the rooms include at least two by Sir Henry Cheere, who carved doves, and an owl devouring a small bird, on the one in the music room and was probably also responsible for the plaque showing cherubs warming themselves by a fire in the study, and for the grand columned doorcase of the saloon. The mahogany staircase inlaid with satinwood and ebony is similarly fine.

Hardly altered since Sir Francis's death, the house still displays his catholic collection of lesser Italian masters, family portraits stretching back to the seventeenth century, and views of the house painted in the 1750s by William Hannan. But much of Sir Francis's fine eighteenth-century furniture, including a state bed embellished with pineapples, was sold in 1922 by the 10th Baronet. Although the 11th Baronet, who inherited in 1963, was able to buy back some of these pieces, many of the present furnishings, all of which seem totally in keeping, are not original.

The house is set off by Sir Francis's serene landscape garden, which he created by remodelling his own earlier, more formal layout. A composition in grass, trees and water, it is focused on an islanded lake and richly embellished with ornamental buildings, many of which are as individual as the house. John Donowell was probably responsible for the gigantic grey arch of flint and stone known as the Temple of Apollo that stands next to the house, and for the octagonal tower carried on flintwork arches. Later eye-catchers designed by Nicholas Revett between 1770 and 1781 include a Doric temple on the largest island in the lake, a cottage disguised as a church and a colonnaded circular dovecote with a pyramidal roof known as the Round Temple. The 11th Baronet added new features to the garden, such as the huge fibreglass equestrian statue on the crest of the hill above the house, and restored others that had been lost, among them the Temple of Venus on a grassy mound in the woods to the west of the lake.

From the north front of the house the ground falls away into a wooded valley, rising again to an extraordinary hexagonal mausoleum and the church remodelled by Sir Francis on the top of the hill opposite. Hidden in the valley is West Wycombe village, which was acquired by the Dashwood family, as part of the estate, in 1698. This is an exceptional place, owing much of its character to the fact that, before the building of the M40, it lay on the main route from London to Oxford, the Midlands and Wales. Timber-framed, flint and brick cottages line the long main street. One of the oldest buildings, the fifteenth-century Church Loft, was originally a rest house for pilgrims, and there are three former coaching inns.

OPPOSITE The huge portico on the west front of West Wycombe was designed as a replica of a Greek temple dedicated to Bacchus.
RIGHT, TOP The Palladian north front of West Wycombe Park is less theatrical than the other sides of the house and looks over the eighteenth-century landscape created by Sir Francis Dashwood.
RIGHT, BOTTOM In 1771, a ceremony at West Wycombe to dedicate the dramatic west portico involved a procession of 'priests ... fauns, satyrs etc ' and further celebrations in boats on the lake.

Wightwick Manor

West Midlands
3 miles (4.8 kilometres) west of Wolverhampton, up Wightwick Bank, beside the Mermaid Inn, just north of the A454 Bridgnorth road

In 1848 seven young men barely out of their teens, including William Holman Hunt, John Everett Millais and Dante Gabriel Rossetti, founded the Pre-Raphaelite Brotherhood, a revolt against the artistic establishment and what they perceived as the emptiness and artificiality of contemporary art. The group was short-lived, but its ideals were enormously influential, feeding into the reaction against mass production and the return to pre-industrial techniques that became identified with William Morris and the Arts and Crafts Movement. Rossetti, Ford Madox Brown and Edward Burne-Jones were among the founders of Morris's design and furnishing company, which started life as an artist's co-operative in 1861.

Wightwick Manor is one of the best surviving examples of a house built and furnished under the influence of the Arts and

ABOVE The east wing of Wightwick Manor, built in the late nineteenth century to resemble a medieval timber-framed house, has richly patterned woodwork and a large gabled bay filled with armorial glass.

Crafts Movement. Morris wallpapers, textiles and carpets and William de Morgan tiles and Benson metalwork supplied by his company set off paintings and drawings by Ford Madox Brown, Holman Hunt, Millais, Burne-Jones and Ruskin. The Jacobean furniture, oriental porcelain and Persian rugs with which the house is also furnished complement rather than compete with the nineteenth-century work, demonstrating how well Morris's work blends with good craftsmanship from other periods. There is a particularly pleasing juxtaposition of antique and Victorian in the drawing room, where rich green tiles by William de Morgan featuring a bestiary of mischievous creatures are inset into an Italian Renaissance chimneypiece.

Built in two stages in 1887 and 1893, Wightwick was commissioned by the industrialist Theodore Mander, a paint and varnish manufacturer, from the Liverpool architect Edward Ould, and was designed in a traditional, half-timbered idiom. The later, eastern half is more richly decorated and is clearly inspired by the Tudor buildings of the Welsh Marches. Decorative black-and-white timbering, in stripes, swirls and quatrefoils, rises from a plinth of local stone, with banks of spiral Tudor-style chimneys crowning the gabled roofline.

In keeping with the late-medieval character of the exterior, the heart of the house is a great parlour in the form of a feudal hall, with an open timber roof painted by the talented Charles Kempe. A minstrels' gallery across one end, a deeply recessed fireplace alcove and extensive use of panelling add to the period atmosphere. Kempe was also responsible for the glowing colours in the painted windows and the deep plaster frieze telling the story of Orpheus and Eurydice that may well have been inspired by that in the High Great Chamber at Hardwick Hall. Orpheus sits with his harp in a forest, enticing a whole menagerie of beasts with his music, from a trumpeting elephant and a kangaroo to a peacock with a golden tail. Morris's last woven fabric design, featuring white and pink blossom on a deep-blue ground, like a meadow full of spring flowers, hangs below the frieze. Wightwick also has a copy of Morris's last major artistic project, an edition of the works of Chaucer, published by Morris's Kelmscott Press in 1896. Burne-Jones, who was responsible for the book's intricate illustrations, is represented as well by his fine late work, *Love Among the Ruins*, which dominates the gallery end of the hall, the tendrils of briar rose in which he has entangled

the young couple recalling those in his cycle of paintings at Buscot Park. Photographs of the Pre-Raphaelites and their associates on an upstairs landing include one showing William Morris and Burne-Jones with their families in which only Janey Morris looks straight at the camera. A drawing of Scarborough by Turner that was recently found in the house and once belonged to Ruskin may also soon be on display.

The attractive 7-hectare (17-acre) garden slopes away from the house into a little valley with a stream and two pools and is shielded by trees and tall hedges from the suburbia around. First laid out on the advice of the painter Alfred Parsons, it was largely redesigned by the Edwardian landscape architect Thomas Mawson, who married strongly architectural formal gardens round the house, marked out with terraces, walls, clipped yew hedges and topiary, with an increasingly informal and natural approach to the layout and planting of the valley, which has orchards and paddocks and winding mown paths. Wisteria and other climbers flower on the house and there is a show of rhododendrons and azaleas round the two pools in the valley. A wooden bridge over the road up to the house was inspired by the Mathematical Bridge over the River Cam at Queens' College, Cambridge.

ABOVE Burne-Jones's *Love Among the Ruins*, painted in 1894, only four years before he died, hangs below the minstrels' gallery in the great parlour.

Wimpole Estate

Cambridgeshire
8 miles (12.8 kilometres) south-
west of Cambridge, 6 miles
(9.6 kilometres) north of Royston

When Rudyard Kipling visited his daughter Elsie here, a few months after she and her husband Captain George Bambridge took up residence at the house in 1936, he was moved to remark that he hoped she had not bitten off more than she could chew. Two years later the Bambridges embarked on the restoration and refurnishing of the largest house in Cambridgeshire, whose red-brick and stone facades, three and four storeys high in the central block, stretch over 76 metres (250 feet) from end to end. A double staircase leads up to the pedimented entrance bay on the south front, which is ornamented with a Venetian window over the front door and a carved coat of arms in the pediment above. From here an immense avenue lined with young limes runs over 2 miles (3.2 kilometres) into the distance. Immediately in front of the house, urns and busts on pedestals flank the courtyard like guards standing rigidly to attention.

The remodelling of the original mid-seventeenth-century house by James Gibbs and, later, Henry Flitcroft, in the first half of the eighteenth century marks Wimpole's golden age. From 1713–40 the house was the property of Edward Harley, 2nd Earl of Oxford, who entertained a brilliant circle of writers, scholars and artists here, Swift and Pope among them, and whose household included a Master of the Horse, a Groom of the Chamber and a Master of Music. Perhaps it was for the latter and his orchestra that Lord Harley commissioned James Gibbs's baroque chapel, Bavarian in its opulence, which is such a striking feature of the house. In Sir James Thornhill's *trompe-l'oeil* decoration, statues of Saints Gregory, Ambrose, Augustine and Jerome stand in niches between pairs of classical columns, their shadows etched sharply on the stone behind. Gregory leans eagerly forward with a book in his hand, as if about to escape his perch, while half-naked St Jerome displays a splendidly muscled physique. The east wall is filled with Thornhill's *Adoration of the Magi*, in which the Three Kings are accompanied by a sizeable retinue of armed men and Mary herself sits amid a romantic classical ruin, her ruddy-faced, bearded husband watching quietly in the background.

Gibbs also designed the long library to house Harley's exceptional collection of books and manuscripts, the largest and most important ever assembled by a private individual in England and later to form the nucleus of the British Library. An oak and walnut pulpit on castors gives access to the upper shelves and a brown, pink and beige carpet picks up the subdued tones of the plaster ceiling. This room is reached through a gallery that was created by Henry Flitcroft in 1742 for Wimpole's next owner, Philip Yorke, 1st Earl of Hardwicke, as a setting for his finest paintings. Now used to display pictures particularly associated with the house, such as *The Stag Hunt* by John Wootton, who frequently visited Wimpole in Lord Harley's time, the room's long sash windows framed by red curtains and the grey-green walls help to create an atmosphere that is both restful and warm.

Wimpole's most individual interior, John Soane's Yellow Drawing Room, was added 50 years later, in the early 1790s, for Philip Yorke's great-nephew, the 3rd Earl. Running from the north front into the centre of the house, the room opens out into a domed oval at the inner end that is lit from a lantern in the roof above. Yellow silk on the walls sets off blue upholstery on the gilt chairs and on the long settees curved round two semicircular apses on the inner wall, with a large painting of cherubs at play above the chimneypiece that divides them. The overall effect is of a chapel transformed into a room of exceptional elegance and grace. Soane's indulgent bath house, with a grand double staircase sweeping down to a tiled pool which holds over 9,000 litres (2,000 gallons) of water, is a delightful reminder of another side of eighteenth-century life.

When the Bambridges moved to Wimpole, they were faced with refurnishing a largely empty house, the contents of which had been gradually dispersed. Aided by royalties from the Kipling estate, which Mrs Bambridge inherited in 1936, they bought on their travels abroad and at auction, and Mrs Bambridge continued to buy after her husband's death in 1943. While he was responsible for two Tissots and a portrait by Tilly Kettle, she acquired portraits connected with the house and paintings by Mercier, Hudson and Romney. Porcelain figures on show are from her collection, and she also added notable books to the library, including some rare editions of Kipling's work.

Wimpole's extensive wooded park fully matches the grandeur of the house and reflects the influence of some of the most famous names in the history of landscape gardening.

The great lime avenue running to the south, its unyielding lines striking through a patchwork of fields like a grassy motorway, was originally created by Charles Bridgeman, who was employed by Lord Harley in the 1720s to extend an elaborate formal layout which already included the east and west avenues to either side of the house.

Remarkably, these remains of what was once an extensive scheme of axial avenues, canalised ponds, ha-has and bastions survived the attentions of 'Capability' Brown and his disciple William Emes later in the century, both of whom set about 'naturalising' the park. The view from the north front, artfully framed by the clumps of trees with which Brown replaced a felled avenue, looks over his serpentine ornamental lake to a hillock crowned with a three-towered Gothick ruin. Built in 1774, this eye-catcher was based on designs by Sanderson Miller made 25 years before. Brown's belts of trees defining and sheltering the park were thickened and extended by Humphry Repton, who produced a Red Book for the 3rd Earl in 1801, but Repton also reintroduced a touch of formality, creating the small flower garden enclosed by iron railings on the north side of the house.

Sir John Soane's home farm to the north of the house, built in a pleasing mixture of brick, wood, tile and thatch, was also commissioned by the 3rd Earl, who was passionately interested in farming and agricultural improvement. Gaily painted wagons and carts now fill the thatched barn, but the surrounding paddocks and pens make up Wimpole's rare breeds farm.

A short distance south-east of the house is the parish church. Substantially rebuilt to Flitcroft's design in 1749, it is all that remains of the village that was swept away to create the park. In the north chapel, the only part of the medieval building not demolished in the mid-eighteenth century, the recumbent effigy of the 3rd Earl with his coronet at his feet dominates a number of grandiose monuments to successive owners of this palatial place, sleeping peacefully in the midst of all they once enjoyed. Banks and ditches in the grass to the south mark the house plots of medieval villagers who tilled the land centuries ago, the ridge and furrow they created still visible on a slope of old pasture.

ABOVE To provide shelving for books which could not be fitted into the library, Sir John Soane created a new Book Room in the early nineteenth century.

The Workhouse, Southwell

Nottinghamshire
8 miles (12.8 kilometres) from
Newark on the A617 and A612

On the eastern edge of Southwell, sitting well back from the road at the top of a gentle grassy slope, is a striking, early nineteenth-century building of mellow red brick. Three storeys tall, it is solid and functional, typical of the many institutional buildings of the period. It was built as a workhouse in 1824 as part of a pioneering approach to poor relief instigated by the Rev. J.T. Becher, a local magistrate. By the early nineteenth century, the existing system, based on the 1601 Poor Law that made each parish responsible for its destitute, was breaking down. Some parishes had banded together to provide workhouses, but the accent was on helping the poor to live in their own homes and this was no longer viable, partly because the scale of the problem had escalated, fuelled by agricultural depression, the return of soldiers from the Napoleonic wars and a rising population, partly because there was concern about a system that provided no incentive to work.

In Southwell, the Rev. Becher came up with a new approach that was designed to deter as well as provide relief. He tried it out first in a small workhouse just for Southwell parish, and then, in 1823, proposed a much larger institution to serve a group of neighbouring parishes. The workhouse was built on what were then open fields outside the town, with a plan that reflected the Rev. Becher's ideas on how denizens should be treated. Intended to house both the able-bodied and the aged and infirm, men, women and children, it was designed so each group would be segregated, day and night. Wives were separated from husbands, children from their parents. Inmates were made to wear a uniform, were fed the plainest of diets, and treated to a daily regime that involved hours of hard and monotonous work: breaking stones, unpicking old rope, digging the garden, or endlessly cleaning the interior and repainting the walls. Above all, they were strictly supervised. It was a narrow and comfortless existence. All this is reflected in the plan of the workhouse, which has separate day rooms for each group on the ground floor, with segregated dormitories above. Inmates passed from one to the other by separate staircases, set side by side, and each day room gives onto a brickwalled yard, for work and exercise, with an open privy, just a hole in the ground, set behind a wall in the corner. From the yard, nothing can be seen of the outside world apart from the tops of the trees in the workhouse orchard.

The interior is shown unfurnished, as a succession of bare rooms with painted and whitewashed brick walls and stone-flagged or lime-ash floors. There are no cupboards or other fittings, just pegs in the walls where the paupers could hang their clothing. In the middle of the main range, marked by a projecting bay with a grand pedimented entrance, are the quarters for the master and the administration of the workhouse. Here the walls are plastered and there is a hierarchy of other refinements, which peaks with picture rails, skirting boards and a wooden floor in the master's office. There are cupboards, and the airy committee room where the workhouse guardians met, and where families could see each other briefly on Sundays, has a mantelpiece and a fender in front of the fire. From his rooms, the master could look down on paupers in the exercise yards, but there were some corners out of his sight, one of which has what may well be a gaming board scratched into the brickwork.

The Southwell Workhouse was studied by a Royal Commission looking into poor relief and became the prototype for a nationwide system as laid down in the New Poor Law of 1834. Hundreds of workhouses were built, each serving a group of parishes, and each operating on Becher principles. As the years passed, the focus shifted away from deterrence towards helping those who needed shelter and nursing, and the numbers needing relief declined. A red-brick building behind Southwell Workhouse was built in 1871 as an infirmary; the introduction of pensions in 1908 and national insurance in 1911 did much to alleviate the poverty of the old and unemployed; and children were moved to separate homes. Despite all this, the workhouse continued to be used into the 1990s and there is a room fitted out as a 1970s interior that would have housed an entire family.

ABOVE This hook on a peeling wall sums up the workhouse's desolate interior.